FAR SWEETER THAN HONEY

SEARCHING FOR MEANING ON A BICYCLE

From the author's original travel diary

FAR SWEETER THAN HONEY

SEARCHING FOR MEANING ON A BICYCLE

WILLIAM SPENCER

The passage on page 7 and on the back cover is from the *Gulistan*, reprinted from Sir Edwin Arnold, trans., *The Gulistan of Sa'di*, which was originally published in 1885.

Photo credits:
UK: Hemel Hempstead *Evening Post-Echo*
Yugoslavia: Trbojević DŽarko-Levin
Iran: Mohammed Davari
Pakistan: H.A. Kay
India: Edite Tolworthy
All other photos: Rudy Buursema
All sketches: The author

Printed in the United States of America
Print ISBN: 978-1-951490-92-8
eBook ISBN: 978-1-951490-93-5

Library of Congress Control Number: 2020922254

Publisher Information:
DartFrog Books
4697 Main Street
Manchester, VT 05255
www.DartFrogBooks.com

Join the discussion of this book on Bookclubz.
Bookclubz is an online management tool for book clubs, available now for Android and iOS and via Bookclubz.com.

Contact the author: WilliamSpencerAuthor@gmail.com

To each of you who fed, hosted, or cared for me: you taught me that goodness lies at the heart of humankind. Thank you.

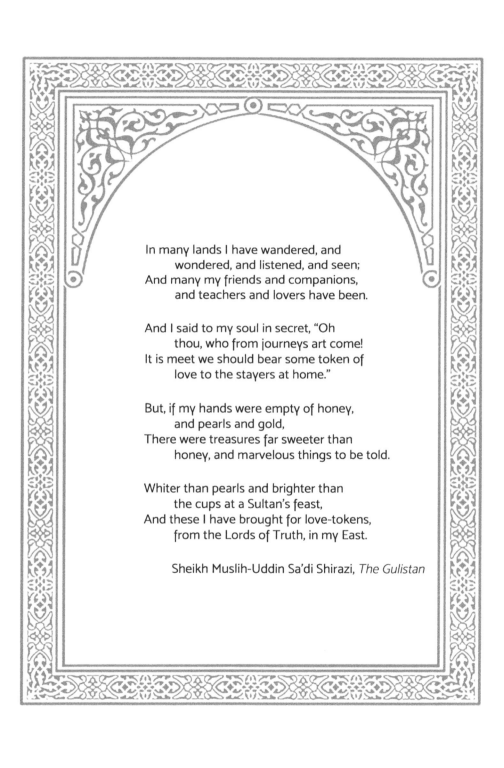

In many lands I have wandered, and
      wondered, and listened, and seen;
And many my friends and companions,
      and teachers and lovers have been.

And I said to my soul in secret, "Oh
      thou, who from journeys art come!
It is meet we should bear some token of
      love to the stayers at home."

But, if my hands were empty of honey,
      and pearls and gold,
There were treasures far sweeter than
      honey, and marvelous things to be told.

Whiter than pearls and brighter than
      the cups at a Sultan's feast,
And these I have brought for love-tokens,
      from the Lords of Truth, in my East.

Sheikh Muslih-Uddin Sa'di Shirazi, *The Gulistan*

CONTENTS

The author's route, from England to India.

One

ENGLAND

June 11th

IT'S A MISTY SUMMER MORNING in Hemel Hempstead, England. I make a few adjustments to my panniers and set out on my bicycle. I'm headed for India. It's an hour later than I had planned to leave. Last night's send-off with a group of friends at a local pub has left me in a hangover fog. I do recall that rounds of beer became rounds of Scotch to mark the significance of the occasion. There were rowdy toasts with innuendos about two young men setting out together. A friend wanted to know how I'd maintain my Bowie-style bouffant hair. He asked, "Who'll carry the hair dryer?"

Even my pounding head cannot dull the exhilaration of this long-anticipated moment. But the first difficulty arrives sooner than expected. A puncture flattens one of my tires and stops me at the first corner, not three hundred yards from home. I can't face another tearful farewell with my mother and sisters, so I push the bicycle a mile to Brian's house. He's my friend from work and traveling companion. When she hears about the flat, Brian's mum offers English solace—a cup of tea. Having just set out on the road to India, it's disappointing to find myself seated now at a kitchen table drinking tea, no matter how sweet, milky and hot it is. Staring at the red and white checkered tablecloth, I'm distracted. I can think only about getting underway.

We fix the puncture quickly and set out. Brian and I will cycle together to Greece, where he'll meet up with his mum and dad. They've coordinated their holiday plans with our route. He'll decide from there whether or not to continue. We say that we are cycling to India, but I'm not sure we will make it. Not all that way. Not on bicycles. The headline in tomorrow's local paper will read, "It's Bombay or Bust for the Two Easy Riders." *Easy riders* because, when we were interviewed, we denied all fear of the unknown. Neither of us mentioned Bombay, yet the headline is prophetic.

India bound. Bill Spencer, left, and Brian Parker before they left on their marathon ride

William and Brian in the local paper on the day before departure.

The idea of traveling together took shape over a period of six months. Brian's quiet enthusiasm helped crystallize our thinking from aspiration into a plan. We became friends while working together as computer operators at BP Oil. We are both twenty-two, but we have different temperaments. Brian is quiet and easygoing. He's sensitive, kind to a fault, and slow to anger. He's usually happy to put his agenda aside and defer to my lead—handy, given my willfulness. He doesn't say a lot; perhaps I say too much. Even his dark hair and heavy eyebrows contrast with my pale skin and fair hair.

A few months earlier, Brian had said, "If we are going to do this, we should set a date." So one evening, seated with pints of bitter at a scarred oak table at the Old Bell pub, we made a pledge. The sound of darts thumping into a dartboard perilously close to my head gave the moment a certain edge. "OK, then. By the end of June at the latest."

The beer lent a happy certainty to the idea. We both enjoyed cycling. We were free of any need to provide for others. In 1970s England, the majority of students did not continue to university. I'd started work at the age of sixteen. Brian and I had both been working for five years. I'd already experienced the trials and the rewards of a steady, high-paying job. Yet the scent of the sixties still hung in the air like patchouli oil. Assumptions about society and class were shifting. Deference was waning. I needed to know what more there was to life than earning and spending my next pound sterling.

I had no savings, but for several months I'd been squirreling away what I could. My mother and stepfather's reaction to my travel plans had been only positive. My mother was a world traveler herself and wanted to show her support. She bought me a small hand trowel. "So you can bury your poo," she explained. I wasn't sure about the precious cubic inches the tool would occupy in my small panniers.

Planning what to take was a project in itself. I laid out all that I wanted to take on my bedroom floor. Space was tight. For long-distance cycling, forty-five pounds of luggage is the maximum; forty is ideal. There were choices to be made. One method is to set out the essentials, then remove half, and then remove half again. I knew not to eliminate any of the several layers of clothing. My favorite heavy woolen sweater and waterproof jacket were must-haves. When all was said and done, clothing formed seventy-five percent of the bulk and forty percent of the weight of my luggage. Tools and essential spares made up fifteen percent of the bulk, but a lot of the weight. A few basic toiletries and medical supplies were the balance. To carry atop the rear rack was a tent, sleeping bag, thin foam sleeping pad, two spare tires, and a collapsible plastic water carrier. And then I added a heavy book, but more on that in a moment.

A month before our planned departure, I was doing contract computer work in London. I was staying not far from the Olympia Exhibition Hall, and I visited the first-ever annual Festival for Mind, Body and Spirit. At one booth, I learned about Auroville, an experimental city in Pondicherry, South India. People there pursue spiritual rather than worldly goals, they explained. The lifestyle is one they hope all mankind might one day adopt. It's a bold vision. They follow the teachings of Sri Aurobindo, an Indian intellectual and mystic. I attended a session with the Aurobindo Society on meditation. I couldn't do it, despite my high expectations. Maybe the high expectations were the problem. A movie and photographs of their idyllic community in the tropics offered the promise of a better meditation experience.

This day at the Olympia Exhibition Hall was significant because, in the months to follow, I started to see the trip more as a pilgrimage and less as a grand adventure. I wanted to experience communal life in a place like Auroville and learn to meditate. To this end, I purchased a book: Aurobindo's epic poem *Savitri and Satyavan*. On the journey I'd shed every ounce of extraneous weight, but I wouldn't relinquish this three-pound, three-inch thick book. The language was too complex for my taste. I would never read it, yet it would become a symbol of the purpose of my journey. This trip would become a journey of the spirit. Traveling on the outside would become traveling on the inside.

And now here we are, en route to India. Brian and I cycle through Hemel Hempstead's industrial area. The roads are mostly free of cars on this Sunday morning. We stop to adjust our luggage. It's the first time we've cycled with it all in place—panniers filled to capacity, sleeping bags, tent, water carriers, and spare tires. The added weight gives my bicycle a very different balance and rhythm. This will take some getting used to.

The cycling is easy enough the first day. We pitch our tent among bushes next to the A2, the main road from London to Dover. A curtain of greenery hides us from the solid flow of traffic. Just yesterday, that was our lot; we rushed from one place to another and then headed home from work, the shops, or the pub. Back home to a warm bed in a comfortable house. But no longer. Brian and I now inhabit a parallel universe, where we're more aware of the cold, the quality of the light, the unpleasant smell of exhaust in the damp air. I tell Brian that this glorious, dry day means that summer is here. It then pours down rain through the night. We awaken in the predawn hours to the rumble of huge trucks on their way to the ferries and the Continent—what we English call the rest of Europe.

I'd learned a lot last year about what to expect on a long cycling trip. I'd cycled three thousand miles around France with my girlfriend, Sharon. We had no particular destination in mind; we wanted only to "cycle around Europe." We detoured into northern Italy, Switzerland, and Belgium. We repaired numerous broken spokes, as our bicycles were not built to carry heavy luggage. We camped with a group of young travelers in a spectacular spot by the River Loire. As workers in the apple and pear harvest, we sat around an open fire each evening. Staring into the flames, we heard stories of travels to India, Nepal, and the Himalayas.

But conditions were not ideal. We had set out toward the end of summer, and we didn't have enough money. The most challenging part was being together day in and day out, seven days a week, in a tent not five feet by seven. Our relationship became strained. I lacked the skills to express the feelings that accompany a full-on commitment. Our itinerary and relationship went round in circles.

That trip taught me that being on a bicycle brings out the best in those we meet. Most people can be trusted, especially those in rural areas. I also learned that covering long distances on a bicycle is easier than I'd imagined. I was surprised by how quickly my body and mind adapted to a more basic lifestyle. We overcame each difficulty as it arose: being unable to wash daily, a broken luggage rack, sleeping in subzero temperatures, coexisting with an insect horde on a hot evening, and more.

On our first night back in the UK, Sharon and I stayed in Dover at the youth hostel. In its small library, I read a hippie guidebook for the trip to India. For many years, traveling overland from England to India had been the alternative thing to do. It signaled an exit from the mainstream. The author asserted in the introduction, "A year spent in India is worth ten years of formal education in the West." A seed was planted as I read that sentence. Six months later, this journey to India is its fruit.

There will be no Dover Youth Hostel comfort for Brian and me. We plan to take the night ferry to Boulogne, France. Approaching the ferry terminus, we're caught in another downpour. We spread our wet things over the radiators in the waiting room. Hours pass. The man in the Automobile Association booth looks at us with disdain, but says nothing. In England, the disapproving glare is intended to put one in one's place. Brian and I are practicing being out of our place.

 Route through England: Hemel Hempstead, St. Albans, Waltham Forest, Barking, Dartford, Rochester, Faversham, Canterbury, and Dover.

Two

FRANCE

June 14th

THE FERRY DEPOSITS US IN BOULOGNE in the early hours. A brightly lit café beckons. We're damp and the warmth is welcome. The hiss of a cappuccino machine provides a lift, even before the coffee arrives. We drink café-au-lait and Pernod, eat croissants, and play the few English rock songs we find on the jukebox. Our tiredness, the Pernod, and the familiar songs in unfamiliar surroundings create a surreal moment. We set off as the first gray light seeps into the sky, cycling beyond the town. We pitch our tent in a shabby campsite, crawl into our sleeping bags, and immediately fall asleep. When we wake, the sun is high in the sky.

At midday we stop in Equihen-Plage and get thoroughly drunk on cold French beer. We pitch the tent at another nondescript camping site. We fall asleep to the sound of rain pelting the flysheet. For the next two weeks it's raining, or about to rain. The sky remains a sullen gray. We cycle along arrow-straight roads lined with poplar trees. The plains of Normandy are as bland as the gray weather.

Our relationship changes as the miles pass. Back home, Brian and I were drinking and working buddies, but not close friends. I'm learning to appreciate his understated ways. His dogged determination is a welcome counterpoint to my impetuousness. Each morning, we agree to a route for the day on identical maps. However, near Amiens we lose each other. I cycle on and then wait for him to catch up. After some time, he still does not appear and I start to worry. An ambulance passes with lights flashing and siren blasting. I imagine the worst; I see Brian in the back of the ambulance with no one there to comfort him. I bolted on his front wheel after a recent puncture. Did I forget to tighten a nut? I decide to cycle on, heavy thoughts filling my head. The more time that passes, the surer I am that the ambulance I saw carried a broken Brian. Sorrow and remorse descend.

Two hours later, I hear Brian's cheery voice coming from behind me. He had some trouble with his luggage rack and stopped to fix it. We sit by the side of the road and I tell him about the day and how I felt when I thought something was wrong. We celebrate our reunion by consuming a huge bar of Belgian chocolate we'd intended to be dessert for several days. I realize that I'd miss him sorely if he were not here. We camp that night near a huge garbage dump outside Amiens. It would seem that even the French produce garbage.

We proceed southward. After two weeks, the weather turns and we cycle beneath cloudless blue skies. The French countryside in summer is all delight. We coast along small country roads that shimmer in the warm air. The French rural way of life is a measured one. There is time for simple things: repairing a fence, having a conversation at a roadside café, eating a meal. There's a smell of dewy earth early in the morning. The leaves of plane trees tremble. Disinterested cows chew the cud in a meadow. The balmy air enhances this ageless glory. The midafternoon silence is amplified by the droning of bees. The surroundings work a spell on us both. Our pace and minds slow. The need to be somewhere else becomes a little less urgent. In the timelessness of nature, I start to see that I am part of a larger whole. I am content to just be; contentment comes in several flavors, and this one is sweet.

France may be the best country in the world to travel by bicycle. There's a network of small roads that's easily found with the excellent Michelin maps. These small roads allow us to ride mostly free of traffic. The country that hosts the Tour de France is a bicycle-friendly place. People wave. Cars slow and follow behind until they can pass safely. Passing motorists call out, *Bon courage! Bravo!* In France, heroes ride bicycles.

Our daily routine settles into a wholesome rhythm. We awake spontaneously a little before dawn. There's magic in these first hours of the day, when we share the world only with cows. The grass around our tent is wet with dew. Spiderwebs along the tent guy lines shimmer with drops of water in the early light. We start our morning routine by washing quickly in cold water, then packing our sleeping bags and striking the tent. If it rained in the night, or there's a lot of dew on the tent's nylon rain fly, we delay so that the morning sun can dry it off. If you pack a tent away while it's still wet, it'll mildew. After some weeks, we perfect this packing and departing routine. We work our choreographed routine in silence. It takes little more than twenty minutes, and we're on the road as the first light of day creeps into the sky.

We talk little for the first hour. A shroud of mist demands silence. We wear gloves, hats, and windproof jackets. The sun rises in the sky, and we peel off a layer at a time. We stop for breakfast after an hour or two. This is often muesli we mix from oats, nuts and raisins with milk from powder. On colder mornings, we stop at a café. Steaming bowls of sweet, milky coffee and made-this-morning baguette with fruit jam warm us from the center out. We cycle without stopping for several hours after breakfast. In the late morning, we stop to buy Camembert cheese, tomatoes, an onion, and a baguette. Brian ties the long loaf across the top of the luggage on the back of his bicycle. With our appetites raging, we look for a place to stop for lunch. By this time, we have already covered two-thirds of the distance for the day.

We wait until just the right place appears. A golden wheat field sprinkled with poppies, where butterflies move among wild flowers at the margins. Or maybe beside a canal, where dragonflies skim black water below pollarded willow trees. Or a bench in a shady village square, watching old men play *boules* in the dust. We wash down the brimming sandwiches with a local table wine served in our enamel mugs. Dessert is several squares of Belgian milk chocolate sandwiched into more of that crispy, cake-like bread. We eat slowly, savoring both taste and setting. Washing up requires only rinsing our mugs and wiping the blades of our pocketknives. If they are still damp from the night before, we spread our sleeping bags and tent in the sun. We wash some clothes by hand if we're near water. We doze in the warm afternoon air, lulled by the music of bees. This is the time for writing letters home, or perhaps a little reading. It's also a good time for fine-tuning the bicycles. I hunt down each rattle or squeak. I put a drop of oil on every cable and every point of movement. Over time, I adjust each screw and nut, each bearing and lever, until the bicycle is a pitch-perfect instrument.

Late afternoon sometimes calls for a cold beer and a game of table football at a roadside café. As the sun sinks in the sky, we look for a place to camp. We need two hours of daylight for the evening routine—set up camp, boil water, make a pot of soup. We look for a pleasant setting that's out of sight of the road and on higher ground. Last year, Sharon and I learned the importance of that last requirement after a miserable experience of being awoken by cold, soaked sleeping bags in the middle of a rainy night.

Traveling through fenced farmland, we knock on a farmhouse door and practice our French. "*Avez-vous un place pour notre tent pour la nuit?*" The farmer smiles that smile one reserves for when foreign mouths mangle the mother tongue. This smile translates roughly as, "*Ah! My cows speak better French. Let the Englishmen sleep near the beasts, so the visitors may learn better pronunciation.*" The light of day drains from the sky. We are in our tent in a cow pasture, comfortably nestled in our sleeping bags. Sleep comes quickly: the blessing of miles of exertion.

Our predictable daily rhythm is interrupted only by rain. If it's raining when we awake, we stay in the tent. We read, write, or make repairs until the rain eases. Should it rain heavily all day, we remain within our nylon universe. This makes me claustrophobic and brings my spirits down. I am a skittish creature, yearning for the road and the wind in my face. If the rain starts while we're cycling, we don waterproof jackets and continue. If it gets heavy, we seek shelter in a shop, bus stand, or under a large tree. Warmth drains from the air. We stand in silence to watch puddles form and wait for the rain to ease.

We cross a stretch of flat country near Gisors. An inland escarpment appears in the distance. We check our Michelin map and see on our route the dreaded triple chevron (<<<), which is reserved for the steepest of hills. They point against our direction of travel, which means the hill goes up, not down—a critical distinction for any cyclist. We study the map for alternatives. With a spider's web of tiny country lanes that cross every corner of rural France, there are usually several ways to get from point A to point B. In this case, the only alternative would take us many miles out of our way. We must tackle the hill head-on.

As we approach this geographic anomaly, it's hard to imagine how the road could cross such a steep incline. We arrive at the base of the climb. Hills are never as steep seen from up close as they appear from a distance. Yet this would surely win a prize in an outrageous gradient competition. The midday heat makes the climb tougher still. I set my jaw, select the lowest gear and concentrate on the road ahead. Twice I consider getting off to push the bicycle, but I don't want to be beaten. I'm hauling two hundred twenty pounds up a one-in-six slope—a bicycle, fully laden front and rear panniers, and myself. After twenty minutes of this self-inflicted torture, I arrive at the top, gasping. The road is as flat as a billiard table up here. Beneath the shade of a huge tree is an area of mown grass with a wrought iron bench. It's an inviting spot. I lean the bicycle on the bench and flop down on the grass, thoroughly spent.

My pounding heart slows, and I open my eyes to see Brian's head appear over the rise. His face is the color of the tomatoes he's carrying for our lunch. He sparkles with perspiration, and he's breathing hard. Slowly, he crests the hill and looks ready to join me on the grass in the shade. He stops pedaling to enjoy a short coast. His bicycle slows, and he throws his leg weakly across the back of the bicycle. But he has forgotten about the long baguette loaf across his rear carrier. His leg and the baguette tangle briefly. He remains on the now-stationary bicycle, his other foot strapped into his pedal. He shoots me a look of helplessness as he hangs there. Then, as if in slow motion, he and the bicycle topple sideways. The sound of metal meeting road and a loud curse break the quiet of the afternoon. I can't help my laughter, and it's some time before I can administer first aid to his bleeding knee.

The days and the miles pass. We discuss how we might supplement our limited funds. When I picked apples and pears in the Loire Valley last year, I learned that it's possible to work through the summer picking fruit. One starts in Spain in early summer with apricots and peaches and then works northward to finish picking grapes in Germany in the autumn. In larger cities, we scour notice boards at the *Agence Nationale de l'Emploi* offices: the government employment agency. But it's too early in the season. So we visit the Vignaults, a family in the Cognac area with whom Sharon and I stayed last year. The family gives us a warm welcome. They grow Folle Blanche grapes that are distilled into cognac. The *vendage*, or grape harvest, is some weeks away, so we help out around the farm. Trying our hand at milking goats, Brian and I wrestle unsuccessfully with the teats. Marcel, the intellectually challenged farm hand, roars with laughter and bellows, "Les Anglais. Ha, ha, ha! Les Anglais!"

After five days of bottomless hospitality, it's time to move on. We set out, laden with several bottles of local brew. There's *pinaud*, mead made with fermented grape juice and honey, and an illicit brew of triple-distilled cognac. They warn us that this will remove varnish from furniture. A tentative sip confirms that it belongs in our first aid kit, its use limited to cleaning wounds.

We push ourselves to meet our target of fifty miles per day. This requires five or six hours on the bicycle. In reality, the distance we cover is determined by hills, the quality of the road surface (a smooth tarmac speeds the way), and—more critically—wind direction. Battling a headwind can cut speed and distance covered by a quarter. In a strong wind, we learn to cycle close, one behind the other. Whichever of us is in front creates a slipstream that the other enjoys; then we periodically switch places. But in these first weeks, the hours we can spend in the saddle are limited by soreness in our southerly regions.

A bicycle is surely the most energy efficient mode of travel. With this simple machine, modest amounts of energy yield impressive results. In the course of a single day, we reach a place far removed from where we started. We cycle through most of the daylight hours, and the miles add up. In the European scale of things, one can cross a country in a couple of weeks. It's a deeply satisfying experience. We create little noise and no pollution. We can enjoy and be an active participant in the scenes through which we travel. No passive observation from the sealed bubble of a car for us! Add sharpened senses from constant aerobic exercise, and a wholesome routine fixed by the sun's rise and fall, and we have the ingredients of a truly memorable experience.

The farther we travel, the clearer my head. My eyesight, hearing, and sense of smell improve. My mind quiets and my appreciation deepens for things about and within me. My awareness of nature increases. I become attuned to daylight and darkness, the sky and clouds, dryness and rain, warmth and cold. The heaviness of an English lifestyle falls away to leave a sense of well-being. Even this city boy, pickled in rock 'n' roll, beer, cigarettes, and late-night discos, can adjust. I learn that we're more adaptable than we might think, and can readily regain our innate connection to nature.

Although I had freelance computer work until three days before we left, I've saved only nine hundred pounds. I don't know how much money I'll need, but imagine I can budget to what I have. In a final attempt to find work, we visit Bordeaux. This is a southern wine-producing area, and we hope that the *vendage* has started.

We cycle through the port area of the city. Ahead is a pair of tram rails. They're recessed into the road surface and cross only at a slight angle. The narrow channel along each rail is treacherous since it can easily trap a wheel. It's impossible to stop in time, given our speed. I think, *Bet Brian comes off.* Brian shares later that he thought the same thing. To cross, I stand up in the pedals and yank the handlebars upward twice in quick succession so that the front wheel momentarily leaves the ground just as it crosses each rail. Since the rear wheel can't turn, it does not drop into the channel.

Brian's front wheel drops into the first track. I turn to see him sprawled on the road, his front wheel badly damaged. The city traffic rushes past in an unbroken stream. I am appalled that no one stops to offer assistance. I help him clean and bandage a badly scraped knee. We sit in this dusty, miserable place and painstakingly repair the wheel. By adjusting the tension of individual spokes, we coax out the worst of the buckle and get the wheel somewhere near to its true form. But from this point on, when Brian brakes, his front wheel plays a rhythm section: *ker-chunk-e-dink, ker-chunk-e-dink, ker-chunk-e-dink.*

Our visit to Bordeaux is fruitless—metaphorically and literally. The *Agence Nationale de l'Emploi* office is in the ultramodern Tour 2000 government complex. With our imperfect French and Brian's small French dictionary, we decipher the many cards posted on huge job boards. There's no fruit-picking work. There's a job as a tractor driver, but neither of us has ever driven one. The other job seekers are Moroccan or Algerian, and, like us, they lack work papers. We browse the boards but can't approach the staff to ask for further assistance. Sitting on the steps outside, a pretty young woman approaches us and introduces herself in a lilting Irish accent. We invite her to join us for a cold beer at a nearby outdoor café.

Mary is from a strict Catholic family. She describes how, through a pen pal, she arranged a job for herself in Lourdes, in the South of France, "selling the holy relics" to visiting pilgrims. She gave up a steady job and said goodbye to a worried family back home. She arrived to find that the job had fallen through. A young woman away from home for the first time, she was at a loss as to what to do next. She dared not tell her family what had happened because someone would be on the next plane to bring her back home. And, after living with her pen pal's family for a time, she felt she could no longer accept their hospitality. She made her way to Bordeaux and got a job in a mental hospital in return for room and board. She's learning French and is here seeking a different job.

We share a beer, offer some suggestions as to what else she might try, exchange addresses, then say goodbye. Some months later, I write to her. A sporadic communication starts up between us. I learn that she did find work, keeping house for an elderly gentleman. I imagine meeting up with her after I return. Her charming Irish ways and pretty face stay with me.

Leaving Bordeaux, we head southeast. We skirt the foothills of the Pyrenees, which separate France from Spain. The countryside changes as we cycle away from the Atlantic. Farms and vineyards slowly give way to scrub-covered hills that are good only for raising sheep. This is an austere place, with little rainfall. Wild thyme perfumes the late afternoon air with a heady scent. The road rises and falls: another stretch of uneventful cycling.

Carcassonne is a medieval, walled city. It looks much as it must have seven hundred years ago, and its rocky outcrop presents an imposing view from a distance. People have lived here since the sixth century BC. This settlement was conquered in turn by the Romans, Visigoths, Moors, Franks and Crusaders. We enjoy a view of the city walls and turrets from the road. We don't stop.

Beyond Carcassonne, we call it a night at a small campground. There are similar municipal campgrounds scattered across France, their blue and white signs easy to recognize. They are mostly bland places with cinder block toilets and laundry buildings. Once a week, we seek out one of these campgrounds and pay a nominal fee to pitch our tent. We take long, hot showers and wash our clothes in hot water.

There's a young Frenchman and his girlfriend staying in a worn khaki tent next to ours. Patrick Vincent is a bear of a man with a bushy, untended beard and a gentle manner. With his limited English and our imperfect French, we talk. It is all we have to offer, so we share some of the Vignaults' devil's brew from the first aid kit. It tastes better after the first mouthful does its work. Patrick invites us to join him tomorrow *chez moi*—at his place. It's not far off our route, about a day's cycle from here.

The following evening, Brian and I set out to find Patrick's house along a series of dusty, unpaved roads. In the small village of Montseret, we ask an old man for directions. He tells us to follow him and fairly jumps onto an antique black bicycle. We follow down a path that becomes progressively narrower. Our guide stops and points a gnarled finger at a scarcely discernible track. We push our bicycles up a low hill, bare but for wild thyme, sage, and brambles. Stepping on the vegetation underfoot releases the pungent fragrance into the air. The hot air of late afternoon is loud with countless bees.

Atop a low, rocky hill ahead there's a small clearing around an old Citroen van. The maroon paintwork of the van is faded with age and painted with mysterious white symbols, yet the place exudes a welcoming air. In one corner of the clearing is a stone oven with a chimney shaped like a kiln. Some odds and ends lay off to one side, but things are otherwise orderly and clean. On the far side of the clearing is a small vegetable garden enclosed by chicken wire. Beside it, a plastic pipe emerges from the sloping ground. From this pipe flows sparkling water. Each of the tree saplings that dot the clearing is also fenced with chicken wire. We're on a small island in a scented sea of thyme.

Patrick greets us warmly and explains that the chicken wire is to keep out the wild rabbits, but that it's a losing battle. He tells us with a laugh that even his carefully guarded patch of marijuana has been eaten to the ground. Apparently, the rabbits are particularly persistent when it comes to reaching these delicate plants. I imagine rabbit stoner parties in tunnels below our feet.

Patrick has been here for four years, living a simple life. He works on a nearby building site, helping to build a *maison de weekend* for a rich Parisian couple. The sun settles into the hills. We sit around a fire and Patrick produces an old turntable that he has somehow wired to the van's battery. The light drains from the sky. The Rolling Stones sing about not always being able to get what you want; the rabbits probably disagree.

Patrick explains that he paid a farmer far above market value for this piece of land, for the chance to live the life he dreamed of. Here, with his wife and child, working and living off the land. The villagers allowed him to tap a nearby spring, and he had all he needed to make his simple dream a reality. With one hoe, one spade, and one garden fork, he transformed rocks and scrub into a level plot. It required many months of hard labor, then some months more to get the van here, cutting a path through the brush a little at a time. His plan is to live in it while he builds a house, using the large, flat rocks that lay all about. He shows us pictures of stone houses that look like igloos, built in France during the Stone Age. This is the design he'll use, eliminating the need for expensive wood timbers.

Patrick is a vegetarian and seeks to kill no living thing. I walk ahead of him along a narrow path near the clearing; he grasps my arm suddenly and tells me to stop. Stooping, he picks up a small snail. He places it to one side and lets me continue. He collects honey from hives set in the brush nearby, but he must soon give up this fragrant treat. He says the bees he kills as he removes the combs are too high a price to pay for the honey. Living this life, Patrick explains, has changed him. Being close to nature helps him see things in a simpler way. He aspires to live here year-round, remaining naked so as not to need clothing and eating raw only what he grows. When he does venture out to visit his family in Paris, he is bewildered by their complex desires. The French place great store in appearance and conformity. So, Patrick has become an outcast. His wife ran away with their young daughter to live with another man. Sitting beneath the stars by an open fire, light dancing across his bearded face, Patrick's eyes fill with tears.

After two nights *chez* Patrick, Brian and I leave in a reflective mood. We also seek simplicity. Does that require giving up cooked food, wine, honey, and clothes? And what about listening to Mick Jagger and the lads? Where does that fit into the picture? Can a person be good and behave ethically in a contemporary life? Does simplicity require moving to a mountain?

We continue east, headed toward the Mediterranean coast and the Italian border. We take a detour from Beziers to Agde to visit the fabled shoreline. A row of swaying palms? No. Perhaps a line of sand dunes? Sorry. It's a bland, flat expanse of caravan parks. On the beach, a line of trash piled eight feet high extends as far as the eye can see in both directions. The seagulls are happy with the arrangement; I am appalled. How many people carrying in how much garbage over how many months does it take to create this insanity? Surely this is a local aberration. We visit the shoreline again ten miles farther east, and a similar scene greets us. The vacation season is ending, and I can only hope that a cleanup is planned.

William and Brian in the South of France.

Mountains are not the cyclist's devil—wind is. It can be a quiet friend or a relentless foe. A strong wind at your back is a joy. In northern France, Brian and I covered a record ninety-six miles in one day on a flat, recently paved road, courtesy of a tail wind. On a flat road with no wind, we manage twelve to fifteen miles an hour; a strong headwind can reduce that to three or four miles an hour. A side wind is merely frustrating, while a strong headwind sucks all joy from a day. Twenty miles by a circuitous route is preferable to ten when you're headed directly into the wind.

We face the worst headwind of the journey in the South of France in les Bouches-du-Rhone, or "the mouths of the Rhone." It is a coastal, marshy delta and is utterly flat. The wind comes off the Mediterranean with great force, and there is nothing to block its path. Not only is the hard work dispiriting, but the constant roar in my ears gives me a headache. We study the map to find an alternate route. We hope to zigzag sideways to our destination, like a sailor tacking across the wind. But few roads cross the marshes, and our options are limited. Tall marsh grass rises on either side, blocking any view beyond. A disused windmill breaks the monotonous scenery. We cycle with our heads close to the handlebars, leg muscles burning, lost in this fight with an invisible enemy. The wind is ferocious. When it gusts, it brings us to a complete stop.

We periodically consult the map and recalculate how many miles to go before the next intersection. Will a turn put us sideways to the wind? Yes, it looks as though it will. We pedal on, each hundred yards a fight. Is this what we left England for? What were we thinking? What if we were to turn around, go back the way we came, and find another route? No, that could add days to the trip. I ponder these pointless questions as we struggle on. Heavy traffic adds to the misery.

Finally, we arrive at the intersection and turn a full ninety degrees to the north. I swear the wind changes then and is again blowing directly in our faces. Hell on toast. A full day of this torture follows. In the late afternoon, another turn takes us in almost the opposite direction from the one we set out on this morning. And we're still being buffeted by a full headwind. The end of the day leaves us dispirited, and our backs sore from pedaling bent over. We have covered twenty-two miles; each was a hard-won battle.

We continue along the Mediterranean coastline. After passing Marseilles, the land folds up once again into hills. The foothills of the Alps marching south, row upon row into the Mediterranean, make for spectacular scenery. But the Cote d'Azure, a playground of the wealthy, was not developed with cyclists in mind. There's a single road that weaves along the water, hugging the hills. Most here drive sparkling Porches or Mercedes coupes. These drivers suffer from a visual peculiarity, which allows them to see only other Porches and Mercedes. We share the road in some imperfectly intertwined dimension. We see them, yet they appear not to see us. They make no eye contact, drive us off the road, and are deaf to our shouted curses. Cannes, Nice, St. Tropez: chic people and expensive yachts pass briskly to the click of derailleur gears. We do not linger.

That overland to India book I read in Dover offered some sound advice. Pay off all debt before leaving on an extended trip, since financial or emotional debt holds one back. Before leaving, I sold everything I owned except what I have with me. I left nothing behind—well, except my collection of LP records, which I couldn't bring myself to sell. That I carry most of what I own is a source of deep satisfaction. And, as the journey progresses, I learn that I need even less than I'd imagined. Wherever there are roads, there are people. Where there are people, the basics of life are to be found: water, food, shelter and warmth. I keep everything clean and organized. I sew patches onto the seat of my shorts. It's the one thing that regularly wears out.

Bicycle parts in mainland Europe and beyond come in metric sizes that don't conform to British standards. So I carry critical spares: a spare chain and extra chain links, a dozen spare spokes, assorted nuts and bolts, and spare inner tubes. Last year, I had problems with tires. Having no spare, I hand-stitched a patch of old tire to the inside of my threadbare back tire. When that trick no longer worked, I had to wait two weeks for a replacement to arrive from England. So now I carry two extra tires. There's a trick to carrying a spare tire. Twist it into a triple figure eight with three equal circles. Fold the outer circles in on the center circle so that the twists cancel themselves out. Hard to visualize, but it works. You're left with a cylindrical tower that's nine inches across and four inches high. Two tires folded in this manner, stacked one on the other, sit on top of my sleeping pad on my rear rack. They form a handy container for carrying food: convenient for the frequent snacking that accompanies the constant calorie burn.

There's pleasure in having and caring for just a few things, each with a purpose. Years later, with the paraphernalia required for babies, children, and life in general, I'll exhale a wistful sigh; there was a time I carried all that I owned on a bicycle.

Brian and I take turns carrying the tent, which is our heaviest item. Our one weight variable is water. I have containers stored in each side of my front panniers to keep the weight evenly balanced. We have chlorine tablets, but we don't need them in Europe since potable water is freely available. We partially fill our containers in the late afternoon for the evening's cooking and washing, and for a flannel bath the following morning. Other than this, we simply fill our bicycle water bottles as needed.

 Route through France: Boulogne, Amiens, Beauvais, Chartres, Blois, Poitiers, Matha, Cognac, Bordeaux, Marmande, Agen, Toulouse, Carcassonne, Beziers, Sete, Aix-en-Provence, Frejus, Nice, Cannes and Monaco.

Three

ITALY

July 10th

WE RECOGNIZE OTHER TOURING CYCLISTS by the luggage they carry. We stop to chat when we encounter fellow members of our clan. On one of our first mornings in Italy, we stop in a village square with an ornate stone fountain. We wash our feet and grimy necks in the clear, cool water; several locals scowl disapprovingly. A tall fellow on a bicycle pulls up and introduces himself. Since he's headed along the same road, all three of us set out together.

His name is Rudy, a Dutchman with curly blond hair; he's cycling from Amsterdam to Israel. He has a fancy bicycle with the latest accessories. It has the narrowest wheels and tires that I've ever seen, which help lessen rolling resistance. He has hand-stitched pannier bags that he designed, with a clever arrangement of straps. The rear panniers convert to a rucksack with shoulder straps. Here's a man who means business.

In the evening, we pitch our tents together in a small orchard in the hills above Mortola. With meticulous attention to detail, Rudy cooks us a wonderful meal on a tiny cooker that burns gasoline, rather than kerosene. It's a proper meal, and no one eats until all the dishes are ready. This is unlike the evening meals we have become accustomed to. With the hunger that comes with a day's cycling, Brian and I usually fall pell-mell on our food. In Rudy's company, we wait patiently as the food is prepared. It's an enjoyable way to eat, savoring both the process and the food. We sit around a small campfire and share stories of our travels. I'm a little in awe of this lean giant of a man: good-looking, organized, and generous to a fault. I like his confidence and openhearted manner. Like most of his countrymen, Rudy is multilingual. He speaks Dutch, excellent English, German, and French.

I tell Rudy about my fascination with the Indian subcontinent. It started when I was six years old. A homework project of mine on India was selected for an exhibition of local children's work. I recall the two pictures I included; one was a sepia photo of a Bengal tiger and the other was of the bathing *ghats* on the Ganges in Benares. That picture kindled a longing to see that place and to bathe in that sacred river.

Rudy describes his plan to cycle through Turkey and the Middle East to Israel and then work at a kibbutz there. Brian shares that he decided some days ago to meet his parents in Corfu, and will likely not continue after that. This leaves me unsure about my plans. Will I continue solo?

But there is an elegant solution; I suggest that Rudy and I combine goals. We could travel together—first to Israel for the winter and then continue on to India. The detour to Israel makes sense. At this pace, I'd find myself in Iran or Afghanistan come winter: not the warmest places in December. It makes more and more sense as we discuss it. The idea of continuing to India appeals to Rudy. His plan is to cycle to Florence, south through Italy, then travel by ferry to Igoumenitsa, a port in the extreme northwest of the Greek mainland. Brian and I think we'll reach Igoumenitsa around September 15th, so we agree that I'll check the post office there daily for a telegram from Rudy. He should get to Igoumenitsa a few days after us, and from there we'll continue on together. We'd both prefer to cross the wilds of Turkey with a companion. This plan is ideal for Brian, too; he can catch a ferry from there to meet his parents in Corfu.

We pitch our tent near Rudy's, and the following day we three cycle together. Brian and I struggle to keep up with Rudy. Later that day, he takes a road to the southeast. Brian and I continue east across northern Italy.

The English cyclist's bible, *Richard's Bicycle Book*, contains a chapter devoted to dogs. Well, *devoted* is the wrong word. Richard Ballantine advises that when a cyclist first sees a threatening dog, he has to make an immediate decision. He can either stop and face the dog, or outrun it. Should the cyclist choose the latter, he needs to be sure he has the speed to get away. A moving cyclist provokes an agitated dog, and it will bite if it can. Richard describes how to keep the bicycle between you and the dog when you stop (which is difficult if there's more than one in pursuit), and that a bicycle pump is a handy weapon. He also describes how, in dire circumstances, you can immobilize or even kill a dog by trapping its neck between the front wheel and the bicycle frame. He does not, however, explain how you get the dog to place its neck just so. *To the left a little, please. OK, hold it right there.*

Following Richard's advice, I carry a heavy steel bicycle pump. This can inflate a tire or deflate a dog's attack impulse. I keep this weapon directly behind my saddle, inside my rolled sleeping pad. Dogs have an unnerving habit of rushing out unannounced from bushes or behind fences. I've perfected my response. I reach behind me as I ride, unsheathe the weapon, and then face the attacker.

As we pass a farm in northern Italy, three large, mean hounds charge us from behind. They're suddenly upon us, barking wildly. Pumps drawn, we come quickly to a stop, skidding in the roadside gravel. The effect on my system is the same as several shots of Italian espresso. We stand back-to-back, pumps raised, ready for battle. The dogs snarl, standing just beyond the range of Excaliburs I and II. They drool, probably in anticipation of succulent thigh muscle. We wait, perspiring heavily in the sun.

Several minutes pass before they break eye contact, lower their heads, and wander away a few feet. One lies down in the shade of a nearby tree. We breathe a sigh of relief and sheathe our weapons. My pulse returns to normal. I take a step forward, and the dogs instantly reassume attack positions. Their hackles are raised, their teeth are bared, and they bark wildly. I stop. After a minute they retreat again. If either of us takes even a single step, the same frenzied threats resume. When we're stationary, they yawn and lie in the shade. Yet they remain close at hand—and leg.

We talk in a low monotone, trying not to move our mouths, as if they might understand our strategizing. "Reckon we could jump on our bikes and pedal like crazy before they reach us?" "No way; they'd be chewing on our bones after ten yards."

Neither of us has a plan. We try waiting fifteen minutes, twenty minutes. Moving slowly, we drink some water and consult our maps. We try to enjoy the scenery while remaining glued to the spot. This is ridiculous; we could be here all day. Man's best friends show no inclination to be anywhere other than here, terrorizing us with their presence. Unlike us, they've no place to go.

When I raise my hand with the pump as if to strike, they cower even though they are well beyond my reach. I recall seeing farm boys throw stones at dogs. Nonchalantly, I bend down and pick up a handful of ammunition. Brian does the same. I throw a stone and miss, but they yelp as if hit and retreat a few steps. We take a few steps before they charge again. We each fill one hand and our pockets with stones. We maintain a steady barrage of fire as we start off, wobbling with only one hand on the handlebars.

I later discover that this works even when there are no stones to hand. I can throw imaginary rocks with the same effect, including the yelps of pain. Dogs remain the biggest threat on the journey. In Europe it is farm dogs, and in Asia it's their wild cousins. Some say it's the sound of the chain passing through the derailleur gear mechanism that antagonizes our canine brethren, but I have my doubts. They react just as wildly to a cyclist with silent internal hub gears. Whatever the cause, the danger is real. Traveling at speed seems to make you a particularly appealing target to dogs, and the threat of crashing is real. In Italy and beyond, the risk of rabies is an added threat.

Apart from dogs, cycling across northern Italy is easy. The scenery is consistently beautiful; the foothills of the Dolomites form a backdrop as we pass through farming communities and small towns. We stop by a river one afternoon for an extended lunch break. I've been frustrated with my hair; a haircut is overdue. We have a small pair of scissors, and I ask Brian to cut my hair. He says he doesn't think this is a good idea. I insist, "Brian, look, I don't care how it turns out. No one is going to see me, and I don't care how it looks. You just take the scissors and cut. In this weather, I want it short. So please just cut it, OK?"

He takes a long time, surveying his work every few snips. He finally announces that he's done. We carry no mirror, so I look at my reflection in the river. A hairdresser friend once told me that the difference between a great haircut and a good haircut is about a week. The difference between this haircut and a good haircut is about two months.

We cover the distance across northern Italy quickly. Venice is close to our route, and we can't pass it without stopping to visit. Along the causeway to reach the area where cars can park, I have my first accident. We're on a narrow road bounded by stone walls. There's no room between the cars and the walls, so we pass on the left side of a long line of cars that are waiting to move forward. A German driver opens his door, and my front wheel goes into the edge of the door and I topple over it. I manage to tuck and roll to escape major injury. The bicycle appears to be fine, but the German tourist can't properly close the door of his car. I'm guessing he'll check his mirror before opening his door in future.

In Venice, the youth hostel is full, so we simply place our sleeping bags on the pavement outside. This is our first night without the tent; it's a delight to be outside on this warm and clear night. When we wake in the morning, passersby give us frosty looks. We meet two girls from England who are staying at the youth hostel and ask them to join us for the evening. We buy a bottle of wine and borrow two glasses from the hostel, then sit in St. Mark's Square and have a wonderful evening impressing the girls with our stories. Our bottle of wine finished, we find a bar for more drinks. When we stand to leave, we take our borrowed glasses with us. The barman objects, believing they are his, and speaks rapidly in Italian as he takes our glasses from my hands. We try to protest, but our Italian isn't up to the task. I tell Brian that we should just take two of his glasses—they're all identical anyway. I do so, and we walk away from the bar. I am proud of the simplicity of my solution.

Moments later, someone comes up behind me and pulls me violently by the shoulder. The barman swings and punches me hard in the face, then grabs the two glasses. Before I can gather my wits, he's gone. His ring leaves me with a chipped tooth that I still have to this day. I later discover that my St. Christopher pendant was lost in the scuffle. It would have been wiser to leave the glasses and not set the record straight. May this lesson in the cost of bravado stay with me as we pass into more dangerous parts of the world!

With promises to meet up again in England, we say goodbye to the girls and to Venice the next day.

Finding a place to pitch our tent at night becomes both a science and an art. Sometimes it's as simple as asking a local farmer if we can use the corner of a field (we are never refused). Alternatively, as the sun sinks lower in the sky, we scan our surroundings for the right spot. A good place is one with a welcoming atmosphere, plus the right arrangement of trees, short grass for the tent, and a rise to hide us from the road. It also has to be a place where we can drive tent pegs into the ground. Trees and bushes on several sides add some sense of safety. Anyone approaching from those directions will make noise and wake us.

A tent offers an illusion of security. People can't see you through the tent's walls, but they offer no real protection. We're careful to not be seen as we leave the road. We feel safer when no one knows we're there; it's a secret delight to peer out from a cover of bushes or rocks to see locals pass by, unaware of our presence. I answer the call of nature in the bushes during the stillness of the night and revel in the secrecy of our camp, lit by the moon and a canopy of bright stars overhead.

We wake at first light, and a morning mist renders the surroundings unrecognizable. As we pack, I silently give thanks for this welcoming corner of God's world that protected us for the night. I feel a twinge of regret at having to leave. The sun rises as we get back to the road. I note with satisfaction that the place is just as we found it except for a rectangle of flattened grass.

Route through Italy: Savona, Alessandria, Pavia, Padova, Venice and Trieste

Four
YUGOSLAVIA
July 19th

WE WERE FRUSTRATED WHILE SHOPPING in Italy for maps of Yugoslavia. Why were there no detailed ones that show the smaller roads? The answer dawns on us after we arrive in Yugoslavia. The maps are accurate; there are few secondary roads and no small country roads where a cyclist can be free of heavy traffic. We didn't realize it at the time, but saying goodbye to Italy also means saying farewell to quiet roads. Our maps show only two choices for a route south through Yugoslavia. One runs through the coastal cities, and the other is an inland route. We think the inland route will allow us to experience the real Yugoslavia. This is the first communist state we have visited, and we're curious to see everyday life. This would be harder along the coast, in the company of German tourists.

At first, our choice appears to be a good one. By the second day, this has changed. We're using the main highway between Zagreb and Belgrade. Most of the traffic in Yugoslavia travels this narrow two-lane strip of asphalt on top of a grassy, elevated bank. Along with Yugoslavian vehicles, there are international trucks from Hungary and Bulgaria. And local farmers in bull-ock-drawn carts piled high with hay. Littered along the side of the raised roadway are wrecks from horrendous accidents: some burned-out, but most mangled beyond recognition. You might think they'd be a reminder to slow down, but the drivers hurtle on, oblivious. There's little margin for error, and there's plenty of error. We see many near misses. Overtaking is the primary danger.

In short, it's a cyclist's worst nightmare. Huge trucks pass with inches to spare, their slipstream causing us to teeter dangerously. Horns blare. At a roadside café, we question the locals and they confirm that the only alternatives are unpaved roads that have been washed out in rainstorms. A police car stops; two jackbooted officers flag us down. In broken English, they state that bicycles are not allowed on this road. Perhaps this explains the potentially murderous behavior of the truck drivers. We nod our agreement, wait for the police to leave, and then rejoin the hellish world of blaring horns and hurtling steel. There's no alternative.

Everything else about our two weeks here is wonderful. The people we meet are the kindest we have encountered thus far. When we stop at a bar for coffee, someone invariably offers to buy us a drink—usually *slivovitz*, the local brew made from plums. The people are warm and open. We explain our highway predicament, and they go to great lengths to direct us to the few short detours off the main road.

A couple of days outside of Zagreb, we leave the main road to follow a long detour. There, we meet Trbojevic Zarko-Levin. We dub him Lord Levin. He is graciousness and hospitality incarnate. His English is fair, and he wants to learn all about us. He wears Levi's he bought on the black market; for him, these symbolize all that is good about Western Europe. He wears his blue jeans with braces, a distinctive fashion twist. He tells us, "You are my brothers, and so you must become my guest. This is the honor I must have. If I do not have this, we will be sad."

William, Lord Levin, and Brian in Yugoslavia.

Lord Levin is fiercely proud of his country and recounts its history for us. He insists that the Yugoslavs enjoy freedom just like the rest of Europe. The only difference, he explains, is that no one here can make large sums of money at the expense of the less fortunate. People may live in a community-owned house, which remains theirs for life, or they can choose to buy their own. A person can work in a state-owned factory or farm, or, he or she can choose to start a private, for-profit business with a limit of five employees. There is no press censorship, and the quality of life (outside of the road network) strikes me as appealing. In the evening, Lord Levin takes us to the local disco, where we meet his many welcoming friends.

Life for these young people is similar to the life that we lead back home. But here, a nationalistic pride and sense of common purpose adds another dimension. Such a welcome for two strangers wouldn't happen in England. Youths back home make it a point to show their unfriendliness to outsiders.

Lord Levin's mother is horrified to learn that the two of us are traveling on bicycles so far from home. She wants to know if we are writing regularly to our mothers. Sheepishly, we admit that contact is sporadic. Then and there, she wants to write to each of our mothers and vouch, mother to mother, that we are safe. She can't write in English, but asks us to promise that we will.

As a parting token of friendship, Lord Levin gives us each one card from a deck. These will bring us good luck, he says. I keep my queen of hearts as a bookmark in my diary. The following morning, he cycles with us for a few miles on his old black bicycle. Then he wishes us a safe trip and turns back.

Departure from Lord Levin's house.

On the main highway, we encounter a remarkable sight. Hundreds of university students, young women and men dressed in government-issue blue overalls, are working in the hot sun. They're helping to build a new motorway from Belgrade to Skopje. We stop to talk and learn that a bus takes them to and from home each day. Food and water are provided at the construction site. I see in their eyes that they're telling the truth when they say it's an honor to volunteer beneath the Yugoslavian flag, and to help build a better future for their country.

We see no evidence of people lacking in industry. We meet no people living oppressed lives. There's a strong sense of community and apparently as much well-being as at home. Where's the bleak communism portrayed in the West?

After five days, we leave hell's highway. Our maps show a secondary road that goes south from Belgrade to the mountains and on into Greece. The map does not tell the truth. The "road" becomes progressively smaller as it passes through the hills. By late afternoon it has become a cart track, obscured and dusty. The rutted way is at times impossible to cycle. Surely we're lost.

Passing through a village, we confirm we're in Prilep. And yes, this track is the red secondary road shown on our map. In England, a secondary road is a three-lane highway. We laugh at a road sign that shows the international symbol for "road narrows" and then another for "no overtaking." The only other traffic is a shepherd with a flock of goats. Is this an example of communist government at work, the signage budget approved prior to the road?

I hurtle down a hill and focus intently on the poor surface. I pass through clouds of small flies in the warm afternoon air; several lodge in my eyes and I have to fight the instinct to close them. The sun has dipped behind the hills, but I put on sunglasses; they offer no protection against inhalation, however. Several flies lodge at the back of my nasal passage and leave a bitter flavor; I don't taste the ones that go straight down.

The balmy days of midsummer and the beauty of the hills of southern Yugoslavia make for enjoyable days. I love the lazy pace here. We both enjoy having the time to do things with care. We repair our clothes and bags, and I fix my rear carrier and mudguards using broken spokes. With patience and practice, a broken spoke can be used to repair many things on a bicycle. Bamboo grows here and from a short stem, I fashion a needle holder for my small sewing kit. With a slightly larger piece, I then make a cap that makes a tight push fit onto the holder.

After Prilep, the road is lined with plum trees that are heavy with ripe fruit. We share the fallen fruit with grazing sheep and goats. We sit eating the sweet, warm flesh and gaze out over wooded hills shimmering in the heat. As afternoon turns to dusk, the setting sun bathes everything in amber honey luminescence.

We travel for days along dirt roads, enjoying the timeless beauty of the region. This was once part of the ancient kingdom of Macedonia, and later the Turkish Empire. The folk in these parts remain distant. There are no offers of tea, no smiles, and no waves. They appear distrustful of these two foreigners passing through. The buildings, farm machinery, and people are rough around the edges. We're in a country truly foreign to us.

Yugoslavian country scene from my sketchbook.

Before we left, I named my bicycle Bilbo, after the main character of Tolkien's *The Hobbit*. The Shire is Tolkien's idealized England: a green and pleasant land inhabited by people who love their gardens, order and pre-dictability. In the Shire, as in England, folks do not take kindly to those who don't conform. That book fed my yearning to travel. There are misty mountains in the distance here, and this vista places me in Bilbo's world. He did not believe he had it in him to make the journey; I'm not sure I do, either. The parallel comforts and inspires me.

Bilbo is a steel bicycle, neither lightweight nor high-tech. It's hob-bit-strong and sturdy. This is the same bicycle I rode around Europe last year. For this trip, I switched to Japanese wheels with reinforced spokes. I also added a chain wheel taken from a child's bike to the crank set; it's only slightly larger than the largest of the five rear gears. This arrangement means I have ten speeds. I also replaced the rear gear changer with a top-of-the-line Shimano to accommodate the widened range of gears. The lowest gear is almost 1:1. This allows me to cycle fully laden up even the steepest hill, but in order to go fast enough to keep my balance, I must pedal at a furious pace.

The struggle up and down dirt mountain roads continues. The dusty track ends and a brand spanking new asphalt surface starts. Incredible. There's no house or village in the vicinity. Why was such a road built in this wilderness? We race downhill, marveling at our speed and the freedom from dust. There's a church or monastery in a fold of the hills. This must explain the road.

Where the road crosses a small bridge over a dry riverbed, there's a vertical step across the road. We're traveling too fast to stop in time. I yank my front wheel up at just the right moment. The back wheel, laden down with weight, gives a stomach-turning crunch as it hits the edge of the step. Brian does the same. A sign for an "inexplicable nine-inch step across road" could have been helpful. Now both of us have a rear wheel that is a cross between a crescent moon and a twist of lemon.

I curse wildly at Yugoslavian planning in general, and Yugoslavian road builders in particular. Brian maintains his composure, and appears undaunted by the reality of two unusable bicycles. He says, "Don't swear so much. This is the stuff adventures are made of. Adventure is what we wanted, and here it is."

He has a point, so I calm down. I inspect the twisted steel of my rear wheel. Brian wanders off along the dry riverbed. He returns some minutes later with an assortment of lumber discarded by the bridge builders. We unload my bicycle and remove the rear wheel, then the spokes along the twisted section. Using a crude arrangement of rocks and timbers, we lever and bend the twisted rim into something approximating its original shape. It's a tedious process that requires some trial and a lot of error.

Hammering and coaxing the rim into shape is essential if the wheel is to spin freely inside the frame again. We replace and rethread the spokes. By progressively tightening spokes on alternate sides of the wheel, we're able to roughly true the wheel until it no longer rubs on the frame. We repeat the process for Brian's bike. The repairs must do until we can buy new rims. It's painstaking work, and it's five hours until we're on our way again.

I reflect on Brian's resourcefulness and my readiness to get upset. We discuss how different our reactions were, relating this to a book we're reading. We're taking turns reading a chapter at a time of *Zen and the Art of Motorcycle Maintenance*. We discuss the ideas as we cycle, testing them against our current experience. We are philosophical neophytes, and the ideas in the book fascinate us. The author describes the classic and the romantic perspective on reality. The romantic perspective sees the outer form and its beauty; the classic mind seeks out underlying function. Brian observes that when we stop to look at bicycles in a city shop window, his focus is on the appearance of the bicycle—the form. I want to understand the strength of the wheel hubs or quality of the gear changer—the function.

I'm eager to make sense of all that is happening, and philosophy in any form is welcome. I particularly enjoy applying the principles we read about to our everyday experiences. The realization that philosophy provides a yardstick to measure and understand personal experience is new to me and excites me to the core. Are we exploring the nature of reality and truth in a way none have before? Is this what everyone experiences as they set out on a quest for inner meaning?

 Route through Yugoslavia: Ljubliana, Zagreb, Belgrade, Nis, Skopje, Veles, Prilep and Bitola.

Five

GREECE

August 3rd

THE MOUNTAINS THAT DIVIDE northern Greece from Yugoslavia form a wilderness of dramatic scenery and a few villages. Crisp mornings, warm days, and cool evenings make for great cycling. The road down out of the mountains and toward Igoumenitsa is exhilarating. From the final pass, we fly like the wind around the switchback curves—mile after mile, with no apparent end to this glorious experience.

I have a cyclometer on the bicycle, a parting gift from my colleagues at BP. It consists of a device fitted near the axle of the front wheel that connects by cable to a speedometer and mile counter on my handlebars. Eighteen miles of downhill road fly by before I need to pedal again. It simply doesn't get any better than this.

Igoumenitsa is a small port tucked away in the northwestern corner of the Greek mainland, just below Albania. It faces the heel of the boot of Italy. Ferries shuttle from here to southern Italy and to the island of Corfu. The town sits on a crescent of flat land, nestled between mountain spurs that tumble into turquoise waters. This is a pleasant place to wait for Rudy. Brian decides after two days to take the ferry to Corfu, where his parents await. I'm sad to wave goodbye to my companion of eight weeks and twenty-two hundred miles as he pushes his bicycle up the steel ramp onto the ferry. We've grown close, and I'm going to miss him. A new phase of the journey is about to begin. Brian has been my link to things familiar. Without him, the needle moves to the right on my inner entering-the-unknown dial.

I pitch my tent in a field not far from town. Each morning, I check at the post office for the promised telegram from Rudy. I also check for letters from home via *poste restante*. This international postal arrangement allows me to receive letters at any post office, even though I've no permanent address there. Correspondents write to *poste restante*, city name, and country. The letters are kept at that post office until one claims them with identification. More often than not, the service is free. Before leaving a chosen city, I consult a map and calculate where I'll be in four to six weeks. I fill out instructions asking this post office to forward any future mail to my next *post restante* city. Of course, if I want my letters, I am then committed to go to that city. Brian and I selected Igoumenitsa as our first *poste restante* address. It's wonderful to receive news from home. There's a letter from my mother, one from my sister Claire in Australia, and one from a friend in England.

There's no word from Rudy after five days. I'm restless, so I cycle back up into the hills. About ten miles from town, I see an isolated vineyard not far from the road. The days are consistently dry, so I don't bother pitching the tent. It's wonderful to sleep out in the open, in my sleeping bag atop the sleeping pad directly on the ground. I fall asleep quickly, not long after the light drains from the sky.

Some hours later, I'm startled from deep sleep by a loud sound. It is a steady crackle, like that of a burning fire. It simultaneously terrifies and confuses me. As consciousness takes hold, I can make no sense of this noise that emanates from somewhere close by. I lie motionless in my sleeping bag, too frightened to look. The noise continues. I sit up and look about.

There's nothing to be seen. All is still under the starlit night. Trellises with dry vines march in straight lines downhill to the darkened road below. I am mystified. There's no movement of any kind, yet there's an unceasing noise from all sides. I fumble and find my flashlight. A foot away from my sleeping bag, a broad, black river flows. Enormous ants march through desiccated vine leaves covering the ground. They munch and carry off dry leaf fragments even as they go. I can only laugh at my terror and the tiny creatures that caused it.

I move my sleeping bag and look up at the stars. The adrenaline in my system keeps sleep at bay for a while, but I eventually drift off. I awake again, unsure if I'm dreaming. The sky is filled with hundreds of shooting stars. This way and that, they slash the sky; there are tens streaking across the sparkling canopy above at any given moment. These celestial fireworks continue unabated for many minutes. I am a spectator in some cosmic realm. Am I witnessing the end of the world? There can be no doubt about it. Here it is: the final grand drama. The heavens are tearing themselves apart. What a way for it all to end, here in the company of an army of insomniac super-ants. I think wistfully of the family I'll never see again, of how I'll miss them. They will never know where I was when The End came.

I learn later that it was an intense meteor shower. I had no idea that they could be so dramatic. Away from city lights, the show has a surreal brilliance. The frequency and brightness of the streaks wane after twenty minutes. The end of days postponed, I fall back to sleep.

I return to Igoumenitsa in the morning and confirm that the world is intact. Still no word from Rudy. We're in the first week of the agreed upon two-week window, yet time is passing. I don't want to get caught in cold weather in Turkey. I fall easily into a daily rhythm. I check the post office every day; the clerks know me now and shake their heads when I enter. I write letters, do some laundry, and eat lunch at a restaurant near the post office. I order the same meal each day. It's a salad that tastes sublime, that is more than the total of its simple parts: tomatoes, olive oil, and lemon juice. A heaping plate of *moussaka*—an oily eggplant dish that is delicious beyond all description—and a side dish of *tzatziki*, which is strained goat's yogurt with diced cucumbers and seasoning.

In the evening, I make my way to a restaurant at the south end of town. I sit at an outdoor patio beneath a trellis covered in vines laden with bunches of purple-black fruit. The young travelers who gather here are mostly German. We dance as a jukebox plays the Rolling Stones. We take our time sipping *ouzo*, a local spirit flavored with anise. We take less time with the *retsina*. This is a white wine flavored with the resin of the Aleppo pine, a local tree. The story goes that the Greeks added the flavor to discourage occupying Romans from drinking the limited supply of local wine. Chewing on a pine bookcase would offer the same flavor, yet it grows on you if you drink enough of it. I drink enough of it.

We watch a blood red sun sink into the Aegean Sea. Mick and the boys complain that they can't get no satisfaction, but I'm just fine in this spectacular setting. There are Greek libations, sweaty dances with German girls, and no shared language to complicate matters. During the days, I hike with these new friends in the hills around town. We stumble upon a deserted village and spend the day there. We feast on grapes and figs that hang heavy on forgotten vines and trees.

Igoumenitsa: the abandoned village.

After two weeks in Igoumenitsa, a telegram from Rudy arrives. It reads, "CUM IN 2 D RU." Now what does that mean? That he's coming today? That he's coming in two days? Or, is he asking me to go to where he is in two days? That afternoon, I meet the daily ferry. No Rudy. Nor does he show up the next day. Two afternoons later, he saunters off the ferry, smiling and tanned. He explains that telegram charges are by the letter, and he didn't want to waste money. He admits that he was tempted to not come at all.

He met a gorgeous Greek girl in Corfu. She came every day to his tent with offerings of food and treated him like a Greek god. He laughs broadly as he tells the story and does not ask what the delay meant for me. We spend the rest of the day in town and visit "my restaurant" in the evening. Rudy says it's a little loud for him after two weeks of writing and being worshipped. I'm disappointed that my new friends don't meet his standards.

We leave Igoumenitsa the next morning. Our route is back up the same mountain road that Brian and I traveled down. When pedaling uphill, I usually have no idea what's around the next bend. I struggle, but remain hopeful for a flat stretch or a little downhill break. That's not the case today. Traveling west, I'd clocked eighteen miles of downhill road. We're now traveling east. If I'm not mistaken, that means eighteen miles of uphill—a nauseating prospect.

I round a corner to see that, far ahead, the road snakes upward. We talk about "climbing a hill" on a bicycle, and climb I do: one pedal turn at a time. I sweat and mentally review my hill climbing philosophy. First and foremost is the tenet I've just broken. Don't look or think too far ahead. Just thinking about a hill can evaporate the stoutest determination. Second, focus exclusively on the next twenty feet of road. Then focus on the next twenty, and the next. As in life, one short stretch at a time is quite different from taking on a mountain. Third, conscious breathing adds enormous power. I coordinate my breathing to the turn of the pedals. Next, give the mind a productive task. I put my attention on my solar plexus. I've heard that this is the point from which energy and willpower arise. I settle into a comforting rhythm and feel the heat emanating from the area below my navel. I've energy to spare.

Another element of hill taming is a technique called ankling. Using my ankles to shift the angle of the pedal away from horizontal, I'm able to apply power around more of the pedal's 360-degree rotation. Since I have toe clips, I can also pull up somewhat with one foot as the other is pushing down. And, if a stretch is particularly steep, I weave back and forth across the available width of the empty road. This creates mini switchbacks within the width of the road and effectively reduces the incline—a trick I learned when crossing the Alps with Sharon last year. With these varied techniques to occupy my mind, the mountain loses it terror. More accurately, I forget that there is a mountain. We continue up and up, so intent on the road that we don't talk. The silent, focused effort is soothing.

In the mountains, we stop to talk with an old man and a pretty young woman. They have a horse-drawn cart unlike anything we've seen in these parts. They are traveling from France to Israel, and have been on the road for several months. They stop overnight at farms to care for the horse; they carry with them a large supply of dried oats. I thought that our mode of transportation was holistic, but this unlikely pair leaves me humbled. Truth be told, I'm happier to travel faster and cross Europe in weeks rather than months.

On a bicycle, a puncture can be a big deal. We take for granted the marvel of pneumatic tires; after all, it's just air. When a tire goes suddenly flat, the bicycle takes on a mind of its own and attempts to steer itself. If it happens at high speed, falling off is a real possibility. A sudden flat brings a sickening sensation as every dip and stone in the road is transferred through metal into my core—it isn't good for the wheel rim.

With time and practice, I've perfected my puncture repair technique. The wheel usually doesn't need to come off, and it's about a ten-minute affair. Run my fingers along the tire tread—carefully, in case there's a sliver of glass—and remove any offending object. Lever off the tire so that there are fifteen inches of space on either side of the puncture and pull out just enough of the inner tube to make the repair. Put some air in the tire to find the hole. If the hole is not apparent, dunk that section of the tube into a bowl of water and watch for the rising line of small bubbles. Dry the area, then roughen with sandpaper to provide the rubber cement a hold. Apply the cement, wait two minutes, and press on the patch. Reassemble, inflate—*et voila!*

The slow puncture and the more frequent ghost puncture are different matters. The slow puncture loses air over several days. Difficult to find, its *raison d'etre* is to strengthen my right bicep—until I concede that it's easier to find and fix it than to pump up the tire four times a day. The ghost puncture seems identical to the slow puncture, except that it does not exist.

The ghost puncture is a puncture I wish I had, as that would explain why pedaling is so difficult. The offending tire does appear flatter than normal. Surely I have a slow puncture; why else would the pedaling be this tough? I get off the bicycle and feel the tire by squeezing from the sides (more telling than squeezing from the top). Strange, the firmness between my fingers feels normal. Just in case, I connect the pump and try a few strokes. The resistance tells me that this tire has all the air it can handle. Disappointed, I realize that what's required is more effort in the legs, not more air in the tires.

Rudy is good-looking, organized, efficient and strong-willed. He is seven years older than me and has worked as a model, raced cars, and sailed to Africa. I am somewhat in awe of him. His demeanor echoes that of my father and elicits in me a complex set of responses. Imagine then, the scene in the hot, dry hills of northern Greece. I get a puncture and want to repair it quickly, lest I cause impatience in my new companion.

I invert the bicycle to stand it on its handlebars and saddle. When fixing a puncture, the most important thing to do is to clean, dry and roughen the area that needs to be glued. My sandpaper is worn, which will slow the process, so I ask Rudy if I can use his. He unpacks his puncture repair kit and carefully removes a small piece of pristine sandpaper, shaped perfectly to fit inside its box. It's rectangular, with rounded corners. *Ah! Who thinks to cut the sandpaper to exactly match the box?* After I roughen the tube, I put the sandpaper on a rock next to me. I spread the glue on the tube and wait the required two minutes before applying the patch. It's a still day, yet a sudden gust of wind lifts Rudy's sandpaper. I watch it sail over the edge of the sheer rock cliff just beyond the road. I peer over the edge and see the sandpaper somersault slowly, gracefully through the air. It disappears among some bushes several hundred feet below.

Rudy hasn't seen this happen. For a moment, I wonder if I can substitute my worn piece of folded sandpaper for the perfectly-shaped piece that's just taken wing. I feel stupid when I tell Rudy what happened. He doesn't say a lot, but the displeasure on his face is clear.

He watches me struggle to reinflate the tire with my heavy steel pump. It's great for intimidating dogs, but its tire-inflating ability is less impressive. He offers me the use of his high-tech, aluminum, made-in-Italy pump, saying, "Just be careful with it, OK?"

I'm loath to keep him waiting longer than is necessary, so I fall to and pump with gusto. I am not accustomed to this design, which attaches directly to the valve. The awkward way I must hold the pump, combined with my desire to not delay Rudy, makes for an interesting combination. After several hurried strokes, the shaft of this top-of-the-line pump simply folds in two, offering no more resistance than a drinking straw would. This time Rudy is watching. He storms over as I stammer an apology. Without saying a word, he grabs his mangled treasure from my hands. As he straightens it, the metal breaks. Bicycle pump designs trade weight with strength, and this is a very light pump. Er, *was* a very light pump.

Rudy moves slowly, as if to counter my haste. In complete silence and without acknowledging my presence, he makes an ingenious repair. Using two smooth rocks, he coaxes the tube back to its circular shape. He selects a small green branch from a tree and cuts an eight-inch piece off. With his penknife, he whittles the stick down until there's a tight fit inside the hollow tube. Matching the two broken parts precisely, he firmly pushes them together. The tight fit holds the repair together beautifully. Taking his other piece of sandpaper, he smoothes the area around the splinted fracture. The tube moves easily in and out of the body of the pump, as it did before.

Before leaving this inauspicious spot, he coolly asks me to please be careful in the future when using his things. It will be some weeks before we're able to talk about the many feelings created by this incident. In time, we'll laugh together about what happened.

We head toward the Pelion peninsula on the east coast of the Greek mainland. Rudy has a friend who vacations there; apparently it's beautiful and unspoiled. And should we wish to, we can catch a ferry to one of the islands from the nearby port of Volos. Here in the mountains, the heat is blistering. We encounter few people in this wild place. Pine forest alternates with drier areas of rocky terrain and low bushes. On one particularly hot afternoon, we come across a sawmill. Enormous sprinklers bathe towering piles of tree trunks. We strip to the waist and run to enjoy the cool water, whooping joyfully. Amid rainbows, we fetch soap from our panniers to make the shower count. This is an opportunity not to be wasted.

After a few days, the road descends, following the course of a mountain stream. It runs ten feet wide and but a few inches deep in a rocky bed. We stop to fill our water bottles and glimpse an expanse of water through a gap in the trees. A high earthen bank, rocks, and trees have forced the river into a tight turn. Here, the water has carved out a dramatic pool, twenty feet deep and fifteen feet wide. Hidden from the road, this natural wonder might as well have been placed here for our benefit. We strip naked and dive in from the overhanging bank. The cool water is perfectly clear. Large fish retreat below the overhanging bank and peer out from behind a lattice of tree roots. After the numbing heat and strain of mountain cycling, this is unalloyed bliss. We splash, scream, swim, and rest in the shade. This extended afternoon idyll will remain a highlight of the trip.

The clarity of mind that comes from daily cycling and weeks spent out in nature manifests in an unexpected manner. We keep a shared fund with which we buy our food. Using a colloquial English term, I've christened this "the pot." Following our afternoon rest one day, I ask Rudy, "How much is there in the *potiri*?" Spontaneously playing with words, I change *pot* to *potiri*, the Greek word for a glass. As I say this improbable sentence, something strange occurs. I ask Rudy what just happened and we both start to laugh. He'd said the word *potiri* at the end of my question. My brain sent the signal to my mouth and vocal cords to say this unexpected word, but Rudy, not I, said it—and the word was perfectly timed to complete my sentence. I haven't experienced anything like this before or since. We enjoy this bizarre moment; perhaps it's a sign of growing closeness.

A night with a full moon inspires Rudy and he suggests that we try cycling in the dark. The country roads are deserted, so I agree to give it a try. Cycling at night isn't common practice for one simple reason. Even with a front light, you can't clearly see the road ahead. A patch of gravel, rocks, or a pothole can send you sprawling, and neither of us has a light. We fly down steep hills through the velvety darkness. In the open, I can make out the road. As we hurtle beneath a canopy of trees, however, we enter a black void. I can barely discern only the broken white center line in the road—I can see nothing else at all. What a crazy and exhilarating experience!

We arrive at Volos, a busy city with a large port. The park at the center of town is a good place to sleep. Our plan is to ask around for work and to explore the different routes eastward. We can take a ferry from here to Turkey. Or, we can visit a Greek island and then continue to Turkey. We might cycle north into Turkey and in Istanbul cross the Galata Bridge over the Bosporus into Asia. We agree to first visit the small fishing village on the other side of the peninsula that Rudy's friend has recommended.

Rudy befriends a stray dog in the park and names him Skilos, which is the Greek word for dog. He loves dogs as much as I am wary of them. It's unclear who adopts whom, but Skilos follows us wherever we go. The days are warm, and it's pleasant to sit in the sun with Skilos lying nearby. We repair our bicycles, stitch our clothes, clean and organize our things. Over some days, the number of dogs grows until there are nine that sleep each night around us in a circle. They bark ferociously whenever anyone approaches their new protectors. Other travelers join our youth hostel beneath the stars. Each morning, we are scrutinized with curiosity (and sometimes disdain) by those on their way to work or school.

In England, itinerant Irish tinkers are promptly asked by the local police to move on. I expect this to be our fate, yet no one bothers us for two weeks. We awake one morning to find the park keeper has set up a sprinkler, and we start the day with a cold shower. I imagine a meeting of town officials, where one asks, "What can we do about this band of undesirables and stray dogs in the park? Ha! Tell the gardener to water the nearby grass while they sleep—that should do it."

And it does. That evening, we move our plastic sheets, sleeping pads, and sleeping bags to a new home: the veranda of the Greek Orthodox Church at the opposite end of the park. The clean marble is a comfortable place to sleep. We stay at our new address until early Sunday morning, when a worshipper tells us we can't sleep here "because this is a church." Was not a church once a place where travelers could seek shelter on the porch?

On the trip with Sharon, I'd adopted her vegetarian lifestyle. It was less expensive, simpler to store food, and went well with the healthy cycling lifestyle. Rudy is also vegetarian.

In Volos, we start to experiment with fasting. Sharon and I had tried three-day fasts, drinking only water and unsweetened tea. Rudy and I are curious to experiment further. We agree to fast every Sunday. A tagline from the sixties was, "You are what you eat." We see this as research into health and awareness. Sundays become a day during which we cycle less, a day of rest and contemplation. For our first Sunday fast, we sit in the sun to write in our diaries and pen letters home.

The fasting yields immediate results. I experience a clarity and lightness of mood. On Monday, my body feels rested and cleansed. The fasting makes us more aware of what we eat the rest of the time. We note that certain foods make us sluggish or ill-tempered. Easily digested foods rarely have this effect. At the start of the fast day, I may be short-tempered. As the day progresses, this gives way to a sense of well-being, a natural high.

Each Friday and Saturday evening, town residents gather along the promenade between the park and the water's edge. They dress in smart clothes, stroll in pairs or trios, and stop to talk to friends. Rudy and I dress in jeans— our best evening wear. It's a delicious sensation to feel clean, blue fabric moving against my legs, hanging down to my shoes. Quite a change from bare legs below grimy shorts. We promenade along the promenade.

We come to enjoy these weekend evenings. From a handcart, an old man sells freshly roasted peanuts and small chickpeas. The chickpeas are prepared and eaten just like the peanuts. For a few drachmas I receive a small newspaper cone filled with these warm, salty delights. They're a little tough on the teeth, but delicious. Just as salty and delectable are the giggles and swagger of the Greek girls, dressed in tight sweaters and even tighter jeans. I've seen the same girls walk by the park in the morning, dressed in navy and white school uniforms. Dressed to the nines, they appear several years older than their weekday personae. Look, but don't touch.

We do become friends with a girl we meet in the park one Sunday afternoon. She's bolder than the others. Her name is Sophia, and she's beautiful. To me, she is Sophia the Greek goddess. I study her as she talks with Rudy in German (unfortunately, she speaks no English). Oh, to kiss that sweet, full mouth... They talk, laugh and gaze into each other's eyes. I feel excluded. The best I can manage is animated sign language and an ingratiating smile. Rudy takes one of the few photographs of the trip. Sophia purses those delicious lips at the camera. Unkempt and suntanned, I stare at her intently.

William and Sophia, Volos Park.

She's a conundrum. At times, she's interested only in Rudy. At other times, she appears to want my company. Unable to fully communicate, this remains an unconfirmed fantasy. Here on Plato's turf, we reluctantly follow his advice on love. Things remain innocent, despite strong signals to the contrary from Sophia. Over the course of several weeks, the three of us spend many enjoyable evenings together. She invites us home for dinner. Her mother is another Sophia who must have been just as drop-dead gorgeous when she was young. Sophia the elder cooks us a delicious meal and clucks over us like a mother hen. These are kind and generous people. Mother Sophia insists on sewing patches onto the threadbare seat of my one pair of shorts. The patches are heavy cotton and she does a meticulous job with her sewing machine. These sturdy patches will last, as do the memories of these Greek goddesses.

We settle into a routine in Volos. During the day, we ask around for work at the docks, hoping to earn passage on a ship to any place east of here. We learn that the hulking pale blue ship that sails into Volos each Wednesday is the *Falstaff*. It carries trucks to Tartus, Syria. We ask around among the truck drivers. We ask if we can be "co-drivers" to avoid paying for passage. The idea meets with zero enthusiasm.

Since we're on a limited budget, paid work would be best. At the edge of town, there are warehouses with a line of brightly painted trucks parked outside. This is the shipping depot to Athens for vegetables and fruit grown in the area. We learn that most evenings, there's work in loading the trucks. We return each day around five to check and are soon working most days. It's heavy work. I stand ready in the back of the truck. Rudy throws me huge, clear plastic bags of bell peppers. I catch and stack them, one by one. Each bag weighs about fifty pounds. Hundreds upon hundreds of bags of this same green vegetable greet us each evening. It's fun to see how fast we can work, especially since we're paid by the truckload. I stack the bags high into the framed canvas cover of each truck. After an hour, my arms ache.

The truck drivers stand about smoking and shouting words of encouragement. They laugh and cheer as we pick up the pace. Sweat drips off me. We make friends with these rough and ready men, despite sharing only a few words. When we take a break, they offer brief Greek lessons. One of them chalks the Greek alphabet on the flat panels of his truck. We repeat the challenging sounds, and they applaud even the smallest improvement. Once the trucks are loaded, we join them in a bleak waiting area, lit by a single light bulb. We share plates of *mezedes*—savory appetizers of olive and anchovy— washed down with plenty of *ouzo*. We eat slowly; there's much talk, laughter and smoking. At ten or eleven, the trucks cough to life, belch black exhaust, and lumber off with their green bounty.

The generosity of these simple people moves me. On this journey, I encounter many like them. People who offer a ready smile, food, or a place to sleep. Many are country folk with little to spare, but who give as if they were kings hosting princes. This sense of fellowship lends texture and joy to the trip. People of the land can be trusted. Relationships are not transactions made to pursue a return on investment. Such large hearts humble me. They reaffirm humankind's essential goodness.

I also find that people reflect back to me my own attitude. If I am uncertain about others, I experience coolness in return. If I approach them with a smile and high expectations, I'm repaid in the same coin. It requires only a willingness to be vulnerable. During many encounters over the course of my journey, this theory is not often wrong. In India, I'll learn of an ancient text that states, "The world is as you see it." Now, there's a contemplation to occupy a long stretch of open road. Is the reality I experience hard fact? Or, does the lens through which I'm seeing all of this create the reality?

The work of loading up the trucks becomes intermittent. We hear about apple picking in the hills above town and leave for the orchards the next day. The road's switchbacks carry us slowly up into the mountains; the Aegean sparkles below. After a couple of hours of serious uphill labor, we crest the hill. We're among apple trees heavy with dark red fruit. We call at the first farmhouse and are greeted with enthusiasm. The apples are ready to be picked, and Nikko the farmer has no help. He's animated as he says, "The gods sent you." I can see that he's sincere. He does not notice the bicycles in place of celestial chariots and grimy shorts in place of flowing robes. Nikko speaks a little German, so he and Rudy can communicate. He hires us on the spot and shows where we can pitch our tents behind the small stone farmhouse.

We stay for eight days, steadily picking whenever there's no rain. This side of the peninsula is much wetter than Volos. So wet that we move into the one-room cottage with Nikko, his wife, father, and young daughter Maria. The family bickers ceaselessly—particularly during the evening meal, when the atmosphere buzzes with tension. Thick smoke from the wood fire fills the room each time the front door is opened. Nikko is a heavy smoker and coughs uncontrollably for minutes at a time. Maria appears accustomed to getting all she wants, when she wants it. When she motions for my pen and I don't hand it to her, she flies into a fury and attacks my legs with her small fists. I awake the second morning to find her standing over me, brandishing a burning stick from the fire, and decide it's time to move back into my tent. We learn in the village that Nikko and his father are the local alcoholics.

Nikko engaged in his favorite pastime.

Apple picking here is tricky work. The apples are the color of black tulips and are huge—some weigh more than two pounds. We use unsteady three-legged ladders called *triskellis* to work in the high trees. Once the lower fruit is collected, we climb into the trees. Rudy has the advantage, with his long arms and over six feet of height. I work the lower branches; Rudy is a fruit-gathering monkey half-hidden in the leafy heights. Nikko praises our teamwork.

There's a small store in the village of Portaria. I freewheel down the steep road to buy laundry detergent. The store stocks an odd assortment. Barbed wire and dog muzzles sit alongside tubes of vanilla flavoring and dusty cans of evaporated milk. I buy a small box of Tide and a toothbrush, and then challenge myself to see how quickly I can cycle back up the mountain. I surprise everyone with my quick return. Nikko promptly dubs me *stein* man, or "man of stone" because of my prominent thigh muscles. He says he will tell stories of his two workers: one so tall that he didn't need the *triskellis*, even for the highest fruit, and the other made of stone, who could cycle up the mountain faster than he came down it.

Nikko shares with us his personal philosophy in the form of a Greek proverb. "When you see food, eat. When you see trouble, run." And we do eat Nikko's food when we see it. We're therefore able to save every drachma we earn. We're glad to earn the money, but we're even happier when the last apple is picked. It's a relief to leave this tense atmosphere.

We continue down the mountain and along the coast to Milopotamus, our original destination. This pretty fishing village hugs a small sandy beach. Each afternoon, guests at the single hotel meet the fishing boats. They choose their evening meal, which the hotel chef prepares. We spend the night on a rock ledge just above the beach, lulled by the sounds of the surf breaking below. The next morning, we lay out our damp clothes to dry on the wide rock shelf. It's a peaceful place: great for a vacation, but of little interest for two cyclists. I agree when Rudy suggests that it's time to leave Greece. Tomorrow we'll return to Volos. From there, we'll explore the best route onward.

Drying out our things on a Milopotamus beach.

Going back up the mountain is tough. Today is Sunday, and neither of us is eating. On the way up, we stop to say farewell to Nikko and family. Climbing the final three miles is the hardest. The lack of food plus extreme physical exertion makes me light-headed. I'm oblivious to anything other than the next turn of the pedal. Is this a wise thing to do with no food in the body? Rudy convinces me to continue. I focus on my solar plexus and before I know it, we're at the summit. Lying on my back by the road, a natural high floods my senses. My experience with fasting is not one of exhaustion. Rather, it grants a temporary heightened state of awareness. What can a person do to experience this euphoric inner state without fasting, I wonder.

Volos lies directly below, and the panoramic view is spectacular. The coast stretches away on either side. Beyond lies a large bay with jigsaw puzzle edges. Small islands dot the shimmering sea. From this height the water appears solid, with a broad band of silver sunlight reflected across it.

Farther away, row upon row of blue mountains recede, then merge imperceptibly with the sky.

William above Volos at the end of the long climb.

A nip in the air suggests autumn is coming. Cooler days and colder nights speak of harder times, of difficulties to be faced. I'm sad knowing that we must move on again, yet I also feel the excitement of heading into the next leg of the journey. Crossing from Europe to Asia will be passing from the known into the unfamiliar, from the everyday into the exotic.

Volos serves up a series of dead ends. A boat to the islands and then on to Turkey costs one thousand drachmas. "Far too much for a few silly islands," says Rudy. At one hundred fifteen dollars, passage on the *Falstaff* ferry to Syria is also too expensive. So, we'll travel to Athens and from there decide the best route on to Israel. We visit the trucking office to say goodbye to our working chums. One offers to take us to Athens that very night, and we accept. We tie the bicycles to the back of an overstuffed truck and join the driver up front. We pull out into a night brilliant with stars.

The stereo blares distorted *bouzouki* music above the roar of the engine. It's a long drive. We doze. We stop for strong coffee at a depressing motorway café. We arrive in Athens at four in the morning, unload our bicycles, and say our thanks. We make our way along the streets of Athens, which is breathless with predawn stillness. We find a small park, lay out our sleeping bags on the ground, and immediately fall asleep.

As we investigate options for a route to Israel, we're unsure if it's better to arrive by sea or land. The overland route passes through Syria and Jordan: Arab countries. We know it can be difficult to enter Israel from an Arab country if you then want to reenter the Arab country. If Arab authorities see an Israeli visa stamped in your passport, they will refuse you entry. But the information we have is sketchy, so we will leave this conundrum for later.

There are many places to go via ferry from Athens, points along the Turkish and Syrian coasts, Lebanon, or maybe directly to Israel itself. Or, we could cycle northeast to Istanbul. With winter approaching, a ferry to the Greek island of Samos appears a good compromise. It's just a mile or two off the Turkish coast. From there, we can head due east into central Turkey. This plan allows us to do all the things we want: see Athens, visit a Greek island (a nice one, says Rudy), and cycle across Turkey.

For the night, we try a large park opposite the Acropolis. We awake in the morning to black clouds of relentless flies. My imagined guidebook of free places to sleep awards this spot but a single star. Great view, steeped in history, but not clean or maintained.

Packing up after a night at the park hotel.

We spend a day among the large yachts at the port of Piraeus. By afternoon, it's clear that the demand for first-time deckhands is low. There will be no free passage onward. We find a park for the night near the port. The evening routine finished, we lay on our sleeping bags in the warm night air. I award these accommodations two stars: clean, with interesting nightlife. Shadowy outlines on park benches occasionally shift and whisper. Their attention on each other, the couples don't notice us.

There are letters for me at the post office in Athens. One is from Mary McGrath, the girl Brian and I met in Bordeaux. She praises my writing and "sense of adventure." A little praise fuels a lengthy response. In reply, I rattle off six pages. Today is our Sunday fast, and I'm relaxed and clearheaded.

Fasting, reading letters, and writing long replies is a happy cocktail. Without having to prepare, down, and clean up after meals, the day is two hours longer—plenty of time for leisurely prose. I enjoy the process of writing these letters. The happy struggle is to find the phrase that perfectly captures a personal, subjective moment.

We stay one night at a small hotel called Diana the Huntress. Fifty drachmas buy a place for a sleeping bag on the flat roof. More importantly, it comes with access to a hot shower and a sink in which to do laundry. Among the rooftops of Athens is a world of red tiles, TV antennae, and small terraces with potted plants. This dimension floats serenely above the craziness below, and the respite from the street is welcome.

Greek drivers are full-fledged members of a lunatic tribe. What we English call the rules of the road do not apply. Joyfully affirming their existence to the ancient gods, drivers honk incessantly. This continues even when there are no other moving objects in sight. They change lanes and turn without warning; turn signals are a meaningless detail. The safest method of moving along the road is to match their considerable speed. I am a leaf borne along by a rushing stream. My focus is absolute, my awareness heightened. Still images emerge from the high-speed action. A patch of sunlight glistens on a truck's green bodywork. Scratches in the yellow paint around a door handle to my right. Three feet ahead of my front wheel, a small dent in the rear bumper of a speeding car. Cycling in this careening flow is an intravenous shot of adrenaline.

Clean, shaved and laundered, we seek new lodgings the next day. A small park tucked away in a residential area fits the bill. At the center of the park, there's a magnificent stone statue of a young girl. I can discern sinew and muscle beneath the skin. The Greek passion for physical grace finds expression in remarkable art. That evening we encounter Greek passion in another form. Looking for a concealed place to sleep, we push through darkened bushes and startle two gentlemen in the shadows. They must mistake us for police because they scurry away, shirttails flapping. On our third night, we awake to find that we were visited by a thief. We had left our belongings arranged on the ground next to the bicycles; oddly, the only thing that was stolen was Rudy's tent.

We take the loss of the tent as a cosmic nudge to make do with less. If you're creative, you can usually find a dry place to lay a sleeping bag. Most apartment blocks have a flight of stairs that lead to the roof of the building. In Athens, we learn that even when the door to the roof is locked, there's almost always a final landing big enough for two sleeping bags and two bicycles. In late evening, having chosen a prime apartment block, we creep up the stairs with our bicycles, the crossbar hooked over a shoulder. More than once, we meet a surprised resident as we descend in the early morning.

Away from the city, there are more options. There are houses or factories under construction, farm buildings or animal barns in fields. If there are no dwellings, there are bridges or dry watercourses that run beneath the road. I mail my tent to Rudy's home in Holland for safekeeping. We'll manage from here on without a tent—another experiment in living an alternative life. And, that's less weight for me to carry.

We each give a half-liter of blood at a nearby hospital and leave four hundred drachmas richer. We pass a lazy afternoon washing clothes under a faucet in a park and waiting for them to dry. In the warm afternoon air, it doesn't take long. On the street outside the main post office, a man sells orange plastic clockwork dogs. They leap in small circles and bark most realistically. The vendor winds one, places it near his feet, and leans over it, as if to watch it closely. But he's making the barking noise. Disappointed children will later learn that they've purchased a jumping mute.

Rudy and I have been bumping heads today. I think we should stock up on supplies for the next phase of the journey since many things are available only in a big city. Rudy thinks the extra weight is unnecessary and has faith that we'll find what we need as we go along. My resentment over this and our earlier disagreements comes tumbling out. It's a relief to talk things out. If we aspire to an examined life, then we must find ways to work these things out. I am as honest as I know how to be about my fears, vulnerabilities and hurts. Rudy does the same. I explain that I worry that I'm not good enough to be in his company, that I'm holding him back, and that my biggest fear is to be seen as a burden. Rudy shares that, while he puts on a strong front, he actually needs and values me as a companion; he would not do this alone.

We share these things and more. We talk in depth for forty-five minutes. We christen this process an "honesty session." There is only one ground rule—tell the truth, as far as you know it, and particularly about your own hopes and failings. My English heritage includes repression of emotions, especially sadness, anger or vulnerability. The freedom to express my feelings is a personal revolution. We agree that either of us can request an honesty session at any time; we will have many of these over the coming months.

I'm energized and inspired because we have found a way to turn conflict into connection. It's alchemy, and it fascinates me. The conversation deepens our bond of friendship. This process of working through difficult interpersonal issues is a stepping stone to what will one day become my profession: improving how teams and individuals work together within organizations.

On our last day in Athens, we visit the Panathenaic Stadium. It's made entirely of white marble and exudes calm permanence. It's open to the unbroken blue of the Greek sky. I love it here; I write letters and sketch. Originally built in 329 BC, it was rebuilt in 1895 for the first of the modern Olympic Games. It can seat sixty thousand spectators, yet we have the place entirely to ourselves. It's a bubble of serenity amidst a frantic modern city.

Athens, from the Olympic Stadium.

Athens, a view from the Panathenaic Stadium.

The sounds of traffic are muffled. I can see the new city sprawled around the base of the Sacred Rock, the hill that holds the Acropolis, or "upper city." Many ancient Greek city-states were built around an acropolis just like this one. On the Acropolis stands the Parthenon. From this distance, the Parthenon appears under construction and almost complete. I lie on the warm stone with my eyes closed, enjoying the sun on my face—the same sun that shone on faces in this stadium two thousand years ago. In my mind's eye, I can erase the blight of concrete and asphalt. I see ancient Athens below the noon sun. The shouts of children can be heard; dark myrtle and olive leaves shimmer as they stir in the breeze.

We return to our park in Piraeus for the night. The next morning we pack quickly and cycle to the port. A hectic scene greets us. Passengers load clothbound bundles, suitcases, chickens in cages, children, and themselves—in that order. There's a lot of shouting: mostly directions between harried crew members. The boat is filled to overflowing and underway before eight thirty. It's a long day spent on a small, crowded ferry with a thunderous motor. There's no escape, and the noise skewers my head. We arrive at midnight, and I'm in a pig of a mood. After finding an alleyway in the town of Samos, we lay down our plastic sheets and sleeping bags and immediately fall asleep.

A bemused local awakens me the next morning so his laden mule can pass. We cycle away from the port, and yesterday's foul mood evaporates. Samos is a beauty among islands in the eastern Aegean. All is quiet and calm. Olive trees and greenery abound. The morning sun is at our backs as we follow the road along the northern shore. We spy an abandoned cottage some distance from the road. It will be the perfect place to stay. It sits atop a cliff, with a stony beach a hundred feet below. The dark gray band of mountainous coastline across a narrow stretch of water confuses us, though. Our maps show no land close to Samos; we should be looking at a stretch of open water. Then it dawns on me. We are looking at mainland Turkey. The Greeks and Turks have fought bitterly over the centuries, and the sovereignty of several Aegean islands is a major source of that conflict. The Greek mapmaker did his patriotic duty by ignoring the existence of Turkey. This is our first glimpse of Asia. It's so close that a steady swimmer could get there.

Samos has several famous sons. One is the mathematician and philosopher Pythagoras, whose theorem tortures schoolchildren to this day. There are also the sculptors Rhoikos and Theodoros, who pioneered the use of bronze to make statues. Samos was at its peak in the sixth century BC, when the infamous Polycrates ruled. A local legend tells that Polycrates used to write to Amasis II, the Pharaoh of Egypt, and describe his wonderful life. One day, his Egyptian friend urged him to change his good fate to something a little less fortunate, lest he risk the wrath of the gods. Polycrates followed the advice and threw his most valuable possession into the sea. A few days later, a fisherman arrived at the palace with a big fish as a gift for the king. Inside the fish's belly, a cook found the jeweled ring the king had discarded. The moral usually drawn from this story is that one cannot change one's destiny; but there's more. When Amasis heard of the episode, he broke off the alliance, believing that any man this lucky was cheating the gods and must come to an unhappy end. In time, the Romans conquered Samos and stripped the island of its treasures. Byzantines, pirates, Arabs, Venetians, Turks, Italians and Germans all overran the island in turn. Amasis may have been on to something. In seeking to change my destiny, I've discarded a comfortable English existence. Should that be returned to me later, will I be cheating the gods?

Other travelers have clearly used this stone cottage before us; snatches of poetry have been written on the walls in charcoal. We take our chances and sleep outside, though the sky is brooding. In the night, huge raindrops hitting the ground wake us. The skies open and we bundle into the cottage. It's a single room, and one corner of the roof is open to the sky. We huddle into the opposite corner, unsure whether or not we will wake up later in a lake. But, we welcome the shelter that the walls offer from the wind. This simple dwelling is a boon now that we have no tent. It will be home for the next ten days. There's a magnificent view through the opening that was once a door. Below and to the left are the waters of the Aegean, with the silhouette of Asia Minor beyond. To the right, the mountainous flank of Samos rises dramatically. The weather here is changeable, and squalls regularly sweep through. The rain falls steadily during our first days here. I arrange my plastic sheet on bushes outside the front door so we can catch rain.

For two days, we cook and prepare food. In France, I wrote to my mother to ask for the recipe for chocolate cake we made when I was a child. I received it in Athens, and we purchased the ingredients there. The recipe uses plain semisweet biscuits, cocoa powder, milk, and sugar, and requires no baking. We also bought brown rice and several types of dried beans. Among these are some I've not seen before; they're huge, brown-green and delicious. They take several hours to cook on our small fire, but they're worth the wait. By late afternoon on the second day, we're cold, damp and happy. Seated on the floor, we eat bowl after bowl of steaming bean stew. The chocolate cake of my childhood is even better than I remember. We eat in silence as sheets of rain fall outside. The sea, Turkey, and the mountains have all disappeared. There's no place to go, no destination outside this moment in time. There is the steady hiss of falling rain, the creeping damp and the stone walls, the warmth of soup in my belly, and the sweetness of chocolate in my mouth.

The skies clear and mornings start with a pale yellow sun rising from its Turkish bed. Night chills dissolve in the welcome sunshine. The stretch of water between Samos and Turkey changes color with the weather: black, then steel, then bright turquoise in the afternoon sun. Using our bicycle tools, we repair what we can of the house. There are two open windows. On one, we coax an old pair of shutters to close. The other we block with discarded pieces of brick and stone. We sweep the floor using branches cut from the bushes outside, and set up a cooking fire in one corner. The floor is part stone, part concrete, and part dirt. We reserve the driest corner to sleep in, using bedding straw and plastic left by prior inhabitants. It becomes a home of sorts.

A paved area extends from the front door to form a small patio that leads to terraced, overgrown gardens. The fig trees and vines have no fruit; the last grapes would have been picked a month ago. The only sounds are of the occasional car passing on the road beyond the empty vines and the distant murmur of the sea below the cottage. In the evenings, we talk over cups of hot cocoa and "Dutch Chocolate Cake," as we have named it.

There's a prominent hill to the west, along the road that follows the coast. We walk to the top and the climb, combined with the heat of the day, tires us out. Atop is a tiny, whitewashed church. It's a serene place. Mountain flanks fall one after the other, directly into the turquoise sea. As the lines of falling mountain progress, they taper off until they merge imperceptibly into the distance. A small crescent bay sits where each pair of mountain shoulders meets the water. Groups of whitewashed houses with terra cotta roofs and cultivated smallholdings fill the sloping area behind each bay. From there, treed slopes rise steadily up the mountainside; this expanse of pale green trees and shrubs is broken by groups of darker green, pointed cypress trees.

I sit in the sun, my back against a cool stone wall, and observe life spread out below. I have God's view. I move my gaze effortlessly from one human life to another. In an olive grove, a man prunes trees and feeds a fire with the offcuts. Over there, two men argue and wave their arms. A car threads its way along the winding coastal road. None of them know they are being observed. The bees in the sage bushes provide a soundtrack. Other than the road and some telegraph poles, the scene is timeless. There's no new building, TV antenna, or machinery to be seen. I return several times over the next few days. I sit in God's lap and sketch the scene, or read from a copy of *Les Miserables* I found lying on the beach below our cottage.

Samos, a view west from the small church.

We cycle the forty miles around the island. The road twists back and forth, following the steep contours. The sparkling waters of the Aegean lie below; above is a cloudless blue sky. The scrubby hills release the scent of sage and wild thyme into the hot air. The glory of the afternoon stills my mind. It's a good day to be on a bicycle; life is simple and sweet. On a down-hill stretch, I focus on the road ahead, watching the surface for loose gravel. We swing back and forth across the full width of the road as we sweep downward. The scrub-covered bank to my left blocks the view around each left curve. We're traveling at over forty miles an hour.

My perception shifts, and I am no longer William Spencer riding on two wheels. A wave of exhilaration washes through me, and my awareness is one with the bicycle. I can feel through my skin the texture of the road passing beneath the tires. The bicycle is an extension of my body. I am one with the machine. I hear each nuance of the sound the tires make. I can feel the tension of the braided steel brake cables within their sheaths. I swoop around yet another bend. I make the finest adjustments to the tension in the cables as if they were the sinews in my legs. I squeeze and then release each brake exactly when I need to slow down just enough to take each bend in the road.

A thyme bush on the bank passes by at head height. There are tiny leaves and small brown patches on the gray stems of the plant. The picture enters my awareness with these small details intact, despite my speed. My cells pulse with the centrifugal outward force playing against the steep inward angle of the bicycle. The wind whips tears from my eyes as I soar down the road. I barrel out of the last bend onto an open stretch of road along the water. My momentum slows. A normal sense of self returns.

The road cuts inland a mile or two from the western end of the island, then heads south and east along the southern shore. We cross the high point in the road, and there's a dramatic change in the surroundings. Prevailing winds and rain keep the northern side of the island moist and green. The mountains block most of the rain from reaching the southern side, leaving it scorched and dusty, threadbare. Rocks jut through dry soil to reveal the island's stony skeleton. There are few houses here.

We visit the fishing village of Pythagorion, named after he of the theorem. It sits facing Turkey on the southeastern end of the island. We explore the small port where fishermen hang nets to dry in the sun; we ask around to see if anyone's willing to take us the short distance to Turkey. We want to avoid the exorbitant price of two tickets for the only ferry that plies the Samos-Turkey route. The fishermen explain in broken English that they won't venture into Turkish waters. Gunboats patrol the narrow stretch of water. Rudy and I discuss the feasibility of building a raft and rowing the short distance, but we imagine that a Turkish gunboat is likely a bit of boat plus a lot of gun. We'll pay the ferry fare.

We sleep near the port on our last night in Samos, ready for the morning ferry that leaves at six thirty.

Route through Greece: Florina, Kastoria, Igoumenitsa, Ioannina, Kalambaka, Volos, Athens, Piraeus, and by ferry, to Samos.

Six

TURKEY

October 25th

OUR LAST DAY IN EUROPE starts with toes numbed by a cold night; winter
approaches. The ferry from Samos to Kusadasi is a *Through the Looking
Glass* experience. A comically short journey carries us into another dimension, carries us from the pleasure park of Europe into the mysterious lab-
yrinth that is Asia.

My belly tightens; I don't understand the rules here. To expect English
fair play is naive. Men on the street have a whiff of danger about them. The
buildings and people are unkempt—just plain dirty, someone from Holland
might say. We choose a modest restaurant, and the waiter brings several
small plates, each holding a single item: delicious pale beans in an oil and
lemon dressing, stuffed green peppers, and a tangy lentil dish. It's a memorable meal. While the dishes are unfamiliar, I can recognize most of the
ingredients. Perhaps life here contains familiar ingredients combined in
unfamiliar ways, cultural seasonings with flavors I can't yet appreciate.

People live and work here. There are places to eat, shops that sell
bread, hardware and clothes. Those walking the street breathe, smile and
talk. The familiar is the weft woven through this woof of strangeness. My
inner voice of reason tells me these things. My emotions pay no heed and
jangle with caution.

We cycle to the Roman ruins at Ephesus. This is one of the early strong-
holds of Christianity. Legend says that buried here are both the apostle
John and Mary, mother of Jesus. Things are geared toward tourism. Plastic
furniture and signs in English lend a tacky familiarity. After three hours,
I'm on overload. I want only to get away from the many Turks and tourists.

We cycle toward Selçuk and pass into the real Turkey. Farm workers
pick cotton in a field by the road. I feel out of place. On a bicycle in Europe,

we merge with the countryside; only a horse and cart does it better. In Selçuk, with our fancy bicycles, we're neon art against timeless Islamic blue tile. This comes as a rude shock. Is cycling really the perfect mode of travel I assume it to be? Why is this all so strange? I try to reason my way through it, but the culture shock is real. This is my first time in Asia. Turkey is the poorest and dirtiest country I've visited. I so want to be comfortable with the Turks, but I'm aware they belong to another tribe.

In Selçuk, we drink tea with two American girls we'd met earlier on the ferry. We depart at eleven that evening and travel east on the main road. It's a road we'll follow for many miles. The night is cold. A full moon provides just enough light to see by, and a steady uphill slope slowly warms me from within. The scenery glides past as indistinct patches of semi-darkness.

Two heavily armed policemen flag us down. They seem startled by two figures emerging soundlessly from the night. After several failed attempts at communication, we exchange smiles and handshakes. They wave us on our way. Some miles later, we arrive at a picnic area. There's an open shelter that appears comfortable enough, but warnings about thieves are fresh in our minds. The safest place is on top of the small shelter's flat concrete roof. We haul everything up, including the bicycles, to our strangest hotel room yet.

The next morning, we awake to a green river valley with dry hills in the distance. As we cycle east, toward the hills, our surroundings slowly change. By day's end, we're in a semi-desert. The following day, we enter the wide valley of the Menderes River. We learn that mandarin orange orchards are an ideal place to sleep. They're generally clean, and the low trees hide us from the road. Being heavy with fruit, they also provide breakfast. We travel steadily along the valley floor, and a distant line of mountains slowly emerges ahead. The road leaves the valley, and we proceed up into the mountains of Anatolia. We're headed due east into the heart of Turkey. When we reach the city of Isparta, our plan is to then turn south toward the Mediterranean. From there, we'll again travel east, following the coast.

We arrive in Denizli, a large Turkish city. To my European sensibilities, it's generally oppressive. The few well-dressed people contrast with many dirty faces and torn trousers. The side streets are made of dirt. There's little that is aesthetically pleasing. Large loudspeakers and trailing wires mar the grace of mosque minarets. The voice of the muezzin calls the faithful to prayer in distorted tones that jar more than uplift. I imagine an amplifier in some dusty corner of each mosque, with its dials turned to the extreme right. How were worshippers reminded of their religious duties in the days before electricity?

The traffic is a malevolent being, and it swallows us. Cars and trucks pass dangerously close, adding aggression to the already unpleasant atmosphere. They sound their horns simply to announce their presence. It's painfully loud. There's no escaping this, and it makes me angry.

Here, there's no minding your own business—that building block of English culture. We stop to buy food and are mobbed by curious Turks. A sea of not-quite-friendly faces and yellow teeth hovers just inches away. They shout at us in Turkish, as if volume will aid comprehension. I discern two distinct races. One is light-skinned and European in appearance; the other is dark-skinned and brown-eyed. The phrase "in your face" perfectly describes this crowd. I have a visceral reaction that sends my emotions reeling. *Oh my goodness, get me out of here. Please.*

Leaving Denizli, we take a short detour north to Pammukkale, which is famous for its ruins and hot water springs. Calcium-laden water from the springs flows down the side of a hill. Over time, the mineral deposits have formed many small, scallop-shaped pools. Steam rises from these pure white terraced pools: an otherworldly, many tiered, steaming wedding cake.

We choose a place to rest below a copse of pine trees in a Byzantine graveyard. Rudy and I argue about something inconsequential. The pattern of our periodic, intense arguments is clear. We argue, then hold onto silent anger for several hours. I mentally rehearse my position on the issue so as to justify myself, and I imagine Rudy does the same. One of us calls for an honesty session, and we talk things through. The air is clear, and we are the best of friends until the next argument. We stay in this charming spot for the night. Sleeping under various trees, I've come to learn the character of each one. This affects the quality of sleep I have beneath it. Like a wise friend, a fig tree offers comfort, and I sleep deeply. Sleep under an olive tree is accompanied by disturbed dreams. Pine trees like these hold mystery and grant me only restless sleep.

Around us, hot water flows through small channels under the trees and across the open ground, sometimes hidden by grass. When we awake, these channels steam in the cold morning air. I wash my hair in the abundant free hot water. What a delicious luxury! A shepherd with a herd of cows stands nearby, curious. He invites us to join him for breakfast, which turns out to be sweetened hot milk. Our new friend repeatedly asks what items we have to sell or what we might want to buy. Thank goodness breakfast is just milk; the conversation would ruin the digestion of anything heavier. Rudy buys a silver coin the shepherd says he found among the ruins. Later, back in Holland, Rudy's hopes of a handsome profit are dashed. The coin is a contemporary copy of an old one. I imagine the shepherd had several to sell to gullible tourists.

We stay a second night and have a magnificent start the next morning. Beyond the trees where we slept lies an open area of springy turf with a deep, natural hot water pool. A thick mist completes the surreal quality of the moment. It's before dawn, and we take a long soak. The morning sun slowly warms the air. After an hour, we reluctantly climb out. It's the end of October; the warm morning and cloudless blue sky are a delight to the senses.

We return to the main road and head east again, deeper into the remote regions of central Turkey. Our map shows this road as the E24, one of three major east-west routes, yet it is narrow and deserted.

We generate strong reactions as we cycle through the large town of Aydin. Young girls look and giggle, women turn their faces away, and men stare aggressively. Rudy suggests that our short trousers and bare skin are the problem. The English equivalent might be visitors walking naked down Oxford Street in London. We must appear as uncaring foreigners, openly flouting their traditions. We decide to wear long trousers from now on. Cycling will be more difficult, but there's little choice as we travel into yet more remote areas.

The long trousers immediately address the problem. We meet a young man who speaks German. He explains that, if we were Turks, our bare legs would be cause for lynching. Bare skin is an affront to local faith and customs. He says that the only reason for restraint toward us is that the police come down hard on anyone who attacks a tourist, but only because the tourist pays the fatter bribe.

But something more is going on, something we don't understand. We have heard about this from other travelers. We pass a group of young boys playing by the roadside. They appear friendly enough, but a few small stones whizz past my head when the boys are behind me. While the stones are not large enough to cause serious harm, the intent is clear. I'm unsettled by this overt act of aggression. We must represent some threat to these people, but we don't know what. Our best guess is that they sense their traditional way of life is threatened by Western values. And they're right, of course. In a paradoxical twist, we're unwitting representatives of the very values we seek to question.

Turkey is a strange immersion into things unexpected and new, simultaneously disorienting and exhilarating. I struggle to understand these people: stones thrown at my head, their anger at bare skin, in-your-face curiosity, and being honked at by drivers who appear to want to force us off the road. This is unsettling and depressing. The deeper we travel into Turkey, the more intense it becomes. The landscape lacks things my eye expects: houses, telegraph poles, pavements, side roads, and road signs.

Yet positive forces buffer the culture shock. Our daily routine is a potent combination of hours of aerobic exercise, wholesome food, fresh water, nature all around us, sound sleep, early starts, weekly fasts, and plenty of time. I feel wonderfully alive and present. My lifestyle in England consisted of questionable food, a steady intake of alcohol, irregular sleep due to shift work, and little exercise. I drove everywhere. I spent a lot of time with electronic media: music, TV and computers. Now I have time to breathe, to see, to feel, and to reflect. What I see and feel at present is difficult, yet I am supported from within.

A bicycle is as much a tool of contemplation as of travel. It provides a lot of time to think. I've read that if I want to change the world, I must start with myself: with my own mind, heart and actions. The idea is both frightening and empowering. It requires a deeper sense of personal responsibility. I can be depressed by the state of the world and the many forces beyond my control. Or I can focus on those things within my control. I can address things in my immediate world. This is why I'm on the bicycle: to learn what I can do and how I should do it.

The road climbs steadily upward. Far below us, a camel caravan moves slowly along the valley floor. There are some twenty camels roped together, with people walking alongside. We round a bend to find ourselves among banana plantations. Camels and banana trees: two firsts in two minutes.

Our surroundings become progressively more barren and burnt. In the distant purple haze, higher mountains begin to emerge. Days are cold and windy. There's a bank of ominous clouds on the horizon most evenings. It gets closer each day. Only the occasional tree breaks mile after mile of straw-colored openness. These trees reveal that autumn is here; their gold and red leaves things of beauty in this stark setting. Finding a place to sleep requires creativity. At the end of a particularly long day on an empty road, we're forced to stop as the last light of day drains from the sky. We're on the lower slopes of a line of craggy mountains. Below us lies a vast salt lake. We choose a place beneath a lone tree of thorns. It offers only a hint of protection from the elements, but there's no better option in this wilderness.

The scene before us is spectacular. A khaki-colored plain stretches away from us; the road is a thin black line across the dun expanse. At the edges of the lake, dried salt forms a wide margin of pure white. Within this belt of white, bands of water reflect neon pink from the evening sky. The broader watery bands mirror the misty mountains beyond. The mountains and their reflected triangles form huge diamonds of gray floating in incandescent pink. We're alone in a kaleidoscopic wasteland. We sit in silence and watch the color drain from the sky. Our map shows this is Lake Acigol, which means, "bitter lake." *Bitter* must refer to the salt. For us, it refers to how bitterly cold it gets as the temperature plummets with the sun's passing. We're in the open, and a sharp wind does its worst. I find no warmth in my flimsy sleeping bag. Rudy says that he heard the howling of wolves last night. The cold, the wind, and thoughts of a night attack keep sleep at bay for a long time. I awake with numb feet before the first light of day. We pack our things as fast as fingers stiff with cold will allow.

It's oddly energizing to not know where we will sleep each night. There's an elemental joy in seeking out shelter. Each evening we cycle and scan the countryside for structures other than houses. Barns are a good choice if the occupants are elsewhere—a small stone hut for sheep with just enough room for two sleeping bags is ideal. We sweep out the dried animal dung and lay our plastic sheets on the floor, then fall asleep after the last light of day drains from the sky.

Dreams of England accompany these cold nights, and I awake confused to find myself in a cold barn in Central Anatolia. Most mornings, we're on our cycles and underway as the sun lifts itself up from the mountains. Only then does the chill leave my core.

As we leave a particularly drafty barn early one morning, we discover that both tires on both bicycles are flat. There are twigs on the ground with needle-like thorns. We hadn't seen them when we arrived under the cover of darkness. We each have multiple punctures in both tires. The morning starts with the many repairs. We work slowly with numb fingers for two hours; clean the inner tube, apply rubber cement, and press on a patch. We carefully check the inside of the tires themselves and remove several thorns. We then carry our bicycles two hundred yards to the road.

Our expenses are low, about two dollars each per day. I hope we can reach Israel with the thirty-five dollars I have in Turkish lira. We supplement our dried goods with bread bought in villages. One day, we stumble upon a gift. Overspreading a sloping bank along the road outside a village is a vine, and among its huge leaves we spy a lone squash. We give thanks for this unexpected blessing. Too large to carry as is, we cut it into pieces and store it in plastic bags. It is just sweet enough to be eaten raw—sort of. For the next ten days, this is our staple. We eat it uncooked, boiled, mashed, and sautéed with a little oil. But rumbling stomachs and rampant farting become too much to bear, and we do the unthinkable. We discard food.

After ten days in Turkey, we reach Isparta. This is our next *poste restante* address. While Rudy heads into the post office to collect our mail, I sit with the bicycles on the steps outside.

In mere moments, a crowd of perhaps a hundred boys and men forms. The few females who pass don't appear to register my presence. The assembled males stand and stare, unabashed. With fair hair, blue eyes, odd clothes, and a strange bicycle, I am a creature from another world. The staring is difficult for me to bear. My English upbringing tells me to be discreet and not look at anyone for too long. I feel awkward and angry that I'm suddenly the center of this silent, unbroken attention. I am a specimen under a microscope. The Turkish sense of personal space is also quite different from the English. The crowd presses in, too close for comfort. They all appear happily unaware of how threatening I find this. I try not to mind, but my reaction is visceral, beyond conscious control.

A man in the crowd speaks in German to Rudy and invites us for tea. He has spent time in Germany as a *gastarbeiten*, or "visiting worker." In the tea shop, our host appears to enjoy the attention from his fellows, who crowd around our table. The staring, the squalor, and the thrown stones are unexpected. But so is this generosity from strangers. Turkey threatens one moment, and welcomes the next. Like the wind we encounter on the open plain, we never know when it will change. An unprompted act of largess may follow an act of hostility. There's no making sense of this platter of emotional scrambled eggs: anger to guilt and back again.

We leave Isparta by the last light of day and cycle a few miles out of town to look for a place to sleep. As the light fades, we see several natural caves in a cliff face across a narrow valley. One of these is a perfect fit for two people and two bicycles. We build a small fire and settle in for the night. Rudy and I have several letters each from the post office. Those who wrote to us would be surprised if they could see us now. We huddle round the guttering light of a single candle in our shallow cave. All is quiet in the starlit darkness outside.

A postcard from my father shows golfers on a serene English golf course. On the reverse, he offers cryptic advice about carrying a gun. He writes that he can personally recommend the Smith and Wesson .38. The card ends with, "Carry a big stick always. All love, Father." When speaking of US foreign policy, President Teddy Roosevelt used the West African proverb, "Speak softly and carry a big stick; you will go far." My dad omits the first part. The phrase mutated into big stick diplomacy, a permission slip for bullying neighbors balking at Uncle Sam's wishes. I'll practice the speaking softly part, thank you. A big stick approach here would quickly land us in hot water. "Carry a big stick always," said in a British major general accent becomes a one-liner sure to inspire a giggle between Rudy and me when the going is tough.

We continue our in-depth metaphysical conversations. After all, we were children who came of age in the waning days of flower power. Letters from home become springboards into deep discussions about family, society, and the values with which we were raised. I seek to better understand my own Englishness. The values I question are burned deep into my being, so this is an exercise in stepping outside my comfort zone.

One letter is from Sharon. She's back home after a trip to Turkey of her own. She complains at length about the Turks' attitude toward women. She spent two weeks in Cappadocia and was constantly harassed—men leering, getting too close, and brushing against her backside or her chest. And then they'd laugh among themselves.

Turks live in a conservative society that bans sexual activity before marriage. But modern media surrounds them. Many popular Western movies and TV shows include scenes where sexual activity is shown or suggested. Young Turkish men have come to believe that Western women are sexually available. They lack awareness of sexual boundaries in the West and how these regulate male-female relationships. Turkish male behavior toward female tourists is often threatening. The respect with which they treat their own women is a paradox. In a debate about women's rights, the Westerner points to the lack of social freedom for Muslim women. The Muslim argues that by limiting a woman's interaction with nonrelated men, they assure her of respect and safety. They say that women in the West have lost their dignity through unfettered sexual freedom. But the issue is not as simple as it first appears. An American or Brit might say, "We have it right, and they have it wrong." But he or she is unaware of the subtle cultural, historical and religious dimensions involved.

More bright, cold days follow. We're headed south through the Taurus Mountains. The morning sun illuminates what leaves remain on the trees. The yellows and reds are a startling contrast to the backdrop of angular gray rock. A group of nomads moves slowly along the road. They have five camels, many children, and countless goats and sheep. They must be an unusual sight since they compete with us for the attention of the few passing cars. We stop to buy milk at a farm, but the farmer will accept no payment. While we wait for the cow to be milked, the farmer and his wife invite us into their house and ply us with tea and apples. I feel guilty about the apples. We already helped ourselves, not half a mile up the road.

A farm tractor slowly passes us on a long, uphill stretch of road. We each catch hold of one corner of the trailer. The driver appears to be about our age. He looks back and smiles, enjoying the joke of two people stealing a ride. We smile back. At the top of the hill, he pulls over and invites us to his home. An hour later, we're in the town of Bucak, seated cross-legged around a low circular table. Our host pours a bowl of rose water for us to wash our hands in and then provides fragrant hand towels to dry them.

We enjoy a sumptuous meal with Mesut and several male friends. We communicate through mime and drawings, describing where we're from, where we're going, how old we are, and that neither of us has a wife or fiancée. We know from experience that these are the usual topics of interest. We can't communicate much more. I'm uncomfortable with the silence and wonder if our hosts feel the same. To be a guest and not be able to share ideas is hard.

Mesut's mother, sisters and grandmother hurry back and forth. They ensure that the men want for nothing. I follow Mesut's lead when it comes to how one should relate to the women. We've been told that contact is limited between unmarried women and men. Women are not often seen in public outside of the cities. We see twenty or thirty males for every female. In Mesut's house, interactions with the womenfolk are formal. He speaks a few words with his mother and sisters, but the women do not talk to the other men, and they do not talk among themselves in our presence. They don't remain in the room for long. We come to learn that this is typical.

We're given the main room of the house for the night. Our host brings us sheets, pillows, and down quilts. The colorful bedding is warm; it smells clean and inviting. We are treated with great respect and honor, as if we were foreign princes on a state visit. We accept Mesut's invitation to stay another day.

The day begins with a wonderful breakfast of bread, olives, cheese, honey, a bowl of spicy chickpeas, and sauce in which to dip the bread. It's all accompanied, of course, by endless cups of tea. If our hosts are surprised by how much we eat, they don't show it. We're taken around the village as honored guests. Mesut's friends include a barber and a tailor. The barber gives us each a detailed shave, the best I've had in a long time. The tailor repairs various holes in our clothes. We offer to pay for these services, but they all adamantly refuse. We sit in the local café, and our hosts insist on paying for the many cups of tea. This freely given kindness humbles me.

The evening finds us back in the tea shop, surrounded by locals who study our every movement. I consider the noteworthy differences between this Turkish tea shop and my local pub back home. Here, the proceedings are sober, cheap and always good-natured. Locals noisily play rummy, but with plastic tiles instead of cards. A variant of checkers takes the place of the dominoes or darts I'd see back home. The playful communal spirit here stands in contrast to the alcohol-fueled camaraderie of a pub. And, of course, there are no women and no beery flirtations.

Smoke-filled air is common to both tea shop and pub. The locals smoke even more than the Brits. To be sociable, I accept a cigarette. Turkey may have the best tobacco in the world. Their unfiltered oval cigarettes taste smoother than any others. I've smoked since I was thirteen years old. A teenage boy in England who doesn't smoke is a social misfit. The health dangers were known but never discussed. I've been trying without success to give up. I assume that it's my lack of willpower; I don't yet understand that nicotine is more addictive than heroin. My smoking continues during this journey. It will be many years before I finally kick the habit.

Over more tea the next morning, we say goodbye. The road drops down and out of the Taurus Mountains toward the Mediterranean coast. We quickly cover the forty miles to Antalya. This westernized city has shops displaying imported consumer goods. Alongside these modern stores are the usual signs of poverty: shabby restaurants, a cooked sheep's head at a butcher's, and small children selling cigarettes. We plan to stay one night at a hotel and, when we leave, to take two blankets. We each want to make ourselves a poncho to protect against the bitterly cold nights. I'm not sure why it doesn't occur to us that we should just buy two blankets, but our penny-pinching protects us from our shameful intentions. The place we choose is so inexpensive that only one blanket is supplied per room, and its absence would be immediately apparent.

However, the rooms do offer an unexpected benefit. With our own lock on the door, we're able to leave the bicycles behind. We have remained with them every moment since we left Samos, afraid they'd be stolen. To walk about without them is a welcome change.

We sample some local food and then enjoy tea in a smart restaurant with wood paneling and modern furniture. My senses tell me I'm back in England. When oddly shaped tea glasses arrive, I'm brought back to the present. Relief unexpectedly washes over me as we emerge from the orderly cocoon and return to the mayhem of the street. Despite the challenges, I'm happy in the rawness of life here. No, I am more than happy. My being hums with satisfaction. This is the adventure I sought.

We spend the next day in a tea shop by the port. This is our day of fasting, a time for introspection. We write letters and talk. We discuss the implications of Westerners traveling through poor nations. Rudy wonders if we're making a mistake by traveling here, transmitting our values and eroding the very thing we've come to see. What are the implications of demanding familiar things, foods and settings? Shouldn't every tourist be sensitive to this dynamic? For better or worse, we are ambassadors of Western civilization. Our actions directly shape perceptions. We understand that being a tourist is a responsibility that calls for conscious awareness.

The recent cold nights serve as a reminder that we must keep going toward Israel or feel the brunt of winter. We leave Antalya in the afternoon. The cycling along the coastal plain is easy. The evening arrives, and we're unable to find a place to sleep in this populous area. We need help in finding a place to camp, but hesitate to ask because we need a break from guesthood. The hours of tea drinking and unsuccessful attempts at communication have been draining. We gently but firmly decline the offer to stay with the man we ask about a camping spot. With true Turkish hospitality, he shows us to a fine place beneath a huge sycamore tree by a river.

Spending three nights in a bed has its price. I don't sleep well, and it's a struggle to get up in the morning. I hope to readjust soon so I can once again rise happily before the sun. Part of feeling safe when sleeping outside is leaving at first light. If we sleep past daybreak, people could see us and then we'd be defenseless. Or, that's how it feels. We've been in Turkey seventeen days, and today we're both homesick. I feel far from England. The longing to be back in familiar surroundings is almost overwhelming. Then the feeling leaves as unexpectedly as it arrived. A friendly tea shop owner and the beauty of the shoreline come together to lift my spirits.

As we continue to follow the shore, all turns green. Mountain slopes are cloaked in pine forests, and the coastal plain holds date and banana plantations. Scalloped bays of sand edge sparkling waters. We're in a Bacardi Rum poster, complete with setting sun, palm trees, beach, and iridescent turquoise water. Near Alana, we settle down on a beach for the night. We cook dinner on a fire of driftwood. The evening is breathless, the sea oddly motionless. We fall asleep to the gentle lapping of tiny waves.

The road follows the shore. It climbs mountain spurs that tumble down into the sea. It then plunges down to the water again. The regular rise and fall of the road, plus a strengthening headwind, makes cycling heavy work. Long trousers and long-sleeve shirts make it harder still; I am sweaty and sticky. Before Turkey, I wore only shorts on days like this. We try T-shirts with long trousers, but angry shouts from passing vehicles tell us that we should also cover our arms.

We stop to eat lunch on the beach at one of the small bays. There's not a soul in sight, so I strip to my briefs to swim. I'm feeling Victorian about my bare skin as I cautiously head toward the water. Shouts emerge from a nearby banana plantation; several workers appear from the wall of green, waving their fists. Begrudgingly, I cover myself.

That night, we stop near Gazipasa. We talk in the dark about social mores and sexuality. Rudy has me in stitches with a story about his mother when he was a teenager. She'd learned somehow that he was masturbating. He got into bed one night to discover a scrubbing brush there. Given her provincial Dutch upbringing, this was the best she could do to let him know that, in her world, what he was doing was unclean.

We get an early start and set a goal for today of one hundred kilometers. The roller coaster shoreline continues as rocky hillsides drop dramatically to the water. There's no coastal plain, only short stretches of beach between steep falls of rock. There's no sign of human habitation among the steep, rocky ground covered in pine trees. The road snakes and clings to the contours. This is the wildest place through which we've passed. I'm surprised to see a herd of black goats with horns twisted into fantastic shapes among the trees above us. Against the odds, they maneuver the sheer mountainside. I glimpse a young girl with the goats. She shouts and throws stones to keep them from straying.

The steep inclines are grueling, dispiriting. We struggle up each sharp hill only to turn a corner and face a crazy descent. The bends in the road are so sharp we must brake and lose the downhill momentum. After each downward plunge, another tortuous climb awaits.

A farm tractor with a low trailer passes, and I grab hold. The driver doesn't notice a thing above the roar of the engine, but this is still tricky business. I hold my handlebars unsteadily with one hand, and the trailer with the other. My face is an arm's length away from the board sides. I can see nothing of the road, so there's no warning before my front tire hits a patch of gravel.

The next moment, I'm sprawled on the road with the bicycle beneath me. I'm winded, and my knee is badly scraped. Loose gravel is the cyclist's lurking enemy. When you hit a patch, the small stones act as rollers, and the bike may as well be on greased paper. Doing anything other than traveling in a perfectly straight line causes the front wheel to slip sideways and the bicycle to fall. A bicycle needs only the narrowest strip of solid surface over which to roll. In Europe, that's a given. The potholes and gravel here mean I must remain keenly attentive. I recall all of this as I lie tangled with my steel steed. I've come off the bike two times in four thousand miles. Could be worse. The only real damage is my pride. I continue up the sharp incline under my own steam.

After one particularly long climb, the road again plunges down to sea level. We hurtle down the twisting road at fifty miles an hour. The wind roars, bringing tears to my eyes—an adrenaline-filled reward after the hard labor of the day. We make camp for the night on a pristine beach. There's not one piece of plastic, paper, or any man-made thing to be seen. How many such clean beaches are left in the world? Not many, I fear.

For dinner, we enjoy a "tea and toast session." We toast bread on the fire and drink many mugs of the local mountain herb tea brewed in one of Rudy's two small pots.

We're awake half an hour before the sun and are greeted by a rust red sky alight with the first glow of day. Across the water, we can just make out a form of mountainous land. This must be Cyprus. We're near Anamur, the southernmost point along this coast. We have been traveling southeast. Now, we'll continue east and slightly north.

A young man invites us to join him for tea at his home. His English is good enough for us to understand. We ask about the greeting we hear repeatedly: *salaa'am a lei'kum*. He explains that this is used throughout the Muslim world. It means, "Peace be upon you." The proper response to *salaa'am a lei'kum* is *w'alei'kum salaam*, or, "And unto you be peace." He also explains that it's a religious duty of Muslims to take care of the traveler in need. If we respond with *w'alei'kum salaam*, the person to whom we are talking is bound by faith to provide us with what we need.

The next day we pass two men winnowing peanuts from their shells. Using rakes with long tines, they toss the peanuts into the air. A strong wind blows away the light shells; the heavier peanuts drop to the ground. As we approach they greet us, "*Salaa'am a lei'kum*." As if we'd been doing it all our lives, we respond, "*W'alei'kum salaam*." We mime that we want to buy some peanuts. One of the men walks to a nearby house and returns with a large bag of the nuts. He also offers us fresh, frothy milk, which we gratefully pour into an empty jar. He refuses payment.

Over time, something in me shifts. I reflect on what it means for two human beings to greet each other in this manner, wishing one another peace. The English "hello" pales by comparison. After some weeks, I can no longer use the greeting to obtain what I want. I use it as it is intended. The sacredness of this salutation does not lend itself to abuse.

I'm happy to leave the mountains behind. There are long stretches of plains with the occasional small hill. The road follows the coastline again, and in many places the beach meets the edge of the road.

We crest a low rise to see a remarkable site. In front of us, to the right of the road, is Mamure Castle. The Crusaders built this structure on the foundations of a former Roman fort. In the eleventh century, a Seljuk Turkish Sultan captured and rebuilt it in its present form. This crenellated medieval wonder sits half on the shore and half out on the water, and is remarkably well preserved. Inside, a walled, grassy courtyard provides shelter from the outside world. The stone walls are pleasantly warm in the still air. There's a hand pump set above a smooth flagstone.

I strip to my briefs and crouch beneath the pump. By working the long lever with one hand, I manage a pseudo-shower while Rudy naps. *Aaah.* After weeks of long trousers and long-sleeve shirts, it feels so good to have the sun on my skin. In one corner of the courtyard stands a large fig tree. There are a few fruits on it. We enjoy the pink flesh, warm with the afternoon sun. A doorway in the southern wall leads to a narrow strip of beach. I swim in the calm water. It's warm for this time of year. We enjoy an afternoon in this tranquil place. I write in my diary and lie in the sun with my eyes closed. I fall asleep and wake feeling completely renewed.

That night we sleep near the empty road beyond Ovacik. It's so warm that it could be summer. In the night, I have a striking dream. Rudy and I are in a large meadow of weeds and long grass. We use our bicycles like scythes. With synchronized, rhythmic motions, we cut broad swathes in the meadow. In time with the cutting, we chant a singing rhyme. In the song, we name each kind of weed precisely at the moment we cut it. A visceral joy floods my body. The dream leaves me feeling vibrant and alive. The mood stays with me through the next day.

The road passes through glorious country. After a pine-clad stretch of rocky wilderness, we emerge onto a plain of banana plantations and orange groves. This is the Cilician coast, the most beautiful coastline in Turkey. It is rich in history. Shakespeare described a meeting that occurred here between Mark Antony and Cleopatra:

For her own person,
It beggared all description: she did lie
In her pavilion—cloth-of-gold of tissue—
O'er picturing that Venus where we see
The fancy outwork nature.

Cleopatra's charms did the trick. Mark Antony gave to her this entire Cilician region as a wedding gift. And what a wedding gift! The land is in turns wild, then benign and fertile. Probably how Mark Antony hoped his new wife would be.

The day turns overcast and cold. The Taurus Mountains again shoulder into the Mediterranean. The road weaves, rises and falls along the rugged hills. As the day advances, a wind stirs and then intensifies. The cycling gets progressively harder. Coming over each rise, the full force of the wind hits us in the face. Pure misery. When it gusts, I have to dismount and push the bicycle, my body braced against the wind. We come to a wide, curved bay framed by two enormous mountain shoulders. These two headlands concentrate the wind into a formidable force.

I place my bicycle on the windward side and lean strongly into it. This walking triangle arrangement offers just enough stability to struggle forward. It's a battle just to remain standing. A schoolgirl in a navy and white uniform clings to an iron post, her arms wrapped tight. A line of twelve more girls hangs on to this anchor by each holding the waist of the girl in front of her. We slowly pass, and they remain there, unable to move on or let go. Their faces are covered with matching navy headscarves that snap wildly in the wind. We can offer no help; the iron post is their best hope. In the evening, the wind dies down somewhat.

We find a low, circular stone enclosure not far from the road. There will be no better place to sleep tonight. We're both exhausted and short-tempered. Rudy says he may be ready to head home soon. Despite the difficulties, I know I want to continue. The benefits outweigh the costs, as they say. In the night, the wind starts up again. I don both my sweaters and all three pairs of socks in an attempt to keep warm. It fails.

The next day is windy, too. We meet a young German couple traveling in a Volkswagen van and stop to chat. They carry with them all the familiar conveniences and interact little with the locals. They are pleasant, but appear not to understand when Rudy and I describe our positive experiences of Turkey. Later, Rudy voices frustration at this insensitivity to local culture. "It's like traveling with ten gold watches on each arm," he says.

As evening falls, we come across another castle by the water. This one is in ruins. Two tumbledown walls meet in a corner that provides some shelter from the wind. Lying in our sleeping bags we discuss the wind that slows us to a walking pace. Why is this so very frustrating? Yes, it foils our expectations. But there's no reason to hurry. We've been caught by the winter, so that's no longer a factor. The frustration comes from within: a consequence of our desire to cover some distance. Will the day come when the miles we cover no longer matter?

The next morning, we leave the mountains and enter a broad plain. We have passed from what the Greeks called Cilicia Trachea—"Rugged" Cilicia—into Cilicia Pedias—"Flat" Cilicia. This is rich farmland; orange and lemon groves host regimented lines of trees heavy with fruit. The mountains were largely uninhabited, but here there are many houses.

Today is our Sunday fast. We fix the front brake on Rudy's bicycle, then cycle into Silifke. It's a pleasant coastal town. We seek out the emptiest café. Drinking cup after cup of dark, sweet Turkish tea, we write long letters home. It takes the whole afternoon to write half a dozen. We leave the café at sunset and cycle out of town to look for a place to sleep. A clump of trees a short distance from the road isn't great but will have to do.

In my dream, I'm in England. I'm three years old. I sit motionless on my red tricycle in the lane outside our house in Boxmoor, Hertfordshire. I can see the far reaches of that lane—two hundred distant yards away. On my left is a high hedge of holly. A hedge that rises so dense and dark I can see nothing of what lies beyond. I imagine a sunlit meadow. An odd sensation stirs in my belly. How dangerous would it be to find out?

Upon waking, it takes several long moments to realize that I'm under a tree in southeastern Turkey. I'm suspended between these two disparate worlds for a minute, but Turkey slowly wins. Since Antalya, our next destination of note has been Mersin, a large industrial city on the coast. For several days, we have been seeing signs for Mersin. In the late afternoon we approach the outskirts, so we look for a place to sleep. An orange orchard off the road is ideal.

In this ancient land, Mersin is a relatively new city. It owes its growth in part to the American Civil War. At that time, there was a worldwide shortage of cotton. Mersin and its port then became a major trade center for cotton; the crop thrives on this coastal plain. Mersin is the most westernized city we've encountered in Turkey. There's not one girl in traditional Turkish dress; they all wear jeans or skirts. Girls in jeans have been a rarity in Turkey. The contrast couldn't be greater between the city and the countryside ten miles away.

We leave through a bleak industrial area. The road is heavy with cars, large trucks, noise and fumes. I'm frustrated and angry with the Turkish truck drivers. They hurtle past, so close to us that their slipstream almost knocks us down. As they pass, they lay on their horns. These demonic banshees send jolts of physical pain through my body. We cycle through the town of Tarsus, the birthplace of Saint Paul, but do not linger. We want only to pass beyond this miserable stretch of road.

We follow a small side road to take a break and make tea. Rudy tinkers with his gasoline stove. It has been misbehaving and may be plotting to blow itself up—and us along with it. Sunset arrives unexpectedly; these winter days are becoming shorter. In a hurry, we follow the road in search of a village. We want to buy bread and fill our water containers before finding a place to sleep. After some miles, we come to the village of Yenice. The villagers' reactions tell us they rarely see foreigners here, yet we know that a well-known foreigner once visited this small town. In 1943, Winston Churchill held a secret meeting in a railway car parked at Yenice's rail station. His aim was to convince Turkish President Ismet Inönü to join the Allies against Germany. The Allies hoped to open a new front against Germany with Turkey on their side. Inönü was resolute in his neutrality, and Churchill came away empty-handed.

There's a single shop in town. With a smile, the young shopkeeper invites us into the back of the shop. He and Rudy communicate in German. We're plied with hot, sweet tea. We ask if there's a restaurant in the village. Our host doesn't answer the question. Instead he asks us to please wait. Ten minutes later, he arrives with a terrific meal: stuffed vine leaves, stuffed peppers, white radishes, and freshly baked flat Turkish bread. We visit a nearby café for a glass of *gazoza*, a delicious sparkling water, and more tea. The patrons switch their attention from the television to the two strangers from *Englant unt Hollant*. Plucked from a horror movie starring fiendish truck drivers, we are welcomed as the second coming of Churchill. No leaving empty-handed for us. That's Turkey for you: from love to loathing and back again in the span of a single day. Expectations and assumptions turn into mush. Cherished notions of right and wrong, good and bad are pried open. They say that travel broadens the mind. What they don't tell you is that it does so via emotional boot camp.

We ask about a place to sleep and our host says he can't allow us to sleep outside. Speaking with some of the others at the café, he asks us to follow him. At the center of the village is a small community hall. He unlocks the building and invites us to sleep there. It is clean and simple. There are mattresses and covers folded neatly in one corner. These people open their hearts without ceremony, as if it were the most natural thing in the world.

We cross the perfectly flat Cilician plain. Rudy says this is the same as cycling in Holland. *Hmmm.* I wouldn't enjoy cycling in Holland.

On a flat, fast road like this, the differences between our bicycles are apparent. Unlike mine, Rudy's bicycle is a professional touring cycle. Beautifully made of special alloys, it weighs half as much as mine does. The wheel rims are unusually narrow, and it has equally narrow tires that Rudy maintains at a very high pressure. The slight weight, plus the reduced rolling resistance from these skinny tires, means that Rudy's bicycle is markedly easier to propel than mine. We occasionally switch for a short time, and the difference is clear. On days like this, when it's hard for me to keep up, my internal chatter kicks in.

Well, if I was on Rudy's aluminum alloy bike, and he was on my steel workhorse, how would he like that? Who'd be waiting for whom, then, eh? Who'd look like the fit, top dog? Exactly how much harder am I working than he is? If I was on his bike, working this much harder, would I be going twenty percent faster than he? Thirty percent? In a way, isn't he cheating with such fancy equipment? And on it goes. My circular thoughts take on the rhythm of the pedals pumping underfoot.

Adana is the fifth largest city in Turkey. It fairly drips with history, having even been mentioned in Homer's *Iliad*. We cycle through the city without pause; the in-your-face presence of this modern Turkish city crowds out any pull Homer might have had on us.

We find a pleasant spot for the night. Between low hills, there's a group of trees next to a nearly dry pond. We unpack and then learn that we are not alone. Hundreds upon hundreds of tiny frogs appear. We eat our evening meal by the last light of day. Frogs sit on our packs, on every part of the bicycles, and on the plastic sheet next to us. They're tree frogs with circular pads on their toes. They jump and stick to every surface, but appear to particularly enjoy man-made surfaces. They sit and study us as we eat. We fall asleep to an odd lullaby: Concerto No. 1 in C-Croak Minor.

During the night it rains. I awake and pull the plastic sheet over me, which works for a light rain. I know that in a heavier rain my sleeping bag will be soaked. I awake in the morning to find the sleeping bag damp, but thankfully not sopping. Before we leave, we cook up a batch of oranges and sugar. The marmalade won't gel and remains thin. In contrast to this sweet orange soup, our mood is heavy. I am damp and filthy. We have cycled every day for three weeks. There's been no opportunity to do laundry. At a faucet by a garage, I wash my hands, face, legs and feet with soap and water. I feel better, but it's still a cold and depressing day.

The sky is overcast, and there's a strong headwind. Here, between sea and mountain, there's a high probability of rain. The map shows us in a pale green area, meaning open countryside or farmland. The map lies. Yacacik is one vast petroleum processing and storage complex. Finding a place to sleep will be tough. By the last light of day, the silhouette of a mosque dome appears. When we get closer, we see it's under construction. This will do. Unfinished brickwork between cast concrete pillars reveals shoddy workmanship. We look out at a bleak industrial expanse. What a thoroughly miserable place. The heavens open and unleash a steady downpour. His house may be unfinished, yet He seems to be about, taking care of us. We would not have fared well under our plastic sheets. I have a dream that I'm back in school. A teacher berates me, saying, "I've never had a student so intelligent, yet somehow so stupid." Which is exactly how Turkey makes me feel.

We awake, and the rain is still coming down. Spending the day here is not a happy prospect. Thankfully, the clouds lighten as the morning advances and we cycle into Iskenderun. *Iskender* is the Arabic rendering of Alexander. Alexander the Great founded the city after his victory over the Persians on the plain we just crossed. We visit the old city, with its dark alleys and dingy shops. We buy half a kilo of *beyaz peynir*, the popular Turkish sheep cheese, for twenty cents. It consists of white lumps preserved in a yellow liquid. I've never smelled cheese this strong. I'm not sure I should trust it, but the price is right for two people on a tight budget.

The mountains ahead of us meet the Mediterranean marshland, so the road south from Iskenderun cannot continue at sea level. It heads steadily upward to the Belen Pass. It's an excellent road in great condition, a rarity in this part of the world. We each catch hold of a slow-moving truck and hitch a ride to the top. There, an incredible view is laid out far below us, to the west. An unbroken patchwork of brown and gray fields marches into the distance. This pass was once known as the Syrian Gate. This gap sits between the Amanus Mountains to the north and the Cassus Mountains to the south. In the past, caravans and armies traveled south from here into inland Syria.

We leave behind the Mediterranean and head toward Syria. Turkey has been difficult and strange. How will Syria be? The name conjures an image of deserts, camels, and dark-skinned Arabs. From the pass, the ride down is exhilarating. The newly surfaced road curves gently and falls steadily. We swoop down at fifty miles an hour. At the bottom, an intersection forces us to stop and refer to our map. A signpost in English tells us that Iran and Iraq are to the east and Syria to the south. We take the southern route.

The sky again looms ominously, and we need to find a place to sleep. As if on cue, rows of small, boxy houses under construction appear a few hundred yards from the road—likely a workman's colony or army barracks. Ah, *shelter from the storm for two cyclists*.

In the morning, we're worried that a watchman might discover us. But the place is deserted. When we sleep in construction sites, we see neither workmen nor guards. Maybe they start late or only work occasionally. It must take a long time to build anything In Turkey. Judging by the many men we see in tea shops at all times of the day, everything must proceed slowly here.

We set out. We're on an elevated plain that makes for great cycling. The skies open, but we don't stop since we're making good time. There's nowhere to take shelter anyway. For the first time since northern France, I'm thoroughly soaked. Our map shows that the Syrian border isn't far. Trucks with foreign license plates pass. This is a major trucking route to Europe.

As the deluge ends, we reach Antakya. In days past, the city was called Antioch. At the time of Christ, it was the capital of Syria. Saint Peter of Antioch started the Syrian Orthodox Church here, and it was here that followers of Christ were first called Christians. Within four hundred years after Christ's death, missionaries from here spread the faith as far as Kerala in South India. Antioch was a western terminus for camel caravans and a key trading point on the Silk Road. The present-day condition of this place belies its exalted history.

A diversion from the main road takes us down narrow dirt streets. The recent downpour and the many trucks have turned a section of the road into mud soup. We watch a convoy of huge trucks from Bulgaria plough through this deep trough. Their passing makes waves in the café-au-lait-colored brew. They don't slow down, and their wheels spray broad arcs of liquid mud against the houses that line the narrow street. Standing with a horse and cart by the road, a farmer watches blankly as these lumbering machines roar past. This depressing scene is an apt metaphor for the struggle between tradition and technology in Turkey.

In the city, unsmiling children shout, "Tourist! Tourist!" The word is said as an insult. A small group of older boys try to hit us as we pass. This last day in Turkey is ending on a sour note; I'll be happy to leave.

Night falls and there's no shelter to be found. But we must get out of the rain. There are few buildings near the border. And then suddenly we are at the Turkish customs post. Unsure of what else to do, we continue through. It's a slow process. Officials study our passports and make notations in large ledgers. They carefully check our bicycles since they were recorded in our passports when we arrived in Turkey. This was to ensure that we didn't sell them and then not pay import duties. As we are about to leave, a guard tells us that the Syrian border is six kilometers away. He adds that it's closed now and will open in the morning. We are in no man's land, between one country and the next. I am thoroughly miserable: wet, cold, and in a foul mood from the mud, the trucks, and the fiends dressed in children's clothing. We make our way slowly through the darkness. Trucks parked for the night line both sides of the road.

A truck with European plates pulls over. Rudy speaks with the driver in German. The Austrian driver is surprised, but after some discussion agrees that we can sleep in the trailer of his truck. So, tonight's residence is five feet off the ground, in a cavernous, empty truck trailer. It's dry, clean, and totally sheltered from the wind. I give it two stars. With carpet and windows, it could have been three. Add a Jacuzzi? Four.

We have cycled nine hundred miles across Turkey in four weeks. It's been a remarkable month of difficulty, tempered by the warmest hospitality. It has not been an easy experience. I'd expected the journey to be physically challenging. I hadn't expected it to be emotionally difficult. One day I'm energized by stark beauty and hospitality. The next, filth or aggression triggers a negative gut reaction in me. My sense of identity has been challenged. I begin to appreciate how English my outlook is. I seek to be open and have harmony with those from other cultures, yet when I feel threatened, I retreat into fear. Visceral reaction trumps aspiration.

Route through Turkey: By ferry to Kusadasi, Ephesus, Selçuk, Aydin, Pammukkale, Denizli, Dinar, Isparta, Bucak, Antalya, Serik, Manavgat, Alana, Aydincik, Ovacik, Silifke, Mersin, Tarsus, Adana, Ceyhan, Dortyol, Iskenderun, Antakya, and Salqin.

Seven

SYRIA

November 20th

DESPITE THE STRANGE SURROUNDINGS, I sleep well. My mood improves. I am in dry clothes and Turkey is now just a memory. We cycle the few miles to the Syrian border post.

We thought Turkish bureaucracy was slow, but we had no idea. The Syrians have perfected slow. Other travelers had warned us that Syrian officials would insist on knowing if we were headed to Israel. Repeated questions about our destination confirm this. We explain that we are going to Damascus and on to Jordan. The Syrian visa fills a full page of my passport. It includes three colorful postage stamps and several rubber stamps, but it's in Arabic, so I've no idea what it says.

Syria is markedly different from Turkey. We cycle among gentle hills. The ground is littered with rocks and devoid of all vegetation. We can't see far, just to a skyline of more low hills. All is a single hue of sandy gray. There are no signs of life of any kind. Other than the strip of dark gray on which we cycle, it's a scene from the Apollo 11 lunar photo album.

For several hours we have the road to ourselves. Slowly, the scenery changes. There are orchards of fig and olive trees. Small trees reveal that these orchards are relatively new. The soil is now a consistent, stony red. The few cars we see are American and from the fifties. They serve as communal taxis, and hurtle past as they belch blue-gray smoke. The drivers wear Arab headdress and honk furiously. It's an exuberant celebration of existence more than a warning of approach. One fine specimen is bright turquoise with enormous tail fins and plenty of rounded chrome. It's a lost soul from 1950s Las Vegas; today, it would not be welcomed back. The car's body sits at a dramatic angle, offset from the wheels as it moves down the road like a crab scuttling sideways. Happy, shouting faces fly past. The passengers appear oblivious to the life-endangering state of their ride.

There are houses with flat roofs and the occasional pointy onion dome. We stop for tea, but don't eat because it's Sunday. The people here seem more laid-back, and I think they'll be easier to deal with than the Turks. They're less sticky, as Rudy puts it. In an olive grove, there's an empty barn. Apart from the smell of manure, it's a pleasant enough room for the night. The day was warm, but the cold evening reminds us that it's winter.

After a day of fasting, our day starts slowly. We pick up momentum as breakfast kicks in. We stop to buy bread at the first village we come to and watch it being made. The baker shapes the dough just as an Italian chef creates a pizza crust. He throws the ball into the air and deftly works it until it is flat and round. Using a large wooden paddle, he tosses the wet dough up into a domed brick oven. It sticks momentarily to the underside of the dome and then falls to the oven's floor. A quick turn with the wooden paddle, and moments later the hot bread emerges. Some are inflated and exhale steam, as if to express relief that it's all over so quickly. The bread is as delicious as cake. We try one that is sprinkled with sesame seeds, then order six. The baker refuses payment.

My efforts to learn the local language start anew. Arabic has nothing in common with Turkish, not even the script. I start by learning the written numerals, as I don't hold out much hope for taking in the alphabet. I'll learn the basic words: bread, water, thank you, money, that sort of thing.

We stop next at a small store to buy sugar and biscuits. We're unfamiliar with the currency, and after we leave town, we calculate what we paid for the sugar and biscuits. We were cheated, and find ourselves once again in a land of contrasts. The unprompted generosity of the baker was followed by the trickery of the grocer. I resolve not to be cheated again and firmly fix the exchange rate in my mind.

The fig and olive orchards continue unbroken on each side of the road. Little else can grow here. The gentle roll of the hills continues until we climb and pass a high ridge. The plain beyond is perfectly flat, the land a patchwork of odd colors; there are a number of small, red-brown or flesh-colored plots of earth. This subtle quilt is broken here and there by a small village. From a distance, each looks like a group of large stones placed on the flat land. The buildings are constructed with mud over frame and are the color of the land itself. In contrast to Turkey, nothing is green here. There are no signs of industrialization, and few people.

In the afternoon, we come to another barren stretch; the surface is an unbroken lump of uneven rock. There are shallow pockets of earth in hollows of the rock. In these grow a few long blades of rough grass. This desolate place is unsuitable even for grazing goats. We do not see a single person, house or animal.

Later, we arrive at the town of Ma'arat An Nu'man. We ask a young man where we can buy bread, and the simple request sets in motion full-blown Islamic hospitality. He insists we come back to his house for chai. We're shown into the living room and meet his father. The floor is carpeted, the walls decorated with tapestries. We're joined by twelve siblings, many grand-children, friends, and sundry others—all male. In Turkey, I felt at times like a circus animal on display. Here, people are friendlier, and I feel more at ease.

We're served a delicious meal, though one item is unfamiliar to me. In the rice, there are what look like whole green bell peppers. They're bright green, a few inches long, and skinnier than any bell pepper I've seen. Other guests eat them whole, so I do likewise. I'm unprepared for what ensues. The fiercest sensation engulfs my face, eyes, throat and stomach. My mouth burns horribly. My face turns bright red, my eyes stream, and my nose gushes water. I hiccup uncontrollably. The others collapse with laughter at my bewilderment. I've just eaten my first raw hot pepper.

One brother speaks a smattering of English. We spend the evening communicating slowly. He shares a few English poems he wrote, and we share some we know. Everyone else watches and listens intently, straining to understand some part of the conversation. When the bilingual brother remembers to translate, the listeners let out a collective sigh of relief. We sip tea and graze on a never-ending supply of sweets, nuts and oranges.

The next morning, our Arab hosts provide a fabulous breakfast. We say goodbye and continue south toward Damascus. We have joined the main road, which runs from north to south and connects the inland cities of

Aleppo, Hamah, Homs and Damascus. After a long day of cycling, we want respite from company. We decline the offer of a place to stay and sleep beneath the stars.

The next day, after only an hour on the road, we stop to buy bread in Talbiseh. While waiting for the bread to bake, we become the focal point for a huge group of boys. A young man who speaks English invites us to join him for chai.

Ahmed studies English literature at Damascus University. His slow and carefully pronounced English is fairly good, yet his phrasing is oddly convoluted. We describe the long cycle up to the Syrian Gate, and he replies, "That is of greatest interest to my own self. I would indeed care to learn more about that. Thou must tell me more about this deed." Having missed the bulletin announcing the demise of Elizabethan English, Ahmed serves up a cocktail of Shakespeare with a twist of modern syntax.

Tea drinking merges into lunch, then drifts into the afternoon, and from there into the evening meal. Ahmed has an older brother, Mahmoud, who teaches English literature. It's odd to hear him quote "famous" English authors of whom I've not heard.

Mahmoud explains further about Syrian society. He describes the dowry system of marriage, in which a young man and his family pay for a prospective bride. He tells us the incredible story of his recent experience. He met a girl at Damascus University and fell in love. After proposing to her, he learned that his family couldn't afford her dowry. Her father had set a high price because she was an engineer. Although the story is surprising, what takes me aback is the absence of emotion in Mahmoud's face and voice as he recounts the story. He relates it not as a tragic personal incident, but as if it's a story from some book he has memorized by rote.

The more time we spend with Ahmed and Mahmoud, the more pronounced their absence of emotion becomes. They talk about passionate pieces of English literature, yet exhibit no feeling—verbally or nonverbally. They describe intense emotion in a flat monotone. I christen them the English Literature Machines. Delightful writing is reduced to intellectual concept. Mice at a banquet, nibbling at paper plates that brim with delicacies.

Stranger still is their arid analysis of our personal stories of trials from the road. I describe when stones were thrown at us in Turkey. I share openly my confusion and dismay at being treated this way. Mahmoud responds in a flat tone, "Thou hast laid at my feet a situation of personal discomfiture. This has arisen as a consequence of unfamiliar surroundings. There has been a gross misunderstanding between you and the Turkish people. Notwithstanding, it would be better if your good person could learn how to avoid umbrage in any future like scenarios." The effect is eerie. They espouse interest in our experiences, yet manage to remain quite distant.

After two days, the tension of mismatched communication is palpable. Rudy and I squabble, then agree to have an honesty session. Ahmed insists that he remain with us while we talk. We relent, secretly hoping it will enlighten him. We talk only of the tension between Rudy and me, of our actions and of our feelings; we don't refer to the brothers' behaviors. Ahmed listens intently as we talk. After fifteen minutes, the air is clear between Rudy and me. Ahmed, on the other hand, appears quite upset and will not tell us why. I assume this open discussion of emotion has disturbed him.

Talbiseh: the conical rooftops.

I have bad diarrhea on our third day in Talbiseh. I'm thankful for spare underwear, as I have several accidents. I feel extremely unwell and want only to be in a familiar bed between clean sheets. It looks like Rudy is coming down with the same thing. In Spain, they say, "Guests are like fish. After three days, they go off." In this case, it is literally true.

On the fourth day, we wonder if we have overstayed our welcome. When we ask Ahmed, he assures us that everything is fine and presses us to stay. He tells us again and again, "You are my brothers. This is your home." In local parlance, another adult male is "brother." It's a noble sentiment, but it doesn't always fit the reality of human interaction. We go with Mahmoud to visit his cousin. We spend a long time playing Bosra, a Syrian card game. Our host is newly married. I'm shocked when he freely tells us that it's a pity he couldn't marry the girl he loved, but that this wife will do. Later, we watch an episode of *Columbo* on TV. Our host's father is clearly an educated man. He says that this TV show is CIA propaganda. At first, I think he's joking, but he's quite serious.

The next morning, we awake to the sound of Mahmoud and his mother loudly arguing. We've never heard an open domestic quarrel in Turkey or Syria. I suspect that this outburst is linked to our continued stay. Although I'm still sick, I press Rudy into agreeing to leave today. We finally say good-bye at two in the afternoon.

We were guests for four days, and our hosts told us more than once that we should stay as long as we wish. They bought me a pen to replace the one I'd lost. They bought me a new bar of soap because mine was finished after their mother used it to wash my clothes. When we asked for directions to a shop to buy milk, they give us a kilo of powdered milk. They didn't want to leave us alone for even a moment, yet there was something missing. They showed indifference to our worsening physical condition. Their nonverbal language and tone of voice never once displayed genuine kindness. Did they offer us hospitality only because it was their religious duty?

Despite the sickness, we cycle twenty miles. The road is level and paved. We stop for the night among a few sickly fruit trees. I awake sometime in the night; the moonlit scene could be a World War I battlefield. Only an occasional dead tree stump breaks the empty skyline. The night is very cold, and in the morning we see snow on nearby mountains, not much higher than where we are now.

We are both weak, so this morning is a slow start. We arrive to where the road is being upgraded to a multi-lane highway and stop at the construction office. It's an Italian contracting company, and the workers treat us to a grand meal of spaghetti, fruit and coffee. The encounter gives us a much-needed lift.

As the light of day wanes and we look for a place to sleep, there is neither shelter nor tree to be found. We notice a dry riverbed that runs under the road. Ensuring that we're not seen, we scramble down the bank and under the road. Below the bridge lies a small, secret world. I relish the fact that the occasional car passes just feet above us, yet no one knows that we're down here. It's a great place to sleep. The parched landscape tells us that rain is rare, so it's very unlikely that that the river will flow in the night.

Weak sunlight in the morning improves my mood, but my diarrhea is no better. Surely it is that cheese from Iskenderun. I later learn that *beyaz peynir* is a documented health hazard because of how it's handled and stored. The issue lies with the yellowish liquid in which it floats. Any food preserved in fluid of that color cannot bode well. I can still taste it in my memory. The strongly acidic flavor was OK at the time with fresh *ekmek* bread. On the plus side, we now have a ready source for tasteless jokes. We've run out of toilet paper, though, and must resort to any other paper we have with us. A perfect candidate is the pamphlet on thin paper I received in England from Her Majesty's Stationery Office, "Health Protection for Travelers." Indeed. Once those sixteen pages are used, the only other paper is letters from home. I don't plan to tell Sharon about the fate of her letters.

The number on my bicycle milometer slowly changes from 4,999 to 5,000. I feel every one of those five thousand miles from home.

Passing through a village, a small group of boys tug at us, trying to pull us from our cycles. They throw stones. No stone finds it mark, though, so it's best to just keep going. In a second village, more stones. Even though I'm weak, I stop. The youths can see how angry I am, and they appear surprised; did it not occur to them that we might face them? I shout and wave my fist, but there are more of them than we could tackle. We cycle away, and there are no more stones. What's the reason for this behavior? Why is this resentment directed at us?

Our residence tonight is a small hut in a parched vineyard. The night is bloody cold. In the morning we make a small fire with what wood we can find. Crouched over the meager heat, it's clear that we must get to Israel quickly. We cannot continue to sleep outside in these temperatures.

Back on the road, we arrive at the Syrian equivalent of a motorway rest area. The patron speaks French and offers us tea. We mention that we want to get to Damascus quickly, and he offers to find us a lift. He returns shortly with the driver of a small truck. We put the bicycles in the back and ride along comfortably over the next forty miles to the outskirts of Damascus. We arrive in the early afternoon.

After the tranquility of the countryside, we now find ourselves in severe traffic. The air is heavy with fumes, filled with the roar of engines and the sound of horns. There are varied neighborhoods. Some are new and could almost be from a European city. The older areas have narrow, winding streets. Small stores that sell the same products are grouped together. Men sit in a row, each patiently waiting for customers behind a large, open sack of tea. How can they possibly make a living from this limited enterprise? Our bicycles draw attention as we walk around the marketplace. It must be the chrome and bright colors. I resolve to paint mine all black when I get a chance.

Evening arrives and we look for a hotel. All of the ones we encounter are too rich for our meager budget. We meet two students from Damascus University who speak English. Their names are complex, and we struggle to say them correctly: Abdulghani and Abdulhakim. When we explain that our finances are limited, Abdulghani insists on paying for a hotel. I feel guilty; he likely has less money than we do. The hotel is a dreary place. The cast iron beds support hard cotton mattresses, but a place to sleep in this large city is a blessing. Before he says goodnight, Abdulghani invites us to stay with him tomorrow. He also asks us to call him by the short version of his name, Abud.

The next day, we leave the bicycles locked to the beds in our hotel room and explore this remarkable city. We try unsuccessfully to find the public baths. It's been a month since I had a bath. In the afternoon, we meet our two new friends as arranged. They have finished their studies for the day and lead us on a city tour. Blocks of shoddily built concrete apartments give way to a medieval scene in the old part of the city. The huge bazaar, Al Hamidir, is a dizzying place. We're in an endless warren of branching tunnels. It's the middle of the day, yet little natural light reaches the covered passageways. Hundreds of small shops sell fancy sweetmeats, gold coins, and everything in between. Merchants sit patiently at their doorways, waiting for customers. Throngs of people mill about in a frenetic, yet oddly ordered manner. In the evening, thousands of small electric lights outline the shops and lend the scene a festive, Christmas-like air. Though Damascus is a biblical city, my Western Christmas imagery would surely be lost on a local resident.

Abud invites us to stay with him, so we collect our bicycles from the hotel and set out for his room. It's hard to find, so Rudy rides the bus with Abud. Abdulhakim rides Rudy's bicycle to show me the way. We pass down empty streets lit by dim electric lights. Abdulhakim appears unsteady on Rudy's bicycle, but against the odds, does not fall off. We cycle in silence for several miles, making many turns down darkened streets. We pass into the oldest part of the city with half-timbered architecture. There are no electric lights. None. We could be in Dickensian England. Evidence of the twentieth century is limited to the two bicycles and the modern clothes we wear.

Abud's place is a single room of ten by fifteen feet on the second floor. At the foot of the narrow stairwell is a smelly, squat-style latrine. Ill-fitting boards form the latrine door. Worn wooden steps and a pervasive gloom complete the oppressive scene. There's no bath or shower. The only running water is from a faucet in the latrine.

We learn about life at the University of Damascus. Abud is studying English literature, and his spoken English is passable. Abdulhakim is studying Arabic calligraphy, and speaks only Arabic. After Abdulhakim leaves to take a bus back to his dormitory, creative sleeping arrangements are needed. Rudy and I share the single bed, lying head to toe, each in our own sleeping bag. Abud sleeps on a mattress on the floor.

We visit a traditional public bathhouse with our two new friends. What a sublime experience! First, we undress in a changing area. Wearing just towels, we walk along a low brick passageway with barrel ceiling. Steam fills the air, and the stone floor is warm on my feet. The baths are hundreds of years old, yet everything is spotlessly clean. There are muffled sounds of water being splashed about and low male voices. Only men use the baths, and all of the attendants are male. The walkway opens into a larger, steam-filled area. An attendant appears and indicates that we should change our towels for fresh ones. We pass into another large, hazy room. We sit on the marble floor, each next to a marble basin.

I take my cues from our two Arab friends. A line of faucets on the wall supplies steaming water. I use a large enamel jug to carry hot water to my basin. I wash with a hunk of hemp fiber, a plastic bowl, and scented green soap. The water runs off through shallow channels at the perimeter of the room. I see that the protocol is to remain seated as you wash yourself. We then pass into another large, steamy chamber. We lie face down on the floor without our towels. The marble floor is deliciously warm against my body, face and hands. An overweight attendant appears, dressed in fifties-style bathing trunks. He gives each of us an invigorating massage down the back and legs. On one hand, he wears a rough mitt that is just this side of painful. *Oh boy! This is fantastic.* I close my eyes and picture four weeks' worth of layered grime being scraped away.

We return to the room with the marble basins and wash again with hot water. In yet another set of clean towels, we return to a room near the dressing area. An attendant motions for us to sit in comfortable wood and leather chairs. He dries me with more fresh towels and then wraps me in two warm and extremely soft towels. I feel thoroughly pampered, like I've returned to the womb. Everything is still, and we talk in low voices. The experience reaches perfection when the attendant brings us small glasses of hot, sweet tea. We wrap up well when we leave, but the cold night is still a shock.

Back at Abud's, the conversation turns to freedom. He says, "Freedom is only having a land—a small land—and having a woman. And no government people in my town." So, a plot of land, a wife and no interference from the authorities—that makes sense to me. But I struggle to explain my idea of freedom of the spirit, mind and heart. It's not easy to explain the idea of a freedom that exists independent of life's circumstances.

We sit in silence, each lost in our own thoughts. Abud and I are the same age, yet our lives have been so different. He was conscripted into the Syrian Army during the Arab-Israeli War. At eighteen, he drove a tank in the Yom Kippur War. It's hard to imagine how such a gentle soul could survive that experience. He's much better qualified than I to understand a lack of freedom.

I describe a scene from the movie *Easy Rider*. The heroes seek freedom on the open road and with the aid of hallucinogenic drugs. They want to discard the fetters of modern life. A farmer and his wife invite the two motorcyclists to the family dinner. As they talk with the farmer, they realize that he has that inner freedom they seek right there, in his mundane farming life. Perhaps what Abud and I seek isn't so different; we just describe it differently. For what is Abud's dream, but to experience the inner freedom I describe?

The rest and warmth are working; I'm feeling better. We decide to stay some days in Damascus. We learn to navigate the bus system and find our way back to Al Hamadir souk. We explore the maze of small streets around the main bazaar. Each shop sells but one type of product. One sells backgammon sets inlaid with mother-of-pearl arabesque designs; another specializes in bolts of silk. There are others selling brass, silverware, antiques, carpets, glassware or sweets.

We stumble upon a street lined on each side with shops that all sell only one item. Twenty shops sell sheep's heads; rows of heads are arranged on iron racks. Lifeless eyes gaze out at more lifeless eyes across the street. A black area beneath each rack tells of countless layers of dried blood. Shiny red patches in the black reveals which of them is the freshest stock. Each severed neck is a buzzing mass of black flies. The shops are dark structures in ill repair, and the smell is indescribable—an onslaught against the senses.

We have entered a diabolic realm of blood, flies and dirt. We leave quickly and I gulp lungfuls of fresh air to rid myself of the bad dream.

We find a small café with a large slab of cake on display in the window. We order with gestures, but there's little room for misunderstanding; they sell only this one type of cake. The proprietor cuts our order from a large, shallow tray in the window and serves it with glasses of warm, sugared milk. These are the only two items on the menu, and it's a great combination. It tastes similar to the Dutch honey cake I ate as a child. Rudy tells me that he's never heard of Dutch honey cake. It's in the same vein as English muffins in America, which a Brit can enjoy only after a trip across the Atlantic. The sweet food is enjoyable, but those dead eyes stay with me. Abud later explains that sheep's head is a delicacy. It's cooked whole, and the eyes are considered the best part of the meal.

I browse Abud's library. Among the books stacked in small piles along the wall are magazines from Russia, Romania and Bulgaria. The periodicals are written in English, a communist *Reader's Digest* of sorts. They contain gloomy art and writing. A line in a poem typifies the somber tone of the writing: "Old memories flicker from nightfall to dawn on the screen of my mind's yellowed pages. And I dream all night long of the snow-birds." There are glowing reports of Russia's support for the proletariat masses in the Arab world. Abud explains that there are close ties between Syria and the Russian communist regime. The Russians supply military hardware, aid and support for large-scale civil engineering projects, and free magazines carrying propaganda.

I attend an evening lecture with Abud at the university. The lecture hall is huge, so I'm able to remain anonymous in the crowd. The lecture is about the poet John Donne. The professor's spoken English is extremely poor, and he appears nervous. He seems unhappy whenever a student raises a hand to ask a question. His response is uniform, regardless of the question; rather than answer the question, he makes a derogatory remark about the person who posed it. "Eef de honored great jantleperson did a better dressing of heemself, zen ee could know zis very hanswer." The few students who understand laugh uneasily. He meets their eyes and smiles, sharing his backhanded insult with the English-speaking elite. It's enough to make me squirm. I wonder about Abud's chances of graduation.

Back in Abud's room, he offers us a lesson in history and in Islam. He explains that Damascus is the oldest city in the world. It was invaded or occupied in turn by Egyptians, Greeks, Romans, Mongols, Tartars, medieval crusaders, Ottoman Turks, and the French. Damascus is an important center of Islam. The Omayyad Mosque is one of the holiest Muslim sites; once a Christian basilica, the mosque contains the tomb of Saint John the Baptist. Some Muslims believe that on Judgment Day, Jesus will descend to one of the minarets of the mosque before he joins the faithful for Friday prayers.

"In old days, this city was the capital of the Sunni," Abud says. He then speaks about the two primary sects of Islam—Sunni and Shia—saying, "We are brothers, but we fight." Although he is Sunni, Abud describes without apparent bias the passionately held differences in beliefs, a split that started with a disagreement about who was the rightful successor to the Prophet Muhammad.

Eighty to ninety percent of Muslims are Sunnis. The name Sunni comes from the Arabic word for tradition, *sunna*. Sunnis believe that the leader of the faith—the caliph—should be chosen based on his human qualities. Muhammad was the One Prophet, they say; therefore, successors are human agents, not divine guides.

Shiites, though a small minority of Muslims overall, make up the majority in Iran, Iraq and Palestine. Some years after Muhammad's death, Caliph Ali was murdered. He was Muhammad's son-in-law and cousin. An Arab council appointed a successor and named that person the next caliph. However, Ali had a son, who some believed was the true successor. This was the start of the two sects. Sunnis accepted the appointed caliph. Following the bloodline, others saw Ali's son as his successor. These were known as the *Shiat Ali*, or followers of Ali. They rejected the Sunni caliph. Abud seems to imply that Shiism was the underdog's revolt against an Arab upper class. Where they are a minority, Shiites tend to be treated as second-class citizens.

Abud goes on to explain that, in Turkey, we would have met mostly Sunnis. Here in Syria, there are many Shiites. Yet, he adds, many Muslims think of themselves simply as followers of Islam and don't think in terms of Sunni or Shiite. These two groups are united in most beliefs. I wonder if the animosity between them is not unlike what exists between Irish Catholics and Protestants. As in Ireland, each side places great store in their own differing history of battles, betrayals and loyalties. This conversation gets me thinking; is the split as much sociopolitical grievance as it is theological divide?

Rudy and I plan an early start for the next day. We must reach the Jordanian border before our Syrian visas expire tomorrow.

In the morning, we pack, eat breakfast, and prepare to leave. Our bicycles are upstairs in the landlady's apartment. Abud knocks on her door, but there's no answer. We try again throughout the morning. Inexplicably, she has gone away, leaving our bicycles locked in her room. She returns later that afternoon, but now we can't possibly cycle to the border in time. Our map shows a train line that runs south out of Damascus and continues most of the way to the border. Luckily, there's a train that leaves early tomorrow morning.

That afternoon, I join Abud at a second John Donne lecture. I'm relieved that I don't share Abud's fate of hunting for meaning in such antiquated writing. After the lecture, we meet another of Abud's many friends. This fellow is a poet. He wants to know more when Abud tells him that I also write some poetry. He listens carefully as Abud translates for him a recent poem from my diary.

Abud then translates for me his friend's response, "You have two blue eyes, but I don't know in what sea you are swimming." I wonder if this is a typical conversation with an Arabic poet. Only later do I think of a clever response. *Ah yes, but these blue eyes see all that swims in this unknown sea—as you swim before me now.* As it happens, in the moment I fall quiet. Yes, *what is the sea in which I swim?*

As a farewell gift, Abdulhakim creates two exquisite pieces of Arabic calligraphy in my diary. He's a gifted artist. I was surprised when I first heard that he studied calligraphy at the university. How can one study *just* calligraphy? Isn't that an overly narrow field for a degree? But Arabic calligraphy is a primary Islamic creative art. It provides a fascinating window into the world of Islam. When used for Quranic phrases, written words gain a beauty that enhances the sacred meaning. Using calligraphy for religious expression helps avoid the risks of idolatry, and is therefore a prized art form in Islamic cultures. Calligraphy adorns surfaces from mosque furniture to the walls of the Kaabah, the most sacred object in Islam. Entire walls may be covered, but an untrained Western eye can mistake the stylized writing merely as pleasing patterns.

Arabic is written from right to left. There are eighteen basic letter shapes in the alphabet, but several of the letters have more than one form, yielding a total of twenty-eight letters. A letter takes a different shape if it appears at the beginning of a word, in the middle, at the end, or if it stands alone. The calligrapher has artistic freedom when forming words. Words need not follow a line, and so can be cast into any artistic form. Letters can be compacted or stretched along any dimension. A word can become any shape imaginable.

There are two styles, dry and moist. Kufic is angular and appears stylized to the Western eye; these square or geometric styles are "dry." An angular modern font of a consumer brand from the Middle East is almost surely Kufic. The second set of styles is cursive or "moist." Common cursive styles are Thuluth and Naskh. Naskh is easily legible and often used for printing. Many Qurans are set in Naskh font. This is a small script with thin lines and round letter shapes. Thuluth is more ornate; it's used for short pieces such as a title or for decorative text. The calligrapher's art here is to balance ornament and legibility. For handwriting, there's a simple form with distinct letters called Riq'a. Each style has many variations.

Abdulhakim's gift to me uses Thuluth. There are two depictions of my name sounded phonetically in Arabic. Looking closely, I can recognize the common elements in each.

A gift from Abdulhakim: my name twice in Arabic calligraphy.

The following morning we rush to get to the train station on time. Unnecessary, since the train leaves thirty minutes late. I'm sad to say good-bye to Abud. We have become fast friends.

On the train, we're in a time machine. A small steam engine pulling four short carriages places us in an old Hollywood Western. We sit on slatted hardwood benches, the only passengers in the carriage. Steam passes by my window, twisting into convoluted shapes before it disappears. The curling, dissolving patterns carry me to another time.

I'm a young boy in Hemel Hempstead, watching a steam train leave for London. I stand with my father on a footbridge above the platform and look down through cast iron railings. A rush of excitement washes through me as the seething beast prepares to move. *Shoo-oosh...* A shaft of dark smoke shoots upward. Then another. *Shoo-oosh...shoo-oosh...* Each massive stroke hits my body. Smoke phantoms curl around our ankles and dissolve as the train departs.

The cold brings me with a jolt back to the present. The carriage windows are without glass. We shiver on the bench as the dry countryside slips by. It takes a few hours to reach Dar'a. The Jordanian border is then only two miles farther.

Route through Syria: Idlib, Ma'arat An Nu'man, Hamah, Talbiseh, Homs, An Nabk, Duma, Damascus, and Dar'a.

Eight

JORDAN

December 5th

LIKE SYRIA, JORDAN LACKS SCENERY. The featureless landscape has little vegetation. With a sparkle in his eye, Rudy explains that in Holland, December fifth is Santa Claus Day, a holiday of note. He must be missing home. So, at a tea shop we splurge on lemon tea to celebrate. I draw a Santa Claus card to surprise him. The proprietor is also the local schoolteacher and speaks good English. He invites us to sleep on the floor of the tea shop that night. We're grateful for the prospect of a warm room. An evening follows with countless cups of tea. Rudy says this is the best fifth of December he's had since he was a child.

Our host leaves for school before dawn; this early start means we're in Amman by midmorning. The city was originally built on seven hills. It now sprawls over many more hills and into the desert beyond. It is westernized, with brand-name stores and plenty of neon. Sometimes called the White City, most buildings are of local white stone. Under the bright Middle Eastern sun, the city has a stark beauty. As part of the Roman Empire, it was Philadelphia. It could not be less like modern Philadelphia in the United States. The inner city of Amman is as light and promising as parts of today's Philadelphia are dark and depressing.

It takes us three frustrating hours to locate a youth hostel we'd been told about. We're given one set of wrong directions after another. We find it, but our frustration increases further. It is closed for the season. We follow more poor directions to the Ministry of the Interior. This is the office that issues permits to visit the West Bank of Jordan—now part of Israel, though Jordan grants permits to visit as if it had not been annexed by Israel. We've been warned not to mention Israel.

The permit will be ready in two days, so we cycle away from the city center in search of a place to sleep. A huge sports complex named Sports City for Youth sounds promising. Two men in an office admit—a little sheepishly—that there's nowhere in the area for young people to stay. Nearby is an open auditorium called the Palace of Culture; we settle in for the night in a sheltered corner. We're enjoying a cup of hot milk when a watchman discovers us. He says we must leave because police are guarding the building in readiness for tomorrow's Party for the Kingdom. Apparently we're not invited.

We cycle through the dark in search of a construction site. But here in the city, each has a watchman. Overcoming my hesitation, I approach a group of men huddled around a fire. With an easygoing sociability, these construction workers invite us to join them. They share their food and ply us with steaming, sweet tea. Now here's the true Palace of Culture, and these are the people I'd invite to my Party for the Kingdom.

The next day we explore the city. At a restaurant in the city center, we chat with some other Westerners. They are the first we've encountered since leaving Ephesus more than a month ago. We stay a second night with our gracious construction worker hosts. I awake early and climb to the flat, unfinished roof. I sit in the early morning sun, relishing the warmth after a cold night. The city of Amman stretches below me, white stone buildings clustered around streets that form webs over many hills. I write in my diary. All is well with me; all is well with the world.

Before leaving Amman, we collect our West Bank permits from the Ministry of the Interior. The sparkling day amplifies the beauty around us. It is greener here than in the north of Jordan. The route rises and falls, following gentle hills. Then the road drops steadily, and we hurtle down amidst rugged scenery. Coming fast around a bend, we're met by a dramatic sight. Far below us lies a huge mass of water that glimmers in the late afternoon sun: the Dead Sea. A roadside marker shows sea level, yet we continue down, moving fast. We arrive in the Jordan Valley, elated. It is a fertile stretch of land with dramatic mountains on three sides. The lushness of the irrigated valley contrasts with a backdrop of angled rock where no living thing can be seen. A setting sun dyes the sheer mountainsides crimson and gray. Again, I am at peace with the world and this journey of mine. A young man invites us to join his family for dinner and offers us a place to sleep. The evening is already cold, and it's a welcome invitation.

We start early the next morning since the Israeli border crossing closes at ten in the morning. To get to the border, we're required to board a decrepit bus. There's a terrible crush of people on the bus, and the high fare bears no relation to the short distance. We enter a war zone as we approach the Jordan River and the Israeli border. Dusty earth is piled high to form barriers, beyond which we can't see. Lines of trenches, sandbags, and barbed wire cross the area. Flat areas appear as nightmare flowerbeds, where an unseen hand has plucked the blooms and left fields of stalks. These are markers that denote a minefield. The many Israeli flags stir in the morning breeze. There are derelict buildings with walls peppered through with artillery fire. There are machine guns posts, armored vehicles, and groups of soldiers.

We arrive at the Jordan River, and it disappoints. As the stuff of spiritual song, I expect a Nile of a river flowing broadly between clumps of palms. This is more stream than river. An Olympic long jumper could clear one bank to the other. The famed Allenby Bridge is but a slab of steel and wood, about forty feet in length.

We unload the bicycles from the roof of the bus to looks of surprise from Israeli soldiers. They tell us that it will be impossible to take our two-wheelers across. For three hours, we negotiate our way up the chain of command, arguing and pleading for the bicycles. Two young soldiers join our cause, but, eventually, the senior officer forbids the bicycles from entry; he fears they may be packed with plastic explosives. The notion is ridiculous; the bicycles have rarely been out of our sight, and no one knew that we were headed to Israel. And what an unfortunate reality the Israelis occupy, fearing even an innocent two-wheeled creature. I'm drained from arguing.

Crestfallen, we wait for the bus to return to Jordan. The best we can think of is to return to Amman, leave the bicycles there, and return next week without them.

We find our way back to our hosts of last night and spend the evening there. We walk to the shores of the Dead Sea as the last light of day drains from the sky. Dark, oily water spreads beneath a pale moon. Not many miles away on the opposite shore, orange and white lights glitter: the lights of an Israeli town. Farther still, lights atop a high ridge must be the outskirts of Jerusalem. We're standing in a geological aberration, the Jordan Rift Valley. This deep depression in the earth's surface runs north to south. To the north lies the Sea of Galilee; the Dead Sea lies to the south. This valley sits between two mountain ranges and is blocked at either end. Just as a child digs a trench near the ocean, elemental forces carved this deep valley not far from the waters of two seas. This is the lowest point on the face of the earth. If the hills to the south were razed, the Gulf of Aqaba would rush in. The water would then be thirteen hundred feet higher, and it would join the Red Sea. Israel would be separated from Jordan by an ocean inlet. From where we stand, the waters of the Mediterranean are seventy miles away and thirteen hundred feet above our heads. A breach to the north would leave the valley a Mediterranean fjord of sorts.

The Sea of Galilee is a large freshwater lake. The Jordan River flows south out of the Sea of Galilee toward the Dead Sea, the lowest point in the valley. From here, the water has no outlet. It leaves only through evaporation. Over millennia, the water has become progressively saltier as minerals washed from incoming streams remain behind. Both Israel and Jordan take water from the Jordan River, and the level of the Dead Sea drops a foot and a half every year. A desiccated, salty end awaits.

The following day, we join our hosts at a celebration for the opening of a new school. Hassan, the youngest brother of King Hussein, and his Pakistani wife attend the occasion. They arrive by helicopter, and we watch the proceedings from behind a small crowd. The royal visitors fascinate me less than a group of Bedouin women does. They're draped from head to toe in black, visitors from another realm. As others applaud, they greet the guests with a high-pitched ululation made in the throat. The sound makes the hair on my forearms stand on end, but our young host dispels this otherworldly aura. He explains that, even while welcoming the royal family, the women are angry because "they haven't given them money for tea and sugar." Did that make the eerie greeting a warning as well as a welcome?

That evening, we share a farewell meal with our hosts. We sit cross-legged in a circle on the floor. In the center, a pyramid of rice and mutton is piled two feet high on a massive circular platter. Eating only with my right hand, I help myself from this communal mountain of food. We offer no money for tea and sugar. There are no complaints. Only goodwill flows.

The next day, we cycle back up that spectacular hill we came down just two days ago. Rudy grabs a passing truck and disappears around a bend. Sometime later, I accept a ride from a driver who pulls over to offer me a lift. We pass Rudy sitting by the road. A second ride in a Jordanian army Land Rover brings me to Amman. A deserted building offers a place to sleep. I settle in for a cold night after a dinner of four radishes. That's all the food I have.

I visit the British Embassy in the morning and ask if they have any suggestions for storing two bicycles. I receive only a look of disdain. Rudy is waiting outside, where we agreed yesterday to meet if we were split up. Last night, he had better luck than I did. He spent a warm night at the home of a young Jordanian man. He told Rudy that we could leave our bicycles in a spare room at his mother's house. After a day in the city, we cycle to the home of Muhammad, our new benefactor. In the evening, I sort and repack. I fashioned my rear panniers in England from two army surplus cotton rucksacks. They have straps so I can carry them. I must leave my other items, including the front panniers.

 Route through Jordan: Zarga, Amman, Allenby Bridge, Salt, Amman, and the Allenby Bridge.

Nine

ISRAEL

December 12th

WE SET OUT THE NEXT MORNING as members of the Universal Brotherhood of Backpackers. It's more work than cycling. The Israeli frontier is only thirty miles away, yet it requires three rides and three hours, plus a lot of walking and waiting by the roadside.

Back at the Allenby Bridge, the two Israeli soldiers who had supported our cause warmly greet us. One is from the US, the other from Holland. After filling out page after page of paperwork, we're granted permission to enter Israel. For a reason that is never explained, we are allowed to walk across the Allenby Bridge. Our soldier friends tell us that this is a rare privilege, since others must reboard the sputtering bus to cross. Once in Israel, we take a taxi into Jericho and argue with the taxi driver about the exorbitant fare. From Jericho, there's a bus ride to Jerusalem.

At first, the city underwhelms, with blocks of featureless concrete apartment buildings. We check into a cheap hotel. In the evening, we stroll around the old city. *Ah! This is more like it.* The market is lively turmoil. The backdrop of ancient stone walls exhales stability. It's a wonderful two-part harmony.

The next morning, it takes several rides for us to reach Nablus. When we were in Turkey, we chose this town by referring to a map of Asia. It seemed, at the time, to be as good as any other. Our unwitting choice reveals our naive lack of knowledge of the region. The map offered no hint that this part of Israel is the occupied West Bank of Jordan, or that Nablus happens to be the epicenter of anti-Israeli sentiment. We couldn't have chosen a worse place.

From the moment we arrive, the hostility directed at us is palpable. The post office clerk starts by angrily describing the "occupation of the Israelis." We elaborate on our travels in Arab lands and how wonderful the Arabs that we have met were—which is more true than not. Without such explanations, I doubt we'd be given our mail, let alone leave the post office upright. The anti-Israeli passion is downright chilling. Policing here must surely be a nightmare. I have to wonder what the eventual cost to Israel of controlling an area that is so vehemently resistant will be.

There are sixteen letters from home. With a delicious sense of anticipation, I put them away for later. We find a cheap hotel in nearby Jenin. There are several kibbutz in the vicinity, where we hope to find work for the winter. We can continue after the coldest weather has passed, but we learn too late that we've made another move of breathtaking naivety. After paying for our room, we learn that Jenin is another hotbed of Palestinian resistance. We stay in our room and keep to ourselves. The uneven walls are painted in peeling green and pink gloss paint. A more ghastly color combination is hard to imagine. I sit on the iron bed to read my letters and write in my diary. Beyond the barred window is a walled courtyard. I feel every bit the hardened traveler.

The next day, we hitch a ride and then walk to Bet Hashitta. This is a kibbutz with twelve hundred residents. We arrive in time for lunch in the glass and chrome cafeteria. We're greeted by the sight of hundreds of people seated on plastic chairs at long tables. They eat brightly colored food from plastic trays. Most are absorbed in eating; only a few are engaged in conversation. What a contrast to the animation of the Arabs—a few miles away, yet another world. I'm quietly relieved when we learn that they do not need volunteers here.

Mu is an intriguing term used in *Zen and the Art of Motorcycle Maintenance*. This Japanese word means "nothing," or "nil." In Zen Buddhism, it's used to describe a state of tranquility. It indicates an atypical approach to a question. The *mu* response asks the inquirer to neither address nor retreat from the subject of inquiry. Instead of focusing on the question, engage in a lateral drift. Expend no effort to resolve. Remain quietly open to further information or experience. Remove any sense of urgency and refrain from expectation. I'm fascinated by the implications. Could we use the *mu* response to approach challenges in a different manner? What might be the results? This part of the journey is a perfect laboratory in which to experiment.

Rudy and I agree to consciously apply the *mu* approach in finding a kibbutz. We will not choose which direction to go or which kibbutz to visit. We'll not seek an outcome or a direction. We'll simply continue along this road and observe what transpires. We're explorers entering uncharted territory within our own perception. I am both intrigued and a bit uneasy at the prospect of letting the winds of chance blow us where they will.

The morning is quiet. The sun is warm on my face and arms. I can hear unseen birds somewhere in the middle distance. I can feel my breath as it enters through my nose. I'm aware of my shoulders rising with the in-breath and falling with the out-breath. I enjoy this moment. And the next.

Twenty minutes pass. A Jeep slows and stops just ahead of us. The driver invites us with a smile to get in. He introduces himself as Czech. He's a Czechoslovakian Jew who works as a border guard. We bounce along on the small roads, and he assures us that he can find us a kibbutz where we can be volunteers. We spend the night at Newe Etan, a small kibbutz where Czech is a member. The people we meet are warm and friendly, but unfortunately, they have no need at the moment for volunteers.

Czech devotes the next day to helping us find a kibbutz. By the end of the day, we have a temporary home. Beit Zera is a medium-sized kibbutz of seven hundred members, which includes fifty volunteers. Founded sixty years earlier, it is a nonreligious kibbutz run on Marxist principles. The community, its assets, and its production are created and shared for the good of all. There are no "owners," or anyone who is privileged above another. The kibbutz has a grapefruit orchard, an avocado orchard, a banana plantation, a large dairy, and an egg hatchery. Incongruously, it also has a plastics factory. It sits two miles south of the Sea of Galilee in the Jordan Valley. The Golan Heights look purple in the hazy distance. The cities of Tiberias and Nazareth are both nearby.

A night spent between cotton sheets is unparalleled luxury. Will this spoil me? Will I lose my appreciation for the raw life of the bicycle traveler? Kibbutz members work at whatever needs doing, according to their abilities. There are jobs in the kitchens, laundry, garden, offices, and so on. They spend leisure hours in their private homes, except for the occasional film or party in a communal hall. They work hard and enjoy the resulting comforts.

Once children reach the age of six months, they live, sleep, eat and learn together. There are residential homes for the younger ones, and a high school with eating, sleeping and living quarters. Children do most activities as a group. Parents reserve the hours between five to nine o'clock each evening for their children. The children visit their parents and they eat dinner together. After, they return to sleep with the other children. Parents argue that this system, with four hours devoted to the children, means that the kids get more attention than do those who live at home. After dinner, parents accompany their children to the dormitory, read them a story, and say goodnight. A child sleeps at home only if he or she is ill. The children appear self-confident and outspoken. The teenage girls I meet are direct, rather than shy and blushing. At eighteen, everyone joins the army: girls for two years and boys for three. After this, they can take a year to "look around" before finalizing a career. They might travel overseas, or work on another kibbutz. Their expenses during this time are paid for by the kibbutz. The following year, they can become permanent members of the kibbutz or choose to leave.

We volunteers live in close quarters, four to a cabin, male and female mixed. The accommodations are comfortable enough. Oddly, it's more of a communal lifestyle than the kibbutz members enjoy. There's a strong sense of camaraderie among the volunteers. They're a tight-knit, yet constantly evolving group. Most are international travelers who choose this as a stop on the way. A few come expressly to be volunteers.

The volunteers exist in a distinct subculture. They are not welcomed or even acknowledged by many of the permanent members. Work supervisors don't always show volunteers a great deal of respect. There are many supervisors, and sometimes one contradicts the instructions of another. One kibbutznik (permanent kibbutz resident) is appointed to oversee the volunteers, and she is our primary contact. Additionally, each volunteer is assigned a kibbutz "mother." This is a nice human touch for us young travelers who see ourselves as so independent, but likely need support from time to time. My kibbutz mother is Shulamit. She has grown children of her own.

I'm kitted out with a set of working clothes: socks, boots, trousers, shirts. Each volunteer starts with a stint of several weeks in the plastics factory. I begin work at noon and continue until six. The work is mindless. I operate a machine making plastic milk crates. After a couple of days, I move on to operate three smaller machines that produce unidentifiable cylindrical objects in military green plastic. I suspect the mysterious parts are for tanks or armored vehicles, so I make a fuss to the supervisor and refuse on moral grounds to operate the machine. I feel foolish when he explains that they will be chromed and then become sink drain downspouts. After some days, I graduate to the big time, producing off-white plastic bench ends on a German machine the size of a house.

Rudy and I travel into Tel Aviv to obtain papers to make our stay in the kibbutz official. I've never been to the United States, but Tel Aviv looks like what I've seen in movies. Indeed, some people here call Israel the Next State. In context of the region, it's sorely out of place. I'd expected Israel to have a distinct culture, but there's no sign of it here. Our papers won't be ready until tomorrow. We have our sleeping bags, so we apply our skills from the road and find a place to sleep. A clean, dry landing at the top of the final flight of stairs in an apartment building is perfect. We sleep well.

After collecting our papers, we return to the central bus station. In light of our unconventional accommodations last night, we discuss what it means to follow the rules. Rudy quotes a Dutch proverb. "The soup is never eaten as hot as it is served." In other words, rules are rarely followed as written. These days, I'm happy to take a more relaxed approach to regulations. I don't try to apply this to my evening shift, however, and we return to the kibbutz on time. In this case, the hot soup is eaten as it is served. I produce a veritable stack of white plastic bench ends, though the noise and fumes from the machine put me in a foul temper. By the time my shift ends at midnight, I'm tired and grumpy.

The kibbutz has many acres. It is a fertile and pleasant place. Thin black drip irrigation tubes in the undergrowth lead to each tree and plant. We've heard of the hard manual labor of the first Jews who came here. Beit Zera was one of the earliest of the kibbutzim, founded in 1927. We've been told that this was once a wasteland. The early kibbutz settlers had a dream, a vision of a paradise on earth. They lived in tents and died of malaria, but they turned this land that the Arabs once ignored into a place they long for. That is how the story is told here, anyway.

I had high expectations of kibbutz life. Given the rich Jewish tradition of faith, I'd assumed that the kibbutz would offer communal living in service of a higher purpose: honest labor beneath the sun, golden wheat dancing in a fresh wind, a farming community populated by salt-of-the-earth types with rough hands and ready smiles, communal meals at a scrubbed wooden table, eating chunks of peasant bread. That sort of thing.

In reality, this is a group of people working to acquire material benefit. I'd imagined life here as a seamless continuation of my recent inner life of discovery. I'm disappointed. Most of the people on the kibbutz have turned their back on their faith. A young man I chat with, who only recently got out of the Israeli army, mocks the idea of meditation. He says that you see things in meditation by rubbing your fists into your closed eyes. I'm surprised. Would you not need to be spiritual at your core to defend your faith against persecution for thousands of years? The secular-religious divide in modern Israel is a reflection of this very question.

The large dining hall serves every kind of processed food one could imagine. I upset those in charge of the food with my many requests for more wholesome food, not to mention vegetarian options. A small drama even builds around the issue of white versus brown bread. Two camps emerge, and those in favor of the brown bread form the minority. A Swiss volunteer takes me to task for being too fussy. It stretches my novice dialog skills to explain my perspective and hear his out. Not much changes, so I must go with the flow or go hungry. Breakfast fairly bristles with temptation. Most mornings, I have two bowls of semolina with cream and honey. In the shower, my view to the south is all belly and toes. I sell my Levi's to another volunteer; it's unlikely the thirty-two-inch waist will ever fit again.

I miss the regular exercise of the bicycle. Work in the plastics factory seasoned with all the temptations of home makes for an unpleasant cocktail. In contrast to the joyous tilt of these past months, I can feel lethargy settling in. Things between Rudy and me become difficult, too. We try to talk, but are unable to reach that same place of honesty and disclosure we had previously established.

Kibbutz Beit Zera: Rudy and William outside their hut.

Six months ago, I left England and family behind. Now Christmas is here—a time for family. I recall Christmases past: decorating the tree, the smell of mulled wine, a day with no cars on the road. Here I am in the land where it all began, yet it does not jive. English greeting cards show heavy snow on the stable over the infant. The nativity scenes feature English farmyard animals—a healthy donkey, a tidy barn—and people with beatific smiles and pale skin. The reality is that it's hot and dry, the animals are scrawny, and the olive-skinned people are busy going about their daily lives. Bethlehem is close enough to visit, and I'm told it's packed with tourists. My version of Christmas is burned forever in my brain. It'd be mind-bending to reconcile that and all of this. I'll skip Bethlehem.

On Christmas Eve, I walk to the Sea of Galilee. The sparkling blue waters and snowcapped Mount Hermon in the distance lift my spirits. Modern Israel still intrudes. Manicured lawns line the shore. Someone water skis across the water—the same water on which Christ walked, and on Christmas Eve, no less.

I return to the kibbutz to join the other volunteers for an excellent Christmas meal. We make a huge fire on the grass square in front of the volunteer huts. Staring into the flames as they leap into the darkness, my melancholy lifts. We talk and drink punch. I go to bed early; my shift starts at six the next morning.

Today, I'm the assistant to the assistant cook. This means I open cans or fetch and weigh ingredients. It's lunch as usual for kibbutz residents. Since it's a Sunday, I still fast. My first food-free Christmas is oddly enjoyable— restraint on a day of excess. I feel festive and whistle Christmas carols. I try to telephone home, but Israeli telephone bureaucracy gets the better of me. After an hour of trying, I relent.

Rudy travels to Nablus to collect our mail and returns with a plastic bag full of letters and a parcel for me. What a great way to start the year! I am a five-year-old enjoying a slightly delayed Noel. There are Christmas cards, letters and a small gift. But the best gift is when my stint in the plastics factory finally ends. I couldn't be happier to start work in the banana plantation. My job now is to pinch the flowers off the end of each bunch of bananas. These fruit are for export and must be perfect. I'm so happy to be outside, even though a canopy of broad leaves hides the sun.

Rudy receives a telegram. His father is seriously ill. After calling home, he decides to leave for Amman the next day. He will collect his bicycle and fly back to Amsterdam. So we find ourselves at a bus stop, unexpectedly saying goodbye. We've spent almost every moment of the past four months together. We've passed through geographical, mental and emotional worlds. We've fought like banshees and had moments of remarkable emotional closeness. I could not have faced the culture shock of Turkey and Syria without him, and he may have needed me just as much. I shake his hand and realize how close we've grown. We embrace, and unexpected, hot tears fill my eyes. I'm going to miss him; his absence will create a vacuum. As the bus pulls away, I send with him good wishes and loving support.

Walking back to the kibbutz, a curtain parts for a few moments, and a larger awareness is revealed to me. One phase of the journey has ended, and a new one has begun. When I left England, I needed a traveling companion. From now on, I am alone. I feel both elated and daunted by the prospect. Can I do it? Am I up to the task?

I move into a new hut. My roommates are a Dutch guy and two English girls. If Elaine is an English rose, perfect and beautiful, then Cathy is a wilted daisy. I'm impressed with how strong, good-hearted and open Elaine is. Is this a growing friendship, or sexual attraction? *Ha! Who am I kidding? With a body like that, in those tight jeans and that top?*

An inescapable part of volunteer life is the intricacies of attraction. This is tricky terrain. I've a history of multiple, freewheeling relationships back home, but there's the emerging wish to be free of that gravity field. I'm a pendulum swinging between two opposing forces. Most of the volunteers are young travelers seeking an alternative lifestyle, to live free of rules that bind. But two timeless laws prevail. Girls attract boys. Boys attract girls.

Despite my unexpressed hankering after Elaine, I spend my spare moments with Ria. She's a sweet, down-to-earth Dutch girl whose company I enjoy. We borrow bicycles and cycle to the Sea of Galilee. When it comes to sleeping arrangements things become complicated. Ria introduces me to a novel idea of spending the night together naked, but having no sexual contact. I agree to try. It's difficult, but I succeed. Sort of. But I'd rather not do that again. Who picks up a glass of iced lemonade on a hot summer's day and agrees not to drink? Back home, sexual desire was something to be fulfilled. It's not been an issue on the open road with all that regular exercise on the bicycle. Here, it's a struggle. The girls are fetching. Promiscuity hangs heavy in the air. My endeavor to understand and control is a brave new world. I've been celibate on the trip, but more by circumstance than by choice. If not in thought, at least in action. I want to understand this force that drives me.

In Western cultures, we think more sex is better than less. But where does the monastic tradition fit into this picture? Why, when a person chooses to fully pursue God, does he or she stay apart from members of the opposite sex? I have come to appreciate the intent behind segregating the sexes in the Islamic world. A society that focuses more on God than on the pursuit of the opposite sex could provide meaning and stability. But must not an individual choose this for him or herself? If imposed, does it elevate or suppress?

A lot of my focus back home was on courting potential sexual partners. Being on the road, focused on other things, I'm more present and have more vitality. There's some evidence that cycling dampens sexual desire—a result of the steady pressure on the pelvic floor. I later learn that, in India, renunciants suppress the urge with a yogic seated pose where one heel is pressed into that same area. These *sadhus* believe that semen is spiritual gasoline that fuels the inner fire; to waste it is to slide backwards in the metaphysical game of snakes and ladders. If a life of celibacy supports the spiritual search, my long hours on a bicycle saddle may have helped me in an unexpected manner.

I'm working in the dish room and loving it. I thrive on the honest labor. It puts me in a great state of mind. I scrub pans and baking trays until they shine. Sweat rolls off me, carrying away any emotional heaviness. I empty the hissing dishwashing machine, which rolls on relentlessly. A steady stream of steaming dishes emerges from behind a curtain of rubber strips on plastic fingers. I remove the hot dishes as the conveyor passes. At the end of the shift, I clean the room with a high-pressure hose and revel in the elemental pleasure of spraying gallons of water all about. I barely master the art when a broken plate ends my promising career. I don't see it coming and slice my finger deeply as I try to grab it.

I'm assigned to the Banana Boys after that. This elite group of young men is mostly made up of kibbutz residents plus a few volunteers. The bananas are an important source of income for the kibbutz, and the Banana Boys are held in high regard. I grab a huge stalk of bananas by placing one hand just above the fruit, and the other below. My partner stands on a ladder, and with a single blow of a machete, cuts the thick stalk from the tree. The stalks are heavy with fruit, some forty to seventy pounds apiece. I carry the precious bundle and lay it gingerly on the bed of a trailer. We work in pairs alongside the tractor, moving slowly between rows of banana trees. It's hard, steady and hot work.

On my first day, I'm not sure that I can make it through the day. But I do, and wind up sleeping like a baby that night. There are only two things that interrupt the work: waiting for the next tractor, and rats. Rats can do a lot of damage to bananas. When one of the team finds a rat's nest, he calls the others over. They each grab a wooden stick from the tractor and strike wildly at the terrified animals, yelling with raw excitement. I'm taken aback by this gleeful attempt to kill. No one remarks on the fact that I don't join in.

I learn of Kibbutz Misgav Am, located in the extreme north of Israel, right on the Lebanese border. It's a community built on spiritual ideals. With a new friend from Canada, Bill, I travel north by bus. The atmosphere in this small kibbutz is markedly different from Beit Zera. We eat dinner in a communal dining hall as one large family. People are animated. They talk and laugh together. They want to know about our lives back home and how we came to be in Israel. Unfortunately, they don't need volunteers.

Bill and I are offered beds in one of the volunteer huts. I awake early next morning and walk outside. A breathtaking view greets me. The morning air is crisp and clear. A patchwork of tidy fields lies in the valley below. The colors are too vivid to be true: a glistening silk patchwork of emerald, pea green, and gold. Beyond, the snowy, broad shoulders of Mount Hermon glisten in the light that follows the dawn. The kibbutz is surrounded by a high fence. On one side, the Lebanese border is just twenty-five meters away. A kibbutz member joins Bill and me for a full day's walk along the border. Heavily armed Israeli troops are evident. Intermittently, we hear the sound of gunfire in the distance. Our guide explains that this gunfire is not directed at the Israelis. The fight is between Christian and Muslim villages in southern Lebanon. Cross-border attacks from PLO factions are the more common cause of mortar and gunfire. Our guide asserts that the odds of being killed here are no greater than when riding in a car. A much-quoted statistic in these parts, I'm guessing. I'm not reassured.

A high fence of barbed wire separates the two countries. It slices the lush farmland in two. An eagle makes slow, wide circles high in the air, soaring back and forth between Israel and Lebanon. Man's reality on the ground offers no hindrance.

Bill points out a flowering cactus with edible fruit. Ever ready for a new experience, I pick one and eat it. I finish the first mouthful and realize something is wrong. My lips and tongue burn. Or, is it more of an intense itch? No, they hurt. We catch up with our guide and he explains what's going on. This is a fruit to pick and peel with gloved hands. It cannot be eaten as is, he explains. Well, I can tell you it can be, but with certain consequences. Over the next two weeks, I pick microscopic cactus spines from my lips and tongue. It's incredibly painful. The cure is to wait until they fall out or dissolve.

Back at Beit Zera, the days are getting longer and progressively warmer. I sit on the threadbare grass square in front of the volunteer huts and write in my journal. With the reassuring regularity of kibbutz life, introspection again becomes my focus. Most of what I write in my diary is self-examination. I continue with my Sunday fasts and a pattern emerges. Sundays recharge my mental and emotional state. As the week goes by, my clarity and focus diminish. On Sunday morning, I can't shake thoughts of that creamy breakfast semolina in the dining hall. So, I walk to the River Jordan instead, which is only a few minutes away.

I take letters that arrived this morning, my sketchbook, and a pencil. The river that some cross with bands of angels is nothing but a stream here. I cross it in three paces. I stand in the shallow water and watch it move past my ankles. I sit on a bank above the gurgling water, warmed and content in the morning sun. The palms rustle in a gentle breeze. I doze, propped against the sloping trunk of a palm tree. I make a pencil sketch of the scene.

Palm tree near the River Jordan.   18 Feb. 78

Kibbutz Beit Zera: palm tree by the River Jordan.

I'm reading Laurens Van der Post's A *Story Like the Wind*. I'm intrigued by his account of the Kalahari Bushmen. They live close to nature, lives defined by their survival in a harsh environment. On this journey, spending extended time in nature has allowed my natural, more spontaneous self to emerge. Van der Post describes how the Kalahari Bushmen's refined senses allow them to communicate telepathically in dreams. Living a Western lifestyle, I often lose the intimate connection with my own body, with my deeper self, and with others.

I read letters from home. My mother reports that my stepfather has brewed a batch of mead for my return. There's a letter from Brian. After we parted in Igoumenitsa, he visited his parents in Corfu. He traveled to Crete and cycled there until his bicycle was stolen. How sad his trip had to end that way. A mutual friend writes that Brian has settled back into the old routine, and I'm relieved that's not my story. The last letter is from Rudy; it is short. His father died fourteen hours before he arrived home. I'm so sorry, and my heart goes out to him. During our travels, Rudy spoke lovingly of his father, who was an engineer with KLM Airlines. I wish I could support Rudy in his grief. The news leaves me sad and introspective.

My English roommates, Elaine and Cathy, discuss their upcoming trip to southern Israel. On an impulse, I ask if I can come along. I'm ready for a break from kibbutz life.

It's early February when we set off. The three of us take a bus to Jericho. From there, we hitch a ride south. The farther south we travel, the more barren the countryside. We travel a road that skirts the western shore of the Dead Sea. On the opposite shore, high cliffs rise vertically from the blue, saline waters. The contrast between the iridescent aqua and the arid surroundings is startling. The road heads due south, parallel with the Jordanian border. We're still in the Jordan Rift Valley. It narrows as we travel south. The road rises to higher ground. The valley and the Dead Sea sit hundreds of feet below sea level. The higher ground we cross is what prevents the Red Sea from rushing in and filling the valley.

We arrive at the tip of the narrow finger of ocean that is the Gulf of Aqaba. Here, there are two cities, almost on top of each other. To the west sits Eilat, in Israel. To the east, in Jordan, sits Aqaba. From Eilat, I can see even from a distance that the city of Aqaba is threadbare in contrast to its modern, brash neighbor.

The Red Sea forms a long arm with two outstretched fingers at the top. These two stretches of water form a huge V. The left finger is the Gulf of Suez; the right is the Gulf of Aqaba, which is where we are. These two bodies of water form the sides of a vast triangular peninsula: the Sinai. These hundreds of square miles of torturous granite and limestone lack any river or water. The mountains of the Sinai tell of colossal geological forces. The collision of the African and Asian continental plates caused buckles that today can be seen as sharp peaks. This is a wild and inhospitable place.

Only three of the noteworthy interior locations are accessible, all via dirt roads: St. Catherine's Monastery, Mount Sinai, and the Feiran Oasis. St. Catherine's sits on the reputed site of the burning bush, and below the mountain where Moses is said to have received the Ten Commandments. There are few other trails, and what life there is clings to the narrow strip of coastline. We're traveling southwest, down the right side of the V. The sky is a cloudless azure blue. Gas stations and tea shops inhabit the occasional untidy cluster of shacks. The land rises up sharply on our right. The shale slopes climb up to high cliffs and crags. There's no vegetation; all is uniformly dry and barren. Beyond the sparkling Gulf of Aqaba to our left sits the smoky blue silhouette of mountainous Saudi Arabia—the very name conjures intrigue. It appears even more rugged and desolate than this side.

Several short rides disappoint, so we catch a bus to Nuweiba. A final ride with an Israeli army truck will take us to our destination: Dahab, a small Bedouin village. From Nuweiba, the road rises and turns inland. We travel across plains of sand strewn with rock. The mountains press in on either side. The wind has blown the sand into drifts. The graceful curves of the dunes create enchanting combinations of color and shadow. The road slices unexpectedly through a pass. Rocky walls rise sharply to meet the unclouded sky above. Some miles farther, the truck drops us outside an area enclosed in cement block walls. Atop the walls is a high fence capped with barbed wire: an Israeli army base.

We thank the driver, say goodbye, and walk the few kilometers to Dahab. *Dahab* means "golden" in Arabic, and the place is probably named for the fine yellow sand here. It's a small settlement on an oasis next to the coast. We walk along the dirt road toward the beach. All around us is sand and rock. Behind, there is a backdrop of fantastical mountains. Ahead, a fringe of palm trees glints in the sun. Beyond this band of brilliant green lies the aquamarine of the Gulf of Aqaba. It's flecked with white and sparkles beneath the midday sun. A brilliant unbroken blue dome above pulls this all together. In the noonday stillness, I think I hear the surf breaking beyond the palms.

Israel annexed the Sinai Peninsula after the Six-Day War with Egypt. Before that, it was Egyptian territory. At the time, the only ones here were the Bedouin, their goats, and their camels. The Sinai Bedouin clans are the indigenous people of the area. They're nomadic, but these days some remain in one place and seek tourist-related income.

We're on a large crescent bay. The Bedouin have built six small shelters of palm branches a little above the high tide mark on the beach. There are no other man-made objects to be seen. The setup is simple and idyllic. The Bedouin encampment is out of sight behind the line of palms. Negotiating a rate for the shelter doesn't take long. Who can argue with seventy-five cents a day? Our landlord wears a flowing cotton robe and a *keffiyeh* headdress held in place with an *igal*, or a black rope made of camel wool. He looks hot to me, but there must be some wisdom to this mode of dress. They've been living in this heat for thousands of years, after all.

Our hut is eight feet square and five feet high. It is a simple wooden frame with palm branches lashed to it. It's just big enough for three sleeping bags side by side. Should it rain (*does it ever rain here?*), there would be no protection at all. Soft beach sand is our floor. Inside, slivers of sunlight form patterns of light across the sand. Once inside, I squint at the brightness outside. From our small doorway, the beach slopes directly down to the

water. Sunlight sparkles off the peaks of incoming waves. Beyond, I see horizontal bands of blue and turquoise. The surf breaks at a reef a few hundred
yards offshore; the ocean seethes at this barrier with a low, steady roar. This
background note provides a steady accompaniment to the brighter sound
of waves breaking on the sand nearby. A steady breeze passes through the
palm leaf walls, rustling the fronds. The leaves intermittently flash as they
catch the sun. The moment has a dreamlike tranquility.

Our hosts come by several times a day, selling *shrak*—a paper-thin flat
bread—and other staples. Elaine and Cathy immediately pay the prices
asked, not knowing that they can bargain. We eat our food and learn that
even in paradise there are flies; the strong breeze doesn't deter them.

In the late afternoon, the light changes dramatically. As the sun dips
behind the mountains, they turn every shade of purple and orange. For
twenty minutes, we're figures in a Maxfield Parrish dream. A soft breeze
rustles our walls. The surf sounds gentler in the hush of the evening. As
the light of day slips away, the coastline opposite appears to move closer.
Individual peaks and crags appear within the silhouette. Night descends,
and stars emerge from the dome of black velvet. I lie on my sleeping bag
and drift to sleep, thinking of Ria.

I awake and am bewildered. Inches from my face, palm fronds shudder
and flash with silver sunlight. Then I remember that I'm in paradise. After a
quick swim, I hike into the mountains. I scramble up steep slopes of loose
rock and sand. It's hard going, and the heat makes it doubly so. I follow a
broad avenue of shale that rises steadily between two high shoulders of
rock. I climb for two hours and don't look back. I want to surprise myself
with the view from on high.

I come across a single, wizened tree. How long has it clung to life in
this remote place? If it does ever rain, this bounded slope must act as a
spillway and leave this tenacious loner with enough precious moisture to
keep going. The trunk divides into two at ground level. One side is dead,
with branch stubs straining skyward. Its horizontal canopy of needle
leaves is more gray than green. Lower limbs have been roughly hacked
off, presumably for firewood. But who ventures up here? Grateful, I stop

in the small pool of shadow it provides. The view is stunning. From where I stand, the ground slopes steadily down, then drops out of view. To my left and right, walls of rock rise and limit my view to a shallow U. Far below, the blue of the Gulf of Aqaba appears lit from within. Whitecaps rhythmically appear and dissolve. From here, I can see the silhouette of Saudi Arabia in more detail. Here and there along the water's edge, I can make out a narrow strip of coast. Beyond that, rows of misshapen mountains fade into a distant haze.

I lay in the shade and sleep a little. The day cools, and I walk twenty paces farther up the mountain. I make a pencil sketch of the solitary tree and the view beyond, then return after sunset from my day in the wilderness. The thinnest of new moons hangs in the sky. In the Bedouin village I can make out shadows moving noiselessly around small fires under clumps of palms. Gray-black mountains are silhouetted against the fading glow of day. Night falls and a gauze blanket of stars emerges against a black sky.

Lone tree in the Sinai   10.2.78

The Sinai desert: lone tree with Saudi Arabia beyond.

Glorious days of walking, contemplating, reading, and writing letters follow. Our small hut provides privacy and shade. I escape the heat of midday there. A hidden observer, I can see through gaps in the palm leaves. My roommates lack all understanding of local culture. They spend their days sunbathing topless. I can't imagine what the Bedouin men must think. Their women are swathed head to toe, according to Islamic edict. Elaine has the most perfect, round breasts; the sunburn developing there must be exquisitely painful. I could offer to tenderly spread suntan lotion where it's needed, but suspect rejection would be mine.

The hut residents gather each night around a leaping fire. Guitar music and our singing mix with the rhythmic breaking of waves close by. I consider form and function. Here in Dahab, I have the form, the outer manifestation of freedom. But what about the function? Is there an inner state that would allow me to be as free in Dartford as in Dahab? How do I learn to be unfettered of mind, no matter where I am? I'm standing at the threshold to this question. It intrigues and energizes me.

I study my maps of the Middle East and plan for the next leg of the journey. The usual way would be to retrace my steps, go northward through Jordan and then Syria into eastern Turkey. This is the way open to tourists, the route described in my overland to India book. I'm unhappy at the prospect of traveling again that dusty road through Syria. And, I've heard stories about eastern Turkey. Truck drivers detour hundreds of miles to avoid the mountains there. Robberies are common. Only the main road across northern Turkey is relatively safe. To reach that road or to travel east through the mountains, I'd be Beanstalk Jack crossing a vast giant's kitchen. If I must travel that region, I should probably take a train.

The shortest route from Israel is east, through Jordan and then Iraq. The map shows a road from Amman to Baghdad. However, Iraq issues visas only for business. There's also a road (on my map, anyway) across northern Saudi Arabia into Kuwait, skirting the south of Iraq. From there, boats cross the Persian Gulf to Iran. I've been told a Saudi visa requires you to travel in a vehicle you own. Would a bicycle qualify? I've seen remarkable things happen on this trip by just trying. The road through Saudi follows an oil pipeline across the desert. Would this be possible to cycle? For how many hours a day could I tolerate the heat? Could I carry enough water? I can see Saudi Arabia across the water. This somehow makes the notion of cycling there seem reasonable.

Regardless, without a tent, I shouldn't leave until the nights are a little warmer. When the tent was stolen in Athens, it turned out to be a blessing in disguise. Rudy and I learned how to find shelter just about anywhere. That proved an exercise in resting in the lap of God. When he left, Rudy took his gasoline cooker with him. Managing without cooked food will be another adventure.

After five days, I must leave this idyll; I'm expected to resume my duties at the kibbutz. Elaine and Cathy will stay some days longer. The trip back to Beit Zera is easy. A decrepit bus— driven by a local intent on meeting Allah sooner rather than later—takes me from Dahab. We hurtle along the small road, raising a long plume of dust. It's surprising that the bus chassis and body don't come apart as we crash through potholes. Against the odds, we arrive unscathed in Eilat. From there, luck grants me a ride with a truck going almost all the way to Beit Zera. The four-hour journey is unalloyed pleasure. I share the back of the open truck with a mysterious piece of large machinery. I lay stretched in the sun, the wind blowing through my hair. The desert slips past. Sun on my skin, the wind rushing in my face: like being on a bicycle. I'm happy.

I have the urge to break into a run as I walk up the long driveway to Beit Zera. It's a homecoming of sorts; I'm returning to my present family, this eclectic band of travelers. I spend the evening with Ria and enjoy just hanging out with her. The next morning finds me peeling vegetables in the kitchen.

In Dahab, I discovered I had crabs, so I visit the kibbutz nurse to ask how to deal with them. She tells me I also have head lice—the uninvited guest jackpot. The nurse describes the Israeli Army's treatment for head lice. Mix together one part hot water with one part kerosene and one part vinegar. I apply the vile-smelling concoction and tie a plastic bag around my head, then sleep overnight with it in place. This leaves the skin on my hairline and neck raw and red. I imagine the lice must be gone. The cure for pubic lice is more straightforward. I shave and use tweezers to remove the visitors one by one. I take every item I own to the laundry room, including my sleeping bag and bicycle panniers. I wash them using the hottest water setting.

Ria discovers that she, too, has both pubic and head lice. I try to make light of it and ask her if the lice speak both English and Dutch. She bursts into tears and runs away. *Oh dear.* The Dutch esteem cleanliness, and this must be a difficult experience for her. The other volunteers embrace the news with gusto. One suggests that I wear a bell around my neck to warn others of my approach. Another asks with a giggle whether Ria and I are expecting the patter of tiny feet soon.

Ria and I attend the Friday evening volunteer party. We dance and enjoy the great music. The fabulous experience of being in the Sinai is still with me, though, and I decide to leave Israel on Monday. The weather the next day confirms my decision. It's an openhearted, cloudless day. I while away a glorious morning at my spot by the Jordan.

Another letter from Rudy arrives on my last day at Beit Zera. This one is longer. He does not write much about his grief or his family's reactions to the passing of his father. I assume that it is still so raw, and so it's easier to write of other things. I'm grateful to him for his companionship and his belief in me. Good old Rudy. The letter reconnects me to the sense of adventure we shared. I pack, and an emotional stew courses through me—excitement and apprehension. What shall I meet on the road and within myself?

From the hut next door, Pink Floyd's song of yearning perfectly matches my mood. For my last evening, Ria has arranged a farewell party. Everyone arrives in Roman dress, using bed sheets as togas. It's a simple, joyous occasion. I'm touched by everyone's presence and the kind words.

My last night in the kibbutz brings a small triumph. I sleep next to Ria, but don't even try to coax her into anything more.

The next morning, several volunteers offer parting gifts. Ria borrowed my black T-shirt a few days ago, and she returns it. Over the heart, she has hand-embroidered a glorious bird in flight above a flaming sunset. There is loving care in the fine stitches; this T-shirt will remind me of Ria and all of the Beit Zera volunteers. I'm sad to leave these good people. Bill walks with me to the bus stop and waits until the bus comes.

The Israeli countryside slips by for the last time. Soon, I'm in Jericho. I walk across town for my next bus. Gnarled evergreens form a solid canopy over an ancient street. Patches of sunlight fall across timeworn curbstones that edge the dirt sidewalk. Somewhere out of sight is the murmur of running water. The stillness of the morning holds me; I stand motionless, not wanting to disturb the glory of the moment. With this blessed morning and an auspicious start to the next leg of my journey, the spirit of the wanderer rises in me again. I am back on the road.

I arrive at the Allenby Bridge around noon. Tall eucalyptus trees sway in the wind, their roots in a field of barbed wire. Their grandeur stands above the ceaseless conflict between Arab and Jew.

Route though Israel: The Allenby Bridge, Jerusalem, Nablus (West Bank), Jenin (West Bank), Newe Etan, Beit Zera Kibbutz, Tel Aviv, Beit Zera, Misgav Am, Beit Zera, Eilat, Nuweiba, Dahab, Beit Zera, Jericho, and the Allenby Bridge again.

Ten

JORDAN, A SECOND TIME

February 20th

THE ANTIQUATED BUS STRUGGLES UP the twisting road from the Allenby Bridge to Amman. The vehicle trails blue smoke as we grind up and away from the Jordan Valley. We crest the top and travel across a dusty plain. I look out the grimy window and watch an old man turn dry, red earth with a horse-drawn plough. The Allenby Bridge marked the crossing back into this other reality. I remember this all from ten weeks ago, yet it's different. I can't put my finger on how exactly.

Then I realize. It's the sunlight. It has a different quality. Winter is on the wane, and there's a breath of spring, a promise of new beginnings. Or is it just me seeing everything with new eyes? I arrive in Amman in the early afternoon. It's hard to believe that I left Beit Zera at seven this morning. The familiar routine starts again. The gaping mouths asking, "What ees your name?" and "Do you speak Eengleesh?" It grates. I hope I'll harden to it. I sit in the sun to write in my diary with the noise and squalor of Amman about me. I look down at Ria's embroidery on my T-shirt. A lump rises in my throat.

It's not difficult to find the house where I left my bicycle. The woman of the house says little as she shows me to the room. It remains unfinished, with cinder block walls and an unframed window open to the outside. I'm delighted to see my trusty steed again. Bilbo looks forlorn, covered in dust and with a flat tire. I run my eyes over the familiar mechanical parts: handlebars, wheels, brakes, pedals, chain and gears.

At dinner with the family, it's uncomfortable to talk about my time at the kibbutz. They know I've been to Israel, so I must offer some account of my time there. I sense pressure to offer a critical account. I do, but then feel shabby. I'm adding fuel to a conflict I don't understand. Muhammad, my host, recognizes my discomfort and ushers me away to another room in the unfinished section of the house. He says I should take all the time I need and that I can stay as long as I wish. He provides a bedroll and covers. The room is bare, yet clean. Last night, I was in a wooden bunk bed in the volunteer's hut at Beit Zera. Tonight, I get a cotton mattress on a concrete floor in Amman.

The next day I work on the bicycle. I want to overhaul it so that it's in good shape for the next leg of the journey. Did Rudy leave me a note? I open the front pannier and there it is. It starts, "Of course there's a message." He ends with, "Take the good direction, where the sun appears in the morning. And be nice to dogs. Look them in the eye and say, 'Hello doggy, doggy. Who's a nice doggy, then?' Or at least carry a big stick!"

Rudy, a dog lover, was always adamant that a friendly approach is reciprocated. That has not been my experience, but I am moved by his thoughtfulness. He wrote the note on his way to see his sick father. Through the open window, I notice again the quality of the Middle Eastern sunlight. Puffs of clouds scuttle across a blue sky. Below, clusters of unfinished concrete buildings appear flimsy and impermanent.

I cycle across town to the Iraqi Consulate to enquire about a visa. This is my first time on the bicycle in almost three months, and it's great. I'm looking forward to loading my luggage and setting out for Damascus. I feel no apprehension at being alone. I'm more at ease than the last time I was here. I'm not successful in getting an Iraqi visa. I'll try again in Damascus.

Back at the house, one of the women walks in on me as I'm shaving. It's an awkward moment. The house is female territory while their husbands are at work. I'll leave tomorrow.

This is the time to service the bicycle, paint it black, and remove the mile counter. As bicycles go, it's nothing particularly special—a mid-priced steel bicycle with the basic ten gears. Yet in Turkey and Syria, it attracted too much attention. It screamed, "privileged Westerner!" I'll feel safer when it appears less sophisticated.

I sit on the bare floor to disassemble it. I clean and oil each part before reassembling and then painting. As I work, memories of my first bicycle arrive, unbidden. That bicycle came into my life as a Christmas present when I was twelve years old. It was a red and white three-speed Philips: a Manhattan model. She had a decal of stylized skyscrapers on the seat tube. I loved that machine. She introduced me to a freedom I did not know existed. I spent hours cleaning her. I used an old toothbrush between the spokes to clean the chrome wheel rims. I worked a rag into her every nook until she shone.

Anything we boys cherish is a *she*. Practice, I suppose, for those of us who'll later take a different *she* to cherish. I join the family for a final evening meal. Together, we watch the evening news. I'm surprised at the news from England, with scenes of roads choked by snowstorms. On this warm evening, I feel a million miles away.

I arise early the next morning. I want to finish my preparations and leave. Everything goes so smoothly, my guardian angel must be working overtime. Even the tricky job of adjusting the crank bearings works the first time. In the past, I've spent hours on this and still couldn't get it right. I said my goodbyes to Muhammad last night. Since it's not appropriate for me to speak to the women, I leave the house without saying anything to them.

The chain rides crunchy and hard. It's time to change it out for the replacement I've carried from England. It's a relatively easy task. A group of grubby kids gathers. One of them runs into a nearby shop and returns with a bottle of cold orange soda. The morning is already warm, and I gratefully accept. I buy a few basic spare parts at a bicycle shop. Most of what I want isn't available since bicycles here use metric measurements. The proprietor brings me an unprompted glass of tea. I'm moved by these good-hearted people and by the glory of this day.

The wind is at my back as I leave Amman. I relish the noise of tires consuming miles. The open road unfolds ahead. I'm better prepared than at any other time on the trip. Joy wells within; I'm back on the road to India.

It's odd not to have a companion occupying the strip of road next to me, but I'm happy to be on my own. I can move at my own pace. There's no one to consult. The journey will surely have its challenges, yet there is inside me a small, steady voice. *Everything will be just fine. You have been cared for. You will be provided for every step of the way.*

When I set out from England, I was tentative. Without Brian, I doubt I would have set off at all. Then Rudy's company and friendship were essential for that next part of the trip. I'll manage on my own from here on out.

As I pass through a village, a young man flags me down. He invites me to join him for cup of tea. He's both a local schoolteacher and a poultry farmer. He takes me on a tour of the sheds where he keeps the chickens that lay eggs. It mimics large-scale egg production in Europe. He shows me with pride the special chicken feed, enhanced with nutrients and medications. So much for my notions of timeless rural culture.

The road crosses an expanse of semi-desert. There's a stark appeal to the empty landscape. The heat of midday rises all around me. The distance shimmers, shredded into strips.

At the border, I expect difficulties leaving Jordan since my visa expired nine weeks ago. The police seem deeply suspicious that I might have been to Israel. My Israeli visa was stamped on a separate sheet of paper that I've removed from my passport. I've also been through my things to remove any evidence of having been in Israel. I've blacked out any reference to Israel in my address book. I talk about my friend Muhammad in Amman, with whom I recently stayed. I describe my long stay in Jordan and the fine time I had here. They accept my story, but there's still suspicion in their eyes. I must pay six dinars for overstaying my visa. This is more than I can comfortably pay. Not altogether truthfully, I claim that I have only five dinars. After much discussion, the police chief reduces the fee to two dinars. Then the moneychanger quotes a usurious rate to convert my remaining Jordanian dinars to Syrian pounds. I simply state that I don't have a lot of money and that he's being unfair. After ten minutes of quiet persistence, he counts out thirty percent more than his initial offer.

 Route though Jordan: Allenby Bridge, Amman, and Dar'a.

Eleven
SYRIA, A SECOND TIME
February 22nd

IN THE SYRIAN BORDER TOWN OF DAR'A, I accept an invitation to stay at the home of a young man. I want to cycle from here to Damascus in a single day. Since it's sixty-five miles away, I set out at six in the morning. I put on all my clothes, including my gloves and scarf. The cold still chills me to the bone. No matter—I can handle the cold if summer is coming. I'll be too hot soon enough.

It starts to rain. I'm now wet as well as extremely cold. This reminds me of the disgusting weather in northern France during the first weeks of the trip. A pale haze of green covers the bare hills and hints that spring is on the way. The road is flat, straight, and thoroughly miserable. It's the only road between Amman and Damascus, and traffic is heavy. I concentrate hard because I share this slender ribbon of tarmac with trucks and cars. Large trucks carrying the telltale large, blue and white TIR (Transports International Routiers, or International Road Transport) symbol thunder past, too close for comfort.

I see two trucks with French license plates parked on the road margin. I stop to chat with the drivers, curious to learn what brings them so far from home. Between my broken French and their broken English, we communicate. They invite me to join them for lunch in the first truck's cab. They offer me coffee, French bread, and cheese. They regularly drive between Paris and Kuwait. They carry all the food they need with them, plus wine and drinking water; they don't want to eat local fare. They are sure I must have had many problems with local people and are incredulous when I tell them how I've been welcomed again and again.

One explains in great detail the infuriating bureaucracy at certain border posts. He becomes angry at just the memory. "These people are all mad!"

he shouts. The other nods vigorously in agreement. I empathize, since I've seen my own anger immediately reflected back to me. Many young men here are ready to pick a fight with a Westerner. I explain as best I can the other kind of experience I've had. When I approach with simple friendliness, it's reciprocated. At times, the remarkable generosity of the locals has taken my breath away. By the end of the meal, I may also have been placed in their "mad" category. I wish them safe travels.

Why is my experience different from theirs? To be sure, human kindness is in shorter supply around major highways. In Europe, I've found cafés and garages on motorways to be rough, unfriendly places. Travel a few miles from the highway, and people tend to be human again.

I'm determined to reach Damascus before nightfall, so I cycle hard. The road crosses a wide plain. I speed through several small villages. A plot of barren earth surrounds each small house. Around each of these "gardens" is a wall of irregular lava stones—the same kind of ugly black stone that is scattered across the plain. There are no trees, no flowers, and no rivers. It's a sad world of dust and soupy puddles. I pity those who live here. Just passing through is depressing.

I'm surprised to see a sophisticated military installation not far from the road. A radar station with a sparkling white dome sits atop a low mountain of tumbledown stones. It looks new, and is a testament to what the government of this poor state chooses to spend money on.

I enter the outskirts of Damascus, and my backside aches after ten hours in the saddle. I'll be happy to stop for a couple of days. I find my way to Abud's. He's surprised to see me and says repeatedly that he can't believe I'm back. He wants to know everything about my travels since we last met. We talk about my experiences in Israel; his face reveals that it's difficult for him to talk matter-of-factly about Syria's archenemy. This is the country against which he fought.

In the night, I'm awoken by hammering and shouting at the door to the street. In the morning, Abud investigates. The landlady's son was drunk and wanted to get into the house. His mother had other ideas. I'm surprised that Abud talks openly about the drunkenness. Isn't this a rare thing, given the

Muslim edict against alcohol? He says that it's not difficult to find alcohol in this anonymous city. There are few police officers to monitor people's actions beyond the city center. Religious belief and the fear of God are the police officers in poorer neighborhoods.

I explore the old city. Damascus is intriguing, and nowhere more so than in the sprawling bazaar. Most sections overwhelm me with their commotion and noise. And then there are unexpected islands of calm. In a side alley, an old man sits in a small workshop that opens to the street. He turns small pieces of wood beading on a hand-driven lathe. He sits cross-legged on the floor, the small lathe in front of him, and applies pressure with his feet on the chisel-like tool he uses to shape each small piece. He rotates the pieces using a bow strung with wet string. Working quietly, he produces intricate objects with these simple tools. I sketch the scene. He glances up at me, but continues working. When the turning wood squeaks, he lubricates it with a drop of water on each of the two iron pivot points. He moves the bow with an even rhythm. The piece turns this way, then that. Each one that he produces appears perfect, despite the constantly changing direction.

There are photographs of President Assad in every shop and on every bus, at every street corner and in every lecture hall in the university. On the escarpment that overlooks the city, there's a huge neon sign in Arabic: "Yes for President Assad." Abud explains that the seven-year presidential referendum will be in a few weeks. Assad is expected to win 99.6% of the vote. If God Himself were running for President, how many would say that He was not the best guy for the job? Methinks more than four in every thousand. The people affirm a choice proposed by parliament in a single-candidate referendum.

Abud explains the election process. There's a photograph of Assad on the ballot. It has two printed circles; one is solid red, the other an empty black circle. Placing an X over the red means yes to President Assad. Placing an X over the black circle means no to President Assad. Votes are cast in front of an election official, not in private. A no vote can inspire an emotional outburst from the loyal clerk. Am I the only one who wonders what might happen if the majority of the populace placed an X over that ominous black circle? I imagine that black ring featured in place of Assad's photo on posters papered across each tea shop and derelict building.

In the old quarter, I stumble across a small park. It provides welcome shade and an unhurried rhythm. An ornate bench provides a good place to sit and write in my diary. I'm packing up to leave when two pretty Syrian girls approach. Other than their headscarves, both are dressed in Western attire: jeans and sweaters. They engage me in conversation with halting English. I remain seated on the bench while they stand. They are nervous, glancing about occasionally as though they're checking to see if anyone is watching. They say they're originally from a Christian village north of here. They seem to see themselves as different from their Muslim peers.

With their limited English, comprehension is iffy. They talk between themselves in Arabic and giggle. Syrian girls that are this forward are a rarity. Painfully shy girls who make no eye contact are the norm. I'm a little uncomfortable, sensing some risk in this exchange. One appears confident in her English, while the other remains largely silent. The chatty one is Dima. She lives right here, next to the park. Her house is beyond one of the mud walls, but I can't understand where exactly. We talk for ten minutes. Glancing about, they leave as suddenly as they arrived.

Later, I tell Abud about the encounter. He also is surprised and warns me to be careful. He's serious and says it more than once. Recently, a French tourist was meeting with a local girl. One night, the young man attempted to climb into her house. The girl's brother cut off the intruder's right hand and the family beat the daughter. I remove *midnight tryst* from my to-do list.

I help Abud with his homework. He is so lost that helping means doing it. On the one hand, it feels good to help him succeed. On the other, he might be better off failing his interim exam and then choosing another subject. The limitation of his English language skills makes this a difficult idea to communicate. He says he's doing as well as his peers. Having attended some of his classes and talked with his classmates, he may, unfortunately, be right.

Damascus: Abdulghani and William.

Our discussion wanders back to the subject of Israel. I suddenly remember the few remaining Israeli banknotes tucked into a seam of one of my panniers. Burning them is the easiest solution. It wouldn't be good to be found with them. This is the first time I've burned money. Abud has done so many times and says, "Only the poor burn money. The rich never do." Am I rich? I'm traveling on a tight budget. But, I'm free to return to England at any point and earn more money. One thing is clear: Abud is generous. He freely shares the little that he has. He thinks first of my needs, and rarely of his own. His generous heart humbles me.

Despite Abud's warning, I return to the park where I met Dima. What can I say? A bee to honey and all that. I wait, but she does not appear. I take a bus into the city. A man on the street invites me to join him for tea in his apartment. He says that he wants to practice his English and I accept the invitation. The room is dim, with a high ceiling. It takes some minutes for my eyes to adjust. Floor-to-ceiling curtains of faded red velvet keep out the noonday heat. The room is airless and has a musty odor. Cheap art deco furniture clutters the place. The upholstery is grimy and threadbare. My host is a sad character, yet educated and fascinating to talk with. We sit in two oversized blocky armchairs that are placed close to each other. Beyond a gap in the drapes, heavy lace curtains move gently. This dreamlike scene is pickled 1940s; the original color and flavor have long since faded.

We talk about politics and the differences between Syrian and English culture. The talk turns to hippies and then to drugs. He asks if I've tried opium. I tell him I haven't, but might if the chance were to arise. He wriggles in his seat and says, "Oh, I wish had some stuff to give you." He leans closer, squeezes my arm, and his voice drops to a whisper. "Whiskey! I have some whiskey!" I thank him politely and explain that I don't drink alcohol—at least not in this situation! His disappointment confirms that he's interested in what might happen after the drinking.

He rises to switch on the light, which will surely break the spell of the place. However, the electric light offers only the dimmest of glows. It's time to extricate myself. I thank him for his hospitality and make a quick exit. Like I've just left a matinee movie, I am hit by the light and the heat the moment I step into the street.

Are these encounters an expression of the pent-up sexuality of a traditional culture in the modern age? After all is said and done, it's sexual attraction at play between Dima and me, and the same could be said for the older gentleman who longs to be with a drunken young man. Is it me and the sun-bleached hair? Or is it in the very air?

There's a diplomatic area of the city, where all of the embassies are bunched close together. I visit the Iraqi Embassy to request a visa again. The road that runs east out of Damascus goes all the way to Baghdad, so in theory, it's an appealing option. The Iraqis tell me it takes eight weeks to obtain clearance from Baghdad for a visa. That's too long a delay. At the Saudi Embassy, the staff is clear that owning a bicycle doesn't qualify for the visa requirement of owning a vehicle. It was worth a try. To skirt Iraq, I must now travel almost a thousand miles to the north. The route will follow the same road as I took before, through Syria and back into eastern Turkey.

I visit the British Embassy to see what advice they can offer. To step from the heat and squalor into a calm slice of England is bizarre. Inside the stately building, it's comforting to look at the notice board and learn of the Thursday evening whist drive. And that, even in Damascus, the British Ladies Society hosts regular tea parties. The middle-aged woman who attends to me has perfected emotional neutrality. She sits beneath large color photographs of the royal family's unsmiling gazes. Ms. No-Nonsense calls me "sir." She has mastered that fundamental skill of British bureaucracy: cordial obstruction. We're sorry. Her Royal Majesty is regrettably unable to provide me with any assistance.

I visit the Syrian government building where I can extend my current visa. I'm ushered into a large office, where an official wears an immaculate military uniform. His bearing is stiff, and the formality makes me nervous. I ask if it's possible to extend my visa. He responds by asking a little sheepishly if I have some time to spare. I'm in no particular hurry, I tell him. Then, could I please help him improve his English? Among towers of dusty paper, we review the basics of English grammar. He frowns in concentration for most of the hour-long lesson. With a charming smile, he then says that I can remain in Syria for three more weeks at no charge. I can probably stay two weeks more in Damascus and still have enough time to cycle north to the Turkish border. And, should I happen to be delayed beyond the three weeks, I now see that Syrian bureaucracy is as pliable as British bureaucracy is rigid.

I return to the Park of Forbidden Love a third time. Dima appears, and she is without her chaperone. I attempt to ask about what she hopes for from our meetings. With maybe fifty shared words, it's a difficult conversation. A man walks by on the far side of the park. Her face falls and she breathlessly says, "My father!" She hurries away, and twenty minutes later, a small girl— likely a younger sister—brings me an envelope. The note is one degree from unintelligible. In addition to the poor English, her handwriting is hard to decipher. I imagine she normally writes in Arabic. I believe she wants me to return tomorrow, but I can't be sure.

On the way back to Abud's, I buy bananas in the market to break my Sunday fast. The merchant places a bunch on one side of a scale. On the other, he places a kilo weight then adds a spark plug so that the two sides balance out. The scale stands on an aging barrow that leans fifteen degrees away from the horizontal position. The science of the arrangement is questionable. The merchant has a weather-beaten face, and it creases into a toothless smile. He's charming. With no pause for calculation he announces that it comes to one Syrian pound and twenty-five piastres. How can I argue?

I wait in line to buy bread at a small bakery. The baker works steadily, placing flat pieces of dough into an open oil-fired oven. People wait patiently in line for their order of steaming bread to emerge. A man tries to jump the queue. The baker is busy, but still notices and sends the man to the rear of the line. An old lady needs only a small quantity, and the baker calls her forward. Those who wait show unspoken acceptance of this compassionate exception.

The next morning, I return to the park. I wait two hours. No sign of Dima or her messengers. I spend the afternoon at the university with Abud and his student friends. They're bright, curious people. We discuss basic issues. Limitations of language frustrate our attempts to exchange ideas about politics, philosophy and religion. Since I speak no Arabic, I do most of the talking, questioning and clarifying in English. After a couple of hours of this, I'm drained. They, however, look as though they could continue all night. Maybe it's their blood nicotine levels. Most young men here smoke constantly. Imported American cigarettes are popular. Those who can afford them smoke Marlboros. I join in to be sociable. Abud says that few here think about the risks of smoking.

Not far from Abud's is Sultan Salim's mosque. This beautiful old building exudes serenity. The mosque itself sits along one side of an enclosed square courtyard. The three remaining sides are lined with a wide veranda, which shades a row of small rooms. Each room has a low doorway and a single window closed with ornate bars. These were cells for dervishes, monks of the mystical branch of Islam. The veranda and cells are formed from a series of domes, repeated arches, and pillars. The fine masonry work shows muted colors of various stones. Above the entrance to the mosque are panels of ceramic tile with intricate designs in turquoise and faded salmon. Large porcelain bowls at each corner of the courtyard contain flowers: a rarity here in the Middle East.

I sit on a smooth, cool paving stone under the veranda. All is muted and calm. The acoustics here reduce the roar of traffic outside to a far-off buzz. A small fountain murmurs in the square pond at the center of the bright courtyard. The cool stone walls emanate countless years of simple devotion. An apartment block that's just visible above the mosque roofline is the only intrusion from the modern world.

I return to the veranda many times over the coming days. I sit each time in exactly the same spot. The light changes from morning to afternoon and then into evening. It reveals different colors in the stone. The shadow of a single tree moves across the smooth flagstones. My place under the overhang moves from shadow to sun and back again. I sit with my back against a pillar that's been worn smooth with time. I can feel the cool stone through my shirt. No one talks to me; most pay me no heed. Those who acknowledge my presence do so with a gentle smile. There's no sense of being an outsider. The sun warms my face and hands. I am utterly content.

Damascus: the courtyard of Sultan Salim's mosque.

The faithful gather several times a day. As each arrival enters and crosses the courtyard, his pace slows. He removes his shoes, washes his face and feet in the shallow pool, and quietly enters the mosque. The unhurried movements are pleasing to watch. Two hundred or more bare-foot men offer prayers. They bow toward Mecca in unison on large reed mats. Several rows of heads touch the ground, and corresponding lines of bare feet show pale soles. The mosque itself isn't open to non-Muslims, yet I feel welcome in the courtyard. Just being here lifts my spirits. A group of French tourists arrives, takes photographs, and leaves. The calm effortlessly repairs itself.

An old woman sells fortunes outside the mosque. She sits at a wooden box that holds hundreds of small, rolled pieces of paper. These form a honeycomb of sorts along the bottom of the box. I hand her a few coins to see how it works. From another box by her side, she produces a guinea pig and places it on the multicolored papers. The animal runs to and fro, then stops to sniff. It removes one of the rolled papers with its teeth and the old lady takes it. Back at his room, Abud translates the slip of paper. "You, man, owner of this fortune: sometimes thoughts go round your head. There are many things which you say you want to do, but you have been disappointed by failure. You must work harder to achieve your dream. It is necessary to travel sometimes. Try to overcome the obstacles which lie in your path."

I return to the Bench of Romantic Possibility in the park. Neither Dima nor an envoy appears. I walk to the city center. The newer section is loud and unpleasant. Ornately decorated buses thunder past, belching black clouds. They sound their horns incessantly, and the noise shoots pain through my temples. This puts me in a foul temper. Abud diagnoses my bad mood as frustrated sexual desire: a direct result of being unable to see Dima. Full access to Dima as a cure for my sourness? An appealing idea, but I'm pretty sure the mood results from a stubborn ear infection, plus the Buses from Hell.

I need a change of pace, so I cycle out of the city on the road to Beirut. A few miles before the Lebanese border, I find a sheltered place away from the road where I can write in my diary. I'm some miles beyond the outskirts of Damascus. The snow-covered mountains that separate Syria from Lebanon are behind me. Semi-desert and scrubby low hills stretch out before me. The Barada river runs out of these hills. It's a desolate place.

I return to the city by the road that follows the river. As it nears the city, the torrent divides into smaller streams that thread through different neighborhoods. This civil engineering of the intricate waterways began hundreds of years ago. Emerging on the far side of the city, the water flows into ever-smaller channels. Supplemented by natural springs, the water irrigates the gardens of the Al Ghouta. This fertile plain stretches for ten miles south and east beyond the city. Here, villagers grow vegetables, oranges, lemons, plums and apricots. The desert starts where the channeled water finally runs out.

I walk the bicycle on a path above a fast-moving stream hemmed between earthen banks. Two lines of pollarded willows line the murky channel. Passing an old mill, rats scuttle from my path. It's a scene straight from Dickens's London. The stream threads its way through the narrow space between two buildings. Farther on, it exhales into a broader flow and then glides out of sight, sparkling and silent, beneath a tunnel of silver winter trees.

I return to the park. How many times has Dima or a messenger come, only to find this bench empty? Today, a young boy approaches. He says nothing, makes brief eye contact, thrusts a note into my hand, and runs off. It's a note from Dima. She writes, "Meet me at cinema at o'clock 1." She doesn't say which cinema. There are several in the city. She doesn't say what day. I assume she means tomorrow.

A little before one the next day, I begin a continuous circuit of the six cinemas near the city center. By two thirty, there's still no sign of Dima. I'm walking back to Abud's when she appears on the street with a young friend. For an hour, we walk and talk as best we can. I'm unable to understand at which cinema she was waiting. A foreigner walking with two Syrian girls attracts many stares. She tells me that she doesn't like Arabs or Muslims. She's also in big trouble with her family for seeing me. She watches nervously for anyone who might know her. Why does she risk so much to meet me? Does she hope to escape from a society she finds intolerable? I can't even guess at the gulf between her world and mine.

I guide the conversation to the subject of marriage. I tell her that I don't want to marry, so she won't have unrealistic expectations. This is unfair of me, since I myself am unclear what expectations I have for the relationship. If there's disappointment in her eyes, she hides it well. She asks if all the girls in London are beautiful. I reply that some of the most beautiful women I've seen are in Damascus. Her face reveals that she doesn't believe me. I want her to know that she is beautiful, but I'm reluctant to be so direct. That evening, Abud offers to visit the park and talk with Dima on my behalf since communication is so difficult. He returns and explains that they didn't talk long because she had to return home quickly. She's eager to continue to see me. Now that he's met her, he gently encourages me. "She's like you and enjoys breaking the rules," he says. He's arranged a date for me at ten-thirty in the morning, three days from today.

I visit a post office to buy stamps and meet a young man. He invites me to his house for coffee. I answer his questions about England and my travels. He mentions, as if in passing, that it's difficult for a gay person in an Arab country. He keeps this secret from his family and most of his friends. I now understand why his family didn't offer me a typical enthusiastic Syrian welcome. He hasn't done as good a job keeping it a secret as he thinks he has. He says he can tell me because everyone in Europe accepts homosexuality. It's kinder to not tell him about the pervasive homophobia in England. Personally, I'm torn between open-mindedness and feeling threatened. Abud is shocked when I later describe this meeting. He warns me darkly to be careful because this is Damascus; there are dangers of which I am not aware. After the story of the Frenchman who lost a hand, I think I'd rather not know the details. I feel less like a seasoned traveler and more like a boy, still wet behind the ears.

Abud's room is simple. The one piece of furniture is a metal bed. His books are arranged in piles along the walls on the floor. To make shelves for his books, I cajole two wooden fruit boxes from a storekeeper. I fashion a basic set of shelves using my bicycle tools and a few wood screws. Without a drill or saw, it takes a long time. After several hours, I have a blister on my right palm from forcing rusty screws into hard wood. I'm satisfied with the end product and happy to be able to do something for Abud in return for his kindness; I hope he'll be happy with my gift when he returns after his classes.

The tranquility of this quiet evening is shattered as the front door bursts open. A man in military uniform rushes into the room, waves a pistol in my face, and shouts wildly in Arabic as he gesticulates frantically. With the gun trained on me, he lifts the mattress, looks under the bed, and goes through the books I've just arranged. He keeps an eye on me the whole time, like he thinks that I might run for it. Does he think that I'll whip out a .38 and get off the first shot? He continues to shout at me, wild-eyed. I've no way to know what he's saying. Adrenaline courses through my system; I'm scared. Is this a drug raid? I pray that Abud has no drugs here. Did the police receive a tip-off about a foreigner fomenting insurgence? Could this be something to do with Dima? I've committed no crime. Or have I? I don't even want to think what Syrian jail is like. *Holy mother of God, this doesn't look good.*

With a wave of the gun he motions for me to follow him. I step outside, my heart racing. In the gloom of the darkened stairwell stands Abud, doubled over with silent laughter. I am angry with him—oh, so angry with him. This only adds to his merriment. I'm in a cold sweat. Abud's laughter subsides and my heart slowly returns to its normal rhythm. He explains that he thought it would be fun to ask a friend from the army to fake a raid. Some say English humor is an acquired taste; I am here to report that Syrian humor is another flavor entirely.

Abud and I stay up late and listen to music. Knowing that he loves contemporary Western music, I recorded some cassettes for him in Israel. He particularly likes the Beatles. By listening to it over and over, we decipher and write down the lyrics to "Norwegian Wood" and accompany John Lennon with great gusto. Perhaps this will help Abud with his English.

My date with Dima is the next day, but the late-night songfest means I don't wake until eleven. I arrive at the park late and she's not there. I wait a long time, but she doesn't appear. I never see her again.

In this conservative society, such meetings are forbidden. Sexual attraction is a smoldering coal that yearns to be a fire. Better not to fan that ember until marriage. Dima and I enjoyed innocent moments together, yet the sexual energy between us was unmistakable. It ends in disappointment for me, and probably heartache for her. I will often think about her and wonder how things might have turned out differently had we met that day.

The weather is as wet and cold as it is in England. After several days in this small room, I'm a caged animal. By the third evening, I'm in a foul mood. Abud's friends visit and I don't try to understand their poor English. I tell one of them that his English isn't good. I can see that I hurt their feelings and that Abud is angry with me. I crawl into my sleeping bag and sleep until late the next morning.

Abud returns that evening with a massive box of sweets. He doesn't say so, but I understand that these are to cheer me up. I am humbled. He has a pure heart and sees the good in everyone. With shining eyes and a ready smile, he's a joy to be around. I'm fortunate to have met him.

To clear my head, I walk out into the wet night. There are no street drains, and I weave my way between the many puddles. The deserted streets are a balm to my stormy disposition. Dark pools of water reflect light from a single electric bulb that swings on a wire in the wind. Yet there's no sense of danger walking these streets at night. I'm safer here than in England. There, groups of youths actively seek trouble. The absence of alcohol goes a long way in making it safer here, along with religious belief that exerts a force field of civility. This social harmony is a testament to Islam.

I want to better understand, so I ask Abud to tell me more about Islam. He starts by saying, "*Islam* is Arabic word. It means, *salaama.* This is peace and obeying will of God." Despite Abud's halting English, I'm pretty sure I grasp most of what he says. If one obeys God's laws, one is in a state of Islam. I fail in my attempt to explain to Abud that Christians might call this a "state of grace."

Abud tells me that the Quran is the sacred book of Muslims. It's written in Arabic, the language spoken by Muhammad the Prophet, peace be upon him. Abud explains that you should say "peace be upon him" because if you are a believer, then you should ask Allah for blessings upon Muhammad each time you say his name. If you don't, it shows that you are miserly in spirit.

The Quran, my friend tells me, contains one hundred fourteen chapters, or *surahs*, and more than six thousand verses. He translates a few short sections of the Quran for me. I surmise that, like the Bible, the Quran is a book of metaphors and parables. It can be understood on several levels simultaneously. So both the fundamentalist and the liberal can quote the Quran to validate their position. There are three main themes: the existence of only one God, the role of prophets, and life after death. The Quran recognizes other prophets besides Muhammad, including Noah, Abraham, Isaac, Moses and Jesus. Muslims believe that these prophets were appointed by God to teach mankind. I tell Abud that seeking to understand and follow God's will is also the essence of Christianity. Perhaps Islam is not as foreign to me as I'd thought.

Faith is woven naturally into the fabric of everyday life here. I can see how the world is a better place because of Islam. It's a force for good in the lives of millions. My respect for their beliefs grows as I travel among these good-hearted people.

Blue skies return. With warmer days, the world is made new. I want to get busy, to move. During my weather-related imprisonment, it became clear that something must be done about the ceiling of Abud's room. It is covered in designs of black soot made with a lighted candle. This visually lowers the ceiling and lends an oppressive air to the tiny space. There's a shop I've noticed that sells large squares of white paper. I spend a satisfying evening papering the ceiling. I prepare a simple meal and proudly welcome Abud back that evening to a lighter, larger room.

I must leave Damascus this coming Monday. That will give me six days of visa in which to cycle two hundred fifty miles of difficult road to the border. I've been living the relaxed Arabic lifestyle of *shway, shway*—slowly, slowly. With limited time now to travel to Turkey, the *shway, shway* must become an energetic *away, away*!

Approaching spring matches my anticipation of change. Bare trees show the first signs of blossoming. I visit a local hospital for a cholera shot. The doctor is in his nineties and looks like someone you'd expect to see selling sheep heads in the souk. I imagine his hands will be unsteady, so I close my eyes and brace myself. It's the least painful shot I've ever been given.

On the day of my departure, Abud needs to wake at eight in the morning. Neither of us has an alarm clock, so he agrees to try my unfailing technique. Just before going to sleep, I visualize a clock showing the time I want to awaken. I tap my head against the pillow, once for each hour. In this case, I tap eight times. I awake the next morning with ten minutes to spare. At eight, I rouse my friend from a deep sleep. He declares the technique useless. I make final adjustments to the bicycle. Bilbo is heavily loaded; the many gifts of food attest to the generosity of my hosts.

We share a glass of tea and pledge to see each other again. We have grown close during these weeks. He's worried for my safety and would prefer to see me return to England rather than continue to India. The subcontinent is as foreign to him as Syria is to me. His parting words are, "Be careful."

The road takes me initially to the west along the Barada Valley before turning to the north. That odd mix of sadness and excitement flows again through my system. When I set out, India was more of a vague notion than an eventuality. Brian and I were "headed east." Rudy and I were "going to Israel." Leaving Israel, Damascus was my destination. Now, there are no more interim destinations. I'm cycling to India.

The long climb into the mountains north of Damascus is easier than I'd expected. Maybe I'm not as out of shape as I feared. These are the Al Jabal ash Sharqi Mountains that divide Syria from Lebanon. There's not much to enjoy in this barren landscape. Patches of late snow relieve the starkness of the scene. Tonight will be cold.

After I've cycled some fifty miles, a Volkswagen beetle passes and then pulls over. The young driver offers me a lift to Homs, fifty miles ahead. That will help with my limited time with a valid visa. It's a struggle to get the bicycle into the back seat. We drive, and he describes his life as a Gillette sales representative in Syria. He's educated and his English is good. It's a pleasure to talk with someone who speaks my language and understands my world. After extricating the bicycle, we say a cheery farewell.

There's a marked difference between the first and second part of my journey today. The bicycle energizes me, and the passing of every mile is a joy in its own right. The ninety-minute car ride leaves me with a tired body and lethargic mind. Feeling a little guilty about accepting a ride, I mentally tally up the sections I didn't cycle: across the English Channel by ferry, Volos to Athens by truck, Athens to Samos and on to Kusadasi by ferry, Damascus to the Syrian border by steam train, and today's ride. That's six hundred miles by motorized transport, and five thousand nine hundred in the saddle.

I can face no more of the dreary scenery of inland Syria. If I travel through Talbiseh again, I might meet the English Literary Machines. *No, thank you.* Traveling west, then north along the Mediterranean will be a welcome change. This will also allow me to visit Abud's family in Lattakia.

So, from Homs I take the road west toward Tartus, a port on the Mediterranean. Syria would be a landlocked country if it not for the one hundred ten miles of coastline between Lebanon and Turkey. As I leave Homs, the scenery changes. This is another world. There are grass and trees; greenery means rain. I expect to see sloped, tiled roofs, but the houses use the same flat roofs found in the dryer interior of the country; they look out of place in this verdant setting. The road follows the northern border of Lebanon. The snowcapped peaks of the Lebanese mountains lie in the distance.

A group of men is seated on the grass near the road. They call out and motion for me to join them. No one speaks English or French. With my thirty words of Arabic, we struggle to communicate. They offer me a cigarette, that universal gesture of friendship. We sit in silence as the smoke of my cigarette curls into the quiet evening air. Serenity reigns. Hoping that it will prompt an invitation of shelter, I ask in mime if it will rain tonight. They reply with gestures that indicate they'll give me a place to sleep. I assume they are resident workers at the sand quarry nearby. They live in simple dormitory accommodations. There are no women, and I guess each worker has a family in another part of the country. They invite me to join their evening meal. I'm touched by this unquestioning generosity.

The pleasant evening changes with the arrival of the first Syrian man I've seen wearing his hair long. He's a big man with a powerful frame, and he smiles often as he talks, but his smile is incongruous. His laughter has a mean edge. He batters me with an appalling version of the English language while he tells me about his "seven boys." He's not old enough for this to mean seven sons.

A few minutes into the conversation, he announces loudly, "Tonight, you will sleep with me." He says this not as a question, but as a simple statement. He continues talking at me, uninterested in my responses. He tells me that I should not smoke because I am a girl. The other workers clearly have no idea what this creepy specimen is saying. I mentally catalog the possible outcomes of this encounter, and none are pleasant. How many others in this group are gay and missing the restraint chip in their brain? I'm afraid, uncertain of how to proceed. Should I pack up my things and head out into the night? That could be just as dangerous. I wrestle with my alternatives for a good half hour.

One of the older men quietly motions for me to follow him. He leads me to an empty room nearby. He takes a key from his pocket, shows it to me and demonstrates how it will lock the door. So, at least one person understood what was happening. I'm relieved.

I remain in the room and decide not to return to my hosts. Unbidden, an English comedy film comes to mind. In it, a medieval merchant offers his wares to departing crusaders. He cries out, "Chastity belts! Chastity belts!" A knight buys one and the merchant waits for the purchaser to leave the market square. The merchant then changes his call to, "Spare keys! Spare keys!"

Before going to sleep I arrange my bicycle and belongings as a blockade against the door. It won't stop someone from entering, but it should wake me if anyone has another key. I sleep without any disturbances through the night. I quickly pack the bicycle and hold my breath as I walk my bicycle away from the quiet dormitory buildings. I don't see a soul. Back on the road, I consider the events of last night. Am I in an environment I can't handle? When I reach Turkey, I could just as easily turn left toward Europe as turn right toward India.

The road to Tartus passes through a small section of Lebanon. There are no border posts, so no visa requirements. The road is lined for these two miles with small shops. Each shop is a mere box, lacking windows or doors. Open shutters reveal merchandise stacked from the floor to the low ceiling—all imported items.

There's no gap between one shop and its neighbors, so they form an unbroken corridor of commerce. In this open, green valley are hundreds of plywood and tin shacks stuffed with washing machines, boom boxes, whiskey, and packs of Dutch beer. Taxes on imported items are much lower in Lebanon than in Syria, I assume. Discarded cardboard boxes litter the surrounding fields. It makes for a sad and sorry sight.

Back again in Syria, the landscape becomes progressively greener. It could be the French Alps with snow-covered mountains in the background. Gray clouds litter the evening sky and the smell of rain is in the air. *Where shall I sleep?* Just as anxiety starts to nibble, I glimpse an open-top truck trailer parked some distance from the road. *Perfect.* I create a makeshift bed on the ground under the trailer. It'll provide a solid roof in case of a downpour. But the trailer chassis is so low that I hit my head each time I turn, so I move my bed up onto the trailer itself. The sides offer some shelter from a gathering wind. The sky is ominous, but there's a large tarpaulin in the trailer that I can pull over myself, should I need to.

I am not far from the sea. The lights of Tartus sparkle below me. The smell of the sea air in the dark, a brisk wind, and those lights in the distance take me back to another time, to Clevedon on the Bristol Channel. I'm with a girlfriend on the small beach of Ladye Bay. It's night, and a steady, incoming wind blows. Beyond the dark water glimmer the lights of Cardiff. Steep cliffs and pine trees stretch high above us. Sleep comes, and the line between the place where I am and the place I remember is unclear. A dramatic downpour awakens me. The tarpaulin is a blessing, but it's airless and heavy after I pull it over me. It's a restless, damp night.

Tartus sits in a huddle of huge, gull egg blue oil storage tanks. I don't stop. The road turns north to follow the coast, and the land rises to my right in a series of terraced areas. The lower tiers hold olive groves; above is farmland, and above that are patches of forest. The ruins of a castle sit atop a high hill. To my left, a patchwork of fields slopes down to the distant blue line of the Mediterranean. I eat lunch in an olive grove and hang my wet things on the low branches to dry in the sun. A farmer ploughs nearby, using a mixed team of a donkey and a bullock. A woman follows, rhythmically casting handfuls of seeds onto the fresh earth. The warm air is heavy with the scent of orange blossoms. This stretch of road is pure cycling pleasure. It gently rises and falls with the coastal plain. There's little traffic, and the miles are a joy.

Lattakia is a large city with a modern port. It brims with ships and dock cranes. The setting sun dips below a bank of gray cloud that sits on the turquoise water. The sun projects three broad bands of blood red light into the sky. It's a Turner painting, and I hold my breath, lest I disturb this perfect moment.

Abud's family's home is easy to find. I deliver a letter from their absent son and am invited to stay with them. Abud's father is a friendly man. He speaks quite an array of languages: Arabic, Sengali, Kurdish, French and Turkish. His is a large and prosperous family. In the evening, the house hosts a stream of visitors: friends, family, and soon-to-be-family. I'm surprised that two of Abud's unmarried sisters remain in the room. They appear comfortable talking with the men—a modern family indeed. Abud's elder brother shows me around the area. We visit a nearby beach, and he explains that the Arabic name for the Mediterranean Sea is the Middle White Sea. It's a name straight from Tolkien, if ever there was one. We return to his apartment. Friends arrive and we drink beer and smoke cigarettes. A David Bowie LP spins on a turntable; the opening lines of "Changes" carry me to another world.

Several relatives own farms near the sea and we take the day to visit. Each farmer has the bright eyes and open face of one who works and knows the land. My blond hair and blue eyes get attention from the girls we encounter. One says I must stay in Syria and marry an Arab girl. She's a real stunner. But the tug of the East is greater than—ahem—the tug of my south. I show my pencil drawings to a visitor back at my host's house. He's persistent in asking where I did the drawing of the Sinai. He ignores my noncommittal answers. I sense that he already knows the answer, so I tell him. Luckily, he's the only one present who speaks English. To not mention you-know-where is difficult. I squirm when the conversation turns anti-Jewish. More than once, I suggest that Israelis may be just everyday people. This notion is met with immediate hostility. A better strategy is to not engage at all in the subject.

After four days in Lattakia, I'm restless. I'm expected to sit for hours with the male family members and discuss at great length politics, money and work. If I ask to go for a walk or be alone to write, my host's eyes reveal that it is taken as a slight.

The family prepares a lavish meal for my final day in Lattakia. There's an array of dishes, and each is delicious. I eat too many of the sticky sweets. A yerba mate tea from Argentina is served after the meal. Each cup comes with an ornate metal straw. At the lower end of the straw is a small strainer bulb to filter the syrupy brew. This tea was a favorite of Che Guevara. Yerba mate was known as green gold for the wealth it brought plantation owners.

Che grew up on his parents' yerba mate plantation. He witnessed his father's principled refusal to mistreat the indigenous bonded laborers. At the time, such abuse was common plantation practice. Che thus learned a formative lesson in social justice for the oppressed. But how did this tea find its way to Syria? The Druze are members of a subsect of Islam that live in southwest Syria. Once powerful, they were later persecuted. A significant number emigrated to Argentina and introduced yerba mate to Syria on their return visits. Syria imports more yerba mate than any other country.

I set out early the next morning. The road between here and Antakya crosses a pass of fifty-five hundred feet. That's a significant climb from sea level, where I am. It's great to be back on the road, working hard. Sunshine, greenery, and the perfume of orange blossoms dissolve my morning sluggishness. The road meanders into the mountains, then gets serious and climbs.

I think of the large book by Sri Aurobindo that I carry at the bottom of one pannier. I have by now shed all extra weight. I've given away any item I don't use on a regular basis, including the small, blue plastic bowl with which I washed my cup, plate and spoon. As socks wore out, I did not replace them. In Israel, I passed on to others at the kibbutz the few pieces of clothing I did not consistently wear. My toiletries kit now comprises one simple razor, a toothbrush, small tube of toothpaste, and a sliver of soap.

I have one pair of shoes—a pair of moccasins I rescued from the trash in Israel. I repaired the frayed stitching with dental floss. My two diaries are too precious to put in the post, so I carry these. At most, I have just enough food for a next meal. The water in my foldable plastic container is the one variable in terms of weight. Other than that, I could not travel with less.

Except this one book. Knowing it is there in my pannier is oddly comforting; it's a tangible, reassuring presence. I'm working harder than I would otherwise in order to carry the book up into these mountains. This reminder of my trip's higher purpose is a source of quiet satisfaction. I do not begrudge that weight.

I cycle among heavy forest interspersed with small farms. A bright green meadow peeks through the darkness of the conifers. The road continues up and up. It's Sunday, and I'm not eating, yet I have a surprising amount of energy. Those sweets last night were not such a bad idea after all. I expect the Turkish border to be at the pass, but it appears many miles before.

 Route north through Syria: Dar'a, Damascus, Homs, Tartus, Mediterranean coast, and Lattakia.

Twelve

TURKEY, A SECOND TIME
March 26th

CROSSING INTO TURKEY, the change is immediate. Brick houses with sloping roofs of faded terracotta tile replace the flat roofs of Arabic dwellings. The road continues through thick forest up into the Amanus Mountains. I finally cross the high pass. I expect that my hard work will be rewarded by a steady downhill all the way to Antakya. I'm disappointed.

After a steep drop, the road heads up, then down and up once again. With each long climb, I tell myself I should stop. I relent at lunch and enjoy two raw carrots, but this is insufficient fuel for fifty miles of steady climb. All my *oomph* is long gone. Knowing that I'll sleep deeply, I need a place for the night where I can be secure. That's going to be difficult in this forested emptiness. After another long climb, I flop down on a patch of grass by the side of the road, exhausted.

From behind the dense wall of trees comes a farmer herding a few cows. With a smile, he invites me in gestures to follow him. The small village hidden nearby is a threadbare place. My host's home is a one-room cottage. Mehmet is simple and hospitable. It appears to not matter to him that we cannot really communicate. He seeks nothing from me. I break my fast and join him and his wife for their evening meal. To refuse food would insult them. His wife crouches over the fire as she prepares the simple meal. The food is hot and tasty.

The room is soon crowded with people curious to see the stranger on a bicycle. I sense a relaxed acceptance. The women sit motionless and stare at me with large, unblinking brown eyes. Two openly breastfeed their babies. These simple farming folk have adopted a functional variation of the Islamic dress code. A hundred miles south, a bare female breast in male company would be unthinkable. We talk in mime for a time. Without prompting, my

hosts see how tired I am and leave me to settle down for the night. I immediately fall to sleep on a warm mattress on the floor.

I awake around six with the rest of the family. Low, dark clouds throw
down sheets of rain. My host provides a hearty breakfast. As we eat, the
rain eases then stops. I'm feeling refreshed and ready once again for the
road. The main street of the village is awash in deep mud. The only way
forward is through. Mehmet insists on carrying my bicycle. He walks ahead
and carries with care my laden bicycle above his head. Wading after him,
knee-deep in the mud, I am suddenly moved to tears. Where else would
one find such unquestioning generosity? At the road, we look into each
other's eyes and share a long moment of nonverbal understanding. I hope
I communicate my gratitude through my eyes and smile. I shake his hand
warmly and leave.

The road crosses an elevated plateau. A following wind pushes me briskly
along the flat road. Beyond Antakya, I pass along the same stretch of road
that Rudy and I traveled five months ago. Construction has not advanced
on the row of small houses where we spent the night. A cousin of Arabic
shway, shway is alive and well, and he resides in Turkey. I cycle below the
Belen Pass, which Rudy and I crossed. I head north now on the road that
the signpost indicates is for Iran and Iraq. In a small town, I buy some bread.
A crowd of men and boys gathers in mere moments. Do they stand hidden
in shadowed doorways, awaiting Englishmen on bicycles? They stand too
close for my comfort and finger my belongings. Ah! *Welcome back to Turkey.*

The large tea shop is empty as I enter. It is soon a veritable sea of male
human beings. They stand in silence to watch my every movement. It's hard
to relax under the gaze of a hundred people. One of them invites me in
broken English to stay at his house, and I accept.

At the home of my host, one of those assembled tells me he's sixteen and
learning English. He suggests that we meet his English teacher in a nearby

town. I agree and we travel to Hassa in my host's car. We sit in a café, and a steady stream of boys appears. My host sends each of them to scour the town for the English teacher. He is found and finally arrives. I dislike him immediately. An insincere laugh accompanies many of his statements, even those that aren't funny. He talks quickly in poor English as he explains that he is a socialist and that all men are brothers. He insists that I stay at his house tonight and says that my bicycle will "arrive tomorrow." No one asks me what I want. My host and the teacher conduct a negotiation in Turkish. I secretly name the teacher Mr. Sticky. He announces that my host thinks this is a good arrangement. My host's eyes say otherwise. Against my better judgment, I stay.

It's an exhausting evening. I wrestle meaning from the barrage of poor English sent my way. Mr. Sticky insists that I must stay three days. I become angry when he won't accept no for an answer. He badgers me to visit his school and talk with his pupils. He's intent on wringing every last advantage from my visit.

The following day, I am an English teacher. From seven until eleven thirty, I'm hurried from one classroom to the next. I talk about England, about my family, and about my travels. I enjoy myself immensely. The kids sit motionless, intent on every word. I share as openly as I'm able. I'd like to show that this tourist isn't a shallow Westerner. I present a simplified account of my family and tire of the subject by the third repetition. There's a generation of children in the town of Hassa who know about the Spencer family—including Korky the cat and Silky the dog—who live in a big brick house in Hemel Hempstead, near London. I make simple drawings on the chalkboard to accompany my account. Mr. Sticky asks questions about money. What is the cost of a loaf of bread? What is the cost of a car? How much does a teacher earn?

In the first class, a young boy asks me to sing a song in English. The class takes up the request with gusto. It's difficult to say no to thirty pleading children. I hesitate for a minute and then surrender. The only song that comes to mind is "Yesterday" by the Beatles. The slow rhythm and my less-than-perfect delivery result in a sea of bewildered young faces. But when I sing "Old McDonald Had a Farm," it's an immediate hit. The children giggle when I make the noise of each animal. News of the singing Englishman spreads and each class ends with a demand for the song about the animals. There are no requests for the slow one by the lads from Liverpool. My fame even spreads to the staff room. The teachers want a command performance. What the heck, if I can sing in front of the kids, then I can sing in front of ten adults. After all, they're just older children. It's liberating to put my self-consciousness aside and sing with gusto. "With a moo moo here, and a moo moo there. Here a moo, there a moo, everywhere a moo moo."

My bicycle is indeed delivered today, but Mr. Sticky wants me to stay. He asserts that the clouds mean certain rain, but I tell him that I'm used to cycling in the rain. He tells me that the night will be cold. I explain that I'm accustomed to cold nights. He then plays his ace. The young biology teacher is single, he says, and "is good to sleep with." He glances about and adds in a low whisper, "She is willing, and ready for you." Does he mean here and now? Is she behind his couch, reclining naked on the floor? If all it requires is a few barnyard verses, she has probably known plenty of *moo moo here and moo moo there*. I decline this generous, yet problematic offer. By early afternoon, I'm back on the bicycle.

Stomach pains and diarrhea tell me I'm back in a region of questionable hygiene. It'll pass soon enough, but it leaves me weak. The days take on an unpleasant, dreamlike quality. The scenery is unbroken monotony; nondescript mountains, rocky terrain, and dreary houses float by. Extreme cold after sundown adds to the misery of wet weather. With an absence of trees and all things green, it's a bleak reality.

I pass through villages with narrow streets. Filthy cars and farm tractors churn the chocolate brown mud of the street into basins of smooth paste. It's a Dante-esque netherworld of ice-encrusted, brown puree. I weave back and forth to avoid potholes in the main street of a large town. Ramshackle shops of wood and corrugated metal sheeting line both sides of the narrow street. A shepherd herds a flock of floppy-eared black goats. Faces peer out at me from the shadows. Every man and boy stops to stare. The younger ones whistle, shout or run alongside my bicycle. The faces manage to both sneer and look hunted. A smiling face is rare. I am desperately cold and thoroughly depressed.

The stories of danger in southeastern Turkey are many, so I'll take a train from here to the Iranian border. In western Iran, I can then join Asian Highway One, which goes all the way to India—at least, that is what my overland to India map shows. From my map of Turkey, I see the nearest train station is Fevzipaşa. Another unexpected plain among the mountains allows the twenty-five miles to pass quickly.

Fevzipaşa is a small town clustered around a rail junction. The town and its railway station are a remarkable sight. Stone buildings cling to the side of a steep mountain. A railway track runs along a narrow shelf cut into the rock face. The track weaves to maintain a level course along the complex contours. I cycle toward town and see the railway is two hundred feet directly above me. The road turns up and away into a hairpin turn. The sides of the mountain carry deep wounds from stone quarrying. Houses made of this same stone cling together on the mountain that gave them birth. The scene is a study in brown and gray. There are no other colors, no hint of human comfort.

The rail station could have been transplanted from nineteenth-century Germany. This is the rail line through Turkey to Baghdad, courtesy of German financiers in the sunset days of the Ottoman Empire. It was built through tortuous terrain; British naval guns could have reached the easier coastal route.

My destination is the city of Tatvan, on the western shore of Lake Van. From there, a ferry crosses the huge lake to the city of Van. A connecting train then runs to the Iranian border. I enquire at the ticket office. The sole daily train is at midnight, says the clerk. Then he says no, it is at 03:00 hours. Then 06:40, then 04:40, then 03:02, then 03:12. My mounting frustration serves only to amuse him. With no better option, I agree to his suggestion that someone from the ticket office will wake me when the train is due. What the ticket office staff lack in precision, they make up for in friendliness. One clerk tells me I can sleep among the packages in the parcel room. Another asks me to join him for chai, and we walk a short distance through the cold, wet night. We sip hot tea at a café-cum-television parlor. Every Turkish town seems to have one of these. Tired-looking men in heavy woolen coats and caps watch a cartoon version of Pinocchio on the television. It's in Chinese. My host and I join a game of cards, whose rules I struggle to understand. From slaps on my back and cups of tea set before me, I gather I have won. No one here speaks a word of English or French, so there's no way to be sure.

Back at the station, the parcel room floor is covered in packages. Sleep will not be easy. The railway clerks share their simple food. The train journey to Tatvan will take twenty-two hours. I gather this from their convoluted sign language and counting fingers. I'm not permitted to take a bicycle with me in a passenger carriage, so they issue a separate ticket for the bicycle and assure me that it will be safe. I have grave doubts, yet there's no alternative. To lose my bicycle would be a tragedy. I resolve to keep a sharp eye on it. With the student identity card that I obtained in Damascus, the fare is forty-six Turkish lire for the five hundred–mile journey, or about two dollars. The bicycle ticket is three lire, which is another fifteen cents. If the bicycle and I arrive safely in Tatvan, it will indeed be a rail travel bargain.

There's a single light bulb in the parcel office. It hangs from a very old brown wire covered in tiny spiderwebs. I doze, seated on some crates. A clerk wakes me at four in the morning. I watch, bleary-eyed, as the bicycle is loaded into the goods carriage. A guard shuts and seals the heavy door. Using a hand tool, he embosses the metal seal with care. This offers me some reassurance about Bilbo's safety. I climb into an empty carriage. The guard blows a whistle. The train slowly pulls out of the station.

As day breaks, bleak mountain scenery slips by under a steel gray sky. We pass muddy villages with no people in sight and continue traveling deeper into this remote area. Shale-covered slopes and rock-strewn valleys lack any sign of life. A lone stork stands in the shallows of a muddy pond, nervously shifting feet. It watches me as the train slowly passes. For a long moment, there's only the two of us—the stork and me—together in a muddy wilderness. I'm separated from the outside by a sheet of glass, yet I can feel the bone-chilling cold and damp. The emptiness depresses and intrigues me. I imagine myself out there on my bicycle, alone and mired in a frozen hell-world of mud.

The train is mostly empty. From time to time, the ticket collector, the guardsman, and other unidentified railway workers come to join me in the carriage. Each somehow knows my name and that I am English. Each offers me a cigarette. We engage in the limited conversation of people who want to be friends but don't share a language. The train stops for an hour or more at each station. Now I understand why this journey will take twenty-two hours. The train is shunted back and forth as the locomotive is changed. We left Fevzipaşa as a diesel train. We're pulled now by a hissing black steam engine. The carriage windows mist from the warmth of the smoke as we move noisily through long mountain tunnels. That a railway line was cut through this extreme topography is remarkable.

The skies clear a little in the evening. We travel deeper into the heart of eastern Turkey before we arrive at the city of Elazig. The conductor explains in gestures that we'll continue at eight tomorrow morning. The other passengers walk to a nearby hotel, but no one objects to my sleeping the night in the carriage. I have only fifty kurus in Turkish money remaining, which is all of about three cents. This arrangement works well. Plus, I prefer to remain close to the bicycle.

I awake from a dream that has me back in Hemel Hempstead. There are a few moments of confusion before I recall that I am on the seat of a railway carriage in the mountains of eastern Anatolia. I'm refreshed, ready for the day. I must have had a long sleep.

There is absolute silence. The carriage is freezing cold. I unlatch the threadbare window shade and it snaps up noisily. There's heavy frost on the inside of the window. I scrape off a patch and peer out. A railway carriage is parked alongside, but there's no sign whatsoever of activity. On the opposite side of the carriage, I open that window shade. Scraping the window again, I see there's another stationary carriage. When I went to sleep last night, the train was at a railway platform. I open the carriage door. The world sparkles with frost in the morning light. Peering over the roof of the adjacent carriage, I can see lines of carriages in every direction. I'm in a massive shunting yard. I'm no longer on the train going to Lake Van. My bicycle probably is, however.

There's a lavatory at one end of the carriage, and I know I'll feel better after I splash my face with water. But the taps are dry. I gather my things and jump down from the carriage. It's a long way down. I trace my way back to the Elazig train station through of a maze of railway cars.

Indeed, the train has left without me. The railway staff assure me that my bicycle will be OK, but I don't share their confidence. Oh well, there's nothing I can do. The next train to Tatvan leaves at five tomorrow morning.

I explore the city. One bank offers foreign exchange. An eager audience of female bank clerks asks questions about England and my work. Anyone canny enough to work in a bank is also canny enough to seek out a better future in England, I'm guessing. Elazig is a large city with muddy streets, many shops and many people. Most stop and stare at me. Several approach and speak to me in German. A foreigner who doesn't speak their foreign language is clearly a disappointment. The men wear their hair very short, which inspires me to do the same. At a barbershop, I ask for a buzz cut. Might short hair make me less attractive to certain Turkish men? I can only hope.

Back at the railway waiting room, I read and write. The other passengers tap their feet or run prayer beads through their fingers. They appear content to sit in silence and study my every move. The room slowly fills, and all hope of sleeping on a bench fades. The attention of the room shifts from one person to another, depending on where the action is. A woman unpacks food from a bag, and all scrutinize each item as it is taken out and arranged on the bench. Attention shifts back to me when nothing else of note is happening. An old man in one corner shouts in a loud voice at a man on the far side of the room. From their tone of voice and charged emotions, they are talking politics. I understand that these conversations are a way to pass time. The old man shouts at me from across the room. *Memleket?* What country? He shouts more questions. Where are you going? What is your name? I call out my answers, pushing the limit of my few Turkish words. Each face in the room turns back and forth to look at us in turn like a Wimbledon audience. I enter into the spirit and return his serves in a loud voice. There's no sleep in my imminent future in this waiting room.

I wander out into the cold to clear my head. A police post with a warm office looks inviting. My opening gambit of *salaa'am a lei'kum* prompts an invitation to sleep on the floor. The unsmiling duty officer clears a place by the fire. He will wake me in time for my morning train.

My police friend wakes me at five in the morning. He warms a little to my efforts at jovial friendship. My train is the weekly express to Teheran. Or, it may be. I'm cautious about anything said to me in Turkish.

The train continues through the mountains. A sign at each station states elevation, and we are gradually getting higher. We stop at the city of Mush, which sits at fifty-one hundred feet. Its name fits. It's the spring thaw, and all that is frozen yearns to melt. Patches of snow with brown, melting edges lay on green-brown earth like enormous pieces of stained parchment. Trickles of water become streams and then form rushing torrents of swirling, muddy liquid. There are remote villages, mere huddles of stone cottages awash in a sea of mud. Imagine having to live out a life in this desolate corner of the world. We pass flocks of brown sheep with long curly hair and a herd of black cattle with long, curled horns. A heavy snowstorm swirls against a battleship gray sky.

At Tatvan, I go straight to the parcel office. My bicycle is there, with boxes stacked against it. The chain has no tension and hangs loose. The rear derailleur that holds the chain taut is broken. I've repaired many things on the bicycle, but I don't believe the derailleur can be repaired. The bicycle is unusable. I'm going to need a good bicycle store. This is an unexpected setback, but at least the bicycle is here. There's little time to worry about it since the ferry across the lake is departing. On the ferry, I see little of Lake Van. Out of a grimy window, all that's visible are swirls of snow, gray water, and a fleeting glimpse of distant snow-covered mountains. Lake Van is one of the largest lakes in the world with no outlet. *Van* means "dead." It's a salt lake, salty enough that it rarely freezes in winter. The journey takes almost nine hours. I settle in the warmth of the first-class lounge.

The roar of the ferry engines is draining, and I am unprepared for the frenetic rush that ensues as we dock at Van. Passengers charge through the dark to secure seats on a waiting minibus. These buses will take us to a train station near the Iranian border. After loading the bicycle onto a roof rack, I take a seat, and we career through the dark night. I am unwell. Is it the many gifts of cigarettes? Or the unbroken diet of bread, olives and scallions?

At Ozalp train station, there's another episode of unbridled mayhem. People run and trip in the dark. Luggage is unloaded from the minivans with wild shouts. It's bitterly cold, and I think that maybe this is how the locals keep the blood moving. Under the platform's fluorescent lights, frost sparkles on the sides of the railway carriages. The train has been waiting eight hours, and it's as cold inside as it is out. It's midnight; I'm exhausted and sick. In an empty carriage, I lay my sleeping bag across four seats. I crawl into the cold bag with my clothes on.

My train ticket was to Van. I'd hoped I might continue on to the Iranian border without being noticed, but this is the weekly Tehran express. The ticket collector angrily demands money. He says that a ticket to the border is fifty Turkish lire. This is a short journey, and that can't be right. My ticket on the same train for a trip that lasted two days cost forty-six lire. The ticket collector grabs me and forces me into a small compartment, where there are three other ticket collectors. I show them my student identity card from Syria and ask for a student discount. They say I must pay full fare. I continue to argue my case. One becomes red in the face and shouts. He makes to strike me, but the others hold him back. Then, two of them restrain me while another goes through my money pouch. He takes my passport. We are at the Iranian border, and I can't continue without a passport. I tell them that the only money I have is forty-two Turkish lire. I've hidden my other currency in the lining of one of my panniers. They threaten me again. Four angry men crowding in on me in this tiny space is oppressive. I feel unwell, exhausted, and unjustly treated. I cry. The ticket collectors sneer. One calls me a girl and begrudgingly accepts the forty-two lire.

The wild minibus ride, my aching stomach, and Beelzebub's ticket collectors leave me debilitated. I can't remember the last time I felt this unwell. I fall asleep in my seat around two in the morning.

 Route though Turkey: Yayladagi, Senkoy, Antakya, Hassa, Fevzipaşa, Malatya, Elazig, Mush, Tatvan, Van and Ozalp.

Thirteen

IRAN

April 1st

A FEW HOURS LATER, Iranian customs officials burst noisily into the carriage. This is a world apart from Turkey. The officials are efficient in an overly dramatic manner. They may have watched too many American TV shows.

They're searching the train for drugs. They've been trained by the CIA, under a US program to intercept drug traffic that flows east out of Turkey. We remain stationary for several hours. I'll take the train only as far as Tabriz, the first Iranian city on the Asian Highway One. The price for a ticket for me and a ticket for the bicycle is high, but I've no strength to argue.

I sleep fitfully for an hour or two more. As day breaks, the few houses are again flat-roofed and mud-walled, as in Syria. We emerge from the mountains onto a vast plain beneath a clear blue sky. The contrast to the mountains of Turkey could not be more extreme. Out of the carriage's left windows, I see that, beyond the plain to the north, there's a distant, unbroken curtain of snow-covered mountains. Out of the opposite window, the plain extends to the south and merges imperceptibly with the sky. The rail line crosses Asian Highway One, the road that's heralded in the overland to India books. Its grand name belies the simple strip of asphalt laid across the plain. The traffic on the road is thankfully light, which bodes well for when I'll cycle on it.

We arrive in Tabriz, and it's a relief to leave the train. My five-day rail journey has carried me all of six hundred miles. Tabriz is a westernized city and holds little interest for me. An English guy I met on the ferry didn't return my overland to India book, which was my guide to cities like Tabriz. What he did leave me with is the flu he had.

I'm able to disassemble the bicycle derailleur, even though I lack the special tools needed. The tensioning spring, which rotates the derailleur assembly rearward to keep the chain taut, is broken. Each end of the spring is turned outward to form a short lug. Each fits into a retaining hole. The body of the spring is intact, but one of the lugs has sheared off, rendering it useless. I scour the city for a bicycle store that might have a replacement spring, but the odds of finding a replacement part for this Japanese gear changer are slim to none. The bicycle is useless in this state. I feel anxious about being unable to continue my journey. I have little energy. My stomach, joints and head ache terribly.

In a ramshackle garage, I show the elderly proprietor the broken spring. We communicate through gestures. I hand him the small piece that broke off. Without a word, he takes the spring, lights a blowtorch, and holds the tip of flame to the broken end of the spring until it is white-hot. This could alter the resilience of the metal and render it useless, but it does me no good as is, so it's worth a try. With a pair of pliers, he gently bends the broken end of the spring outward ninety degrees to mirror the original profile. In less than five minutes he repairs that which I had assumed was beyond repair.

I reassemble it, and the derailleur works like new. The repaired spring gives no further trouble on the journey. He charges twenty cents for his work and then says that he must buy bread and motions for me to wait. He returns with a glass of hot tea and a piece of cake for me. What can you say to this openhearted generosity? I'm buoyed, my spirits lifted by this unassuming man, and I'm relieved that, against all odds, the bicycle is now usable again.

However, I need to rest for a few days. I ask around for the cheapest hotel in town. I'm directed to a camping site with large frame tents. Each tent is set on a concrete base and contains ten metal cots. There's no one to share the per-tent fee with me. This may be more expensive than a hotel, but I lack the energy to search further. I desperately need to sleep and be warm. I feel desolate; I want only to be home, tucked into my bed, with my mother fussing over me. I set my sleeping bag on one of the beds. I pull on every piece of clothing I have, including my woolen hat. I climb into the sleeping bag and add the two blankets provided. I place my plastic sheet on top of those. I'm chilled to the bone. The tent is unheated. The mist of my breath is clear in the freezing air. I fall into a feverish sleep.

I pass the night in a hot fever and awake spent. I panic at the prospect of bitterly cold nights and wide expanses of uninhabited country. I may be unable to continue. I'd return to England if it were easier; I am ready to turn back. The only thing stopping me is that it was even colder in eastern Turkey. This is the lowest point of the journey. I recognize my illness is the cause of this desperation. But knowing this offers no comfort. It's a struggle to decide what to do next. It's too expensive to stay here, but I lack the energy to move.

I meet a Belgian couple returning overland from India. They tell me that the freezing nights will last until June, and I shouldn't expect warm weather until Pakistan. Teheran is a place to avoid at all costs, they say. But I've already chosen it as my next *poste restante* address. They confirm that prices in Iran are high: five times higher than in Afghanistan. This dose of bad news is somehow homeopathic. I am at rock bottom, yet a raw energy arises from somewhere within. It's daunting, yet I shall carry on. There's no other option.

A small boy from a neighboring tent brings me an orange. It's sweet and delicious. I'm not sure which does me more good, the fresh fruit or the simple act of kindness. I slowly gather my things, check out, and cycle to the main road. I try for a lift to Teheran. Many people stop, but none are going far. A bus to Teheran is the only answer. I return to the bus station in town. All of the many buses are booked up several days in advance. Desperation seizes me. A train from Tabriz to Teheran is the only remaining option. In a feverish haze, I find my way back to the rail station. I explain to the ticket clerk that I don't have enough local money for both the bicycle and me. More Iranian kindness follows. He suggests an Iranian student ticket at a fifty percent discount. A wave of weary relief washes over me.

A group of young men who speak some English invite me to join them in their compartment. They're students at a college in Tabriz. They are pleasant, intelligent people. The train rushes through desolate countryside as we talk of politics. They pull the window shades and speak of their disagreement with the status quo in hushed voices. Anything said against the Shah of Iran invites police attention and jail time. They talk of the feared secret police and the suppression of anti-government sentiment among students.

The train stops at a small station. The conductor states that we'll be here for four hours. Four hours become eight, then ten, then twelve. It's unclear when the train will continue. Anti-government rebels shot at the previous train, apparently. They also blew up the rail tracks, which must now be repaired. Night arrives. All compartments are full, and there's only one place to sleep. A luggage rack above the seats is barely wide enough to hold me, but it's not a bad arrangement. Though narrow and restricted, my crow's nest by the ceiling is warm and comfortable enough. Another feverish night filled with strange dreams. I awake to find that the train hasn't moved. My friends explain that we may be here most of the day. They buy me breakfast. Seeing that I'm ill, they talk softly and refrain from smoking. Their kindness is balm. I drift in and out of sleep. The train starts.

The day weaves itself into a quiltwork of memories, the here and now, and feverish dreams. I'm back in England. I'm twelve years old. On my beloved red and white Manhattan bicycle, I explore the network of quiet country lanes that range beyond Hemel Hempstead. I take a favorite route through the rambling National Trust property of Ashridge. This is a happy time; I forget the feuding parents at home. The warm summer air fills with the unmistakable scent of ferns, which blanket the ground here. That fragrance closes about me as I lie down to rest. The fronds fold aside to form a soft bed, curving away and up on all sides. These living walls offer a safety that my family home lacks. Yellow-green light filters down through the transparent leaves of early summer. Perhaps I can stay here for the night. Or forever. The silver birches around me could be my steady family.

If there is any self-pity left in me, it burns off in the heat of pedaling up a particularly long climb. My leg muscles burn. I know I can get off the bike and push it uphill, as I have in the past. I also know that I can persevere. I've learned that persevering never turns out to be as difficult as I imagine. If I don't dwell on the *thought* of how difficult it is, then I can handle the present moment. And it is only ever one moment, then another, then another. Hard by the yard: a cinch by the inch. At the crest of the hill, elation awaits. I stand astride my bicycle, heart pumping, mind glad. I soak in the moment. The water in my bicycle bottle is warm and tastes of plastic. It's a delicious reward for someone who has resisted the urge to give up.

The windswept chalk hills of Dunstable Downs are my destination. These make up a line of hills that fringe one edge of the Chilterns. The low hills support grassland and bushes of hawthorn or gorse. I ride Manhattan along narrow chalky paths that form deep ruts in the ground. I stop on the brow of the downs. From here, they plunge to farmers' fields and a small airfield below. I fling myself onto the springy turf. I take greedy lungfuls of gorse-scented air. Above is a blue sky hung with cotton-ball clouds. The sun is on my face. The heat of the afternoon combines with the hum of wild bees among the yellow gorse flowers. I'm at peace with the world. This is my place, my time. I've earned this with many turns of the pedals. There's no doubt about the purity of spirit that breathes within me.

From this dream, I drift back to a train in Iran. Time is a rubber band, taut at some moments, slack at others. In a window below the cream-colored roof of the railway compartment, austere scenery noiselessly slides by. I catch snippets of whispered conversation and am confused as to why I don't understand the language. Delirium and reality merge. At the very edge of my awareness, I somehow know that I am being rocked to sleep by a giant beast that sighs its way across endless arid scrubland. Time passes. I'm lost to this world.

One of my new friends gently shakes me awake. The others each say a fond goodbye. The train has arrived at Zanjoun, their destination. Several of them invite me to stay with them if I return to Tabriz. I slip back into my netherworld.

The train pulls into Teheran station at three in the morning. There are few people around. I try to find a cheap hotel, but no one I ask speaks English. I cycle through deserted streets and see flames licking out from behind the closed metal shutters of a shop. I throw stones at the shuttered windows above. Five or six noisily hit home. A bleary-eyed man opens a shutter and stares out at me. He's angry and shouts at me; he can't see the flames below. I shout and gesture. I struggle to communicate through mime the idea of fire. I don't know why he doesn't smell the smoke; the fire is fifteen feet from the window at which he stands. He moves to close the shutters, to ignore this deranged foreigner and return to sleep. I add more drama to my waving and shouting. He then shouts with alarm to someone in the house. Now that he understands, I leave. I can't deal with the complications that will surely follow if I remain. I pedal on through empty streets. I feel bad that I didn't help to fight the fire, but there's little I can do in my state.

Teheran is a large city. A small café offers a retreat from the cold of night. I plan to be at the post office when it opens to collect my letters. After that I'll look for a hotel. I struggle to remain awake, despite several cups of hot tea. The other patrons stare blankly at a wall, make no eye contact, and do not talk to each other. The shopkeeper speaks few words to his customers. This could be early morning city life anywhere in the world.

There are two letters for me at the post office: one from my mother, the other from Rudy. With failing energy, I see a sign announcing a tourist hotel, the Hotel Amir Kabir. I later learn that it's famous with the overland to India crowd. This hardy bunch has seen life's underbelly. They're not easily daunted. But this hotel receives special mention; some call it The Arsehole of the World. Toilets without doors overlook the restaurant. The filth and the smell are beyond all description. A one-eyed cook in a greasy apron prepares what another guest tells me is the hotel's one redeeming feature: a fried egg atop hot French fries. But that's too rich for me at the moment. In the market, I buy fruit and nuts. I hole up in my room for two days of sleep. News from England and Rudy's long letter provide a much-needed boost.

By the third day, some of my strength returns, but still I have no appetite. I apply for a visa at the Afghan Embassy. The visa will be ready in two days. I hope to be strong enough to leave by then. Despite the crazy drivers and polluted air, the city is not as bad as the Belgian couple described it. Maybe it is my good cheer at my returning health. I enjoy the tree-lined avenues in the wealthier parts of the city, which are a bit like Paris, but with the snowcapped Elburz Mountains as backdrop.

I leave the hotel early on Saturday morning. I want to be well out of the city by nightfall. First, I visit the Afghan Embassy to collect my passport with the Afghan visa. Below the visa stamp is written, "Duration of Stay: Up to April 30." It's odd for a visa to expire on a given date, rather than remain valid for a period of time. Today is April 8. There are seven hundred miles to cross in Iran, plus another five hundred in Afghanistan. Twenty days simply isn't enough time for twelve hundred miles. I ask them to cancel the visa and refund the fee. I'll try again for an Afghan visa when I arrive in the city of Mashhad, closer to the Afghan border. Starting from Mashhad with a twenty-day visa should be OK.

The Afghan Embassy sits high on a hill overlooking the city. I move fast down the hill, along a broad avenue. There's the usual heavy traffic. A line of cars is stopped at a red light a hundred yards ahead. The light changes to green and the cars start to pull away. I don't want to use my brakes; this is precious momentum. It's a steep hill, and I am traveling over forty miles an hour. I pass by on the inside of a taxi waiting to leave the light. A passenger in the taxi opens a door. The bicycle slams into the edge of the door and stays there. I, however, fly twenty feet through the air and come to rest in a concrete gutter next to the street. The gutter is two feet wide and two feet deep, bridged by narrow concrete walkways for pedestrians.

After some dazed moments, I sit up on the concrete curb and struggle to get my wind back. Amazingly, my only injury is two cut fingers. My clothes are intact. There are no holes in the knees or elbows. I must have gone instinctively into a roll, though I remember nothing. My feet were strapped securely into the pedal toe clips, which can be released only by pulling up on the buckles. It's unclear how my feet were released. Onlookers gather.

Badly shaken, I return to the bicycle. It lies on the road next to the taxi. My heart falls. The front wheel is now shaped more like a comma than a period. The front forks are bent backward twenty degrees. The damage to the bicycle shows the force of impact. It's incredible that I'm not seriously injured, especially since I wear no helmet. But, my journey is clearly at an end. I am devastated.

A remarkable series of events now unfolds. A young man in the crowd speaks English, and he takes charge of the situation. He tells me to wait until the police arrive and not to accept any offer of money from the taxi driver. My self-appointed advocate explains that in an accident between a car and a bicycle, the car is automatically at fault. The taxi driver accepts that the responsibility is his. I'm not so sure. Flying by on the inside of a stopped car is never a good idea. There's a doctor among the onlookers. Wordlessly, he produces a medical kit, then cleans and dresses the deep cuts on my fingers.

We wait, and a policeman arrives in half an hour. Another member of the Unprompted Generosity club, he berates the taxi driver at length. The policeman, taxi driver, and my guardian angel walk with me to a cycle shop, not five hundred yards away. The policeman carries my disabled bicycle over one shoulder. This cast of unlikely characters is focused solely on my care.

But there's more. Outside of England and its former colonies, the standard for bicycles is metric, which isn't compatible with the imperial measurement system. No metric screw, nut, or bearing will fit an English bicycle. No repairs to my bicycle can be made here. The nearest imperial measurement bicycle parts are probably in England, four thousand miles to the west, or in India, two thousand five hundred miles to the east. Yet this bicycle store stocks imperial size spares. How is this possible? I never get a clear answer. The storeowner says parts and repairs will cost fourteen hundred rials, or about twenty dollars. The taxi driver pays in full under the watchful eye of the policeman. The bicycle store owner gets to work. Several young men from a grocery store next door invite me to join them for a meal and a bottle of Coca-Cola.

I cycle out of the city in the late afternoon. The front forks have been repaired and appear as good as new. I have a new front wheel of better quality than the original. My injuries are expertly bandaged. I'm well fed and thoroughly cared for. A spontaneous laugh arises from within. This is a story I could not have invented. It may sound overly grand, but it's as if some destiny carries me unfailingly forward.

I'm headed some miles west to Karaj. From there, a road heads north across the mountains to the Caspian Sea. The suburbs of Teheran seem endless. Factories and warehouses line the road. Not far off the road, I see tonight's accommodation—a large building that's under construction. It has a roof and walls, protection from rain. I choose a corner shielded from the wind.

The night is less cold than I'd expected. As I settle in, I hear sounds; I'm not alone. Tentatively, I scout around and find a group of Afghan workers in a room at the far end of the building. After the initial surprise and some laughter, they invite me to join them for a meal. The warmth of a fire, some simple food, and an unquestioning acceptance provide the fitting close to a remarkable day.

I continue west early the next morning. At Karaj, it's a relief to turn off the busy main road and head north into the Elburz Mountains. The road weaves back and forth between steep rocks before a vista opens up. High mountains loom ahead; I have to strain my neck upward to see where they meet the sky. I now better understand the phrase "feeling weak at the knees." My legs want to give up. I'm tempted to agree. How can a road cross mountains this high? I brace myself, expecting it to become even steeper. But it rises slowly and steadily, following a mountain river.

The civil engineering is remarkable. River and road pass through gorges of sheer rock. The canyon amplifies the roar of rushing water. Where the ravine widens a little, trees grow along the river. Bare branches carry a fluorescent yellow-green haze that speaks of spring. I pass a cluster of modern houses. Pink and white blossoms on fruit trees lend the scene a familiar, European air. The happy illusion dissolves as I pass again into barren mountains. The road continues to climb. I cross the snow line.

The Karaj hydroelectric dam towers far above me. The road climbs steeply now, snaking back and forth. A strenuous thirty-minute climb draws me level with the top of the dam. I stop, my heart pumping wildly. There are some pistachio nuts on the ground, left behind after a roadside picnic. Evergreen pistachio trees thrive in the elevated plateaus of Iran. They hold a place of pride in the Iranian heart. The nuts are offered to guests, eaten at celebratory meals, and are the stuff of legend. The Queen of Sheba was so fond of them, it's said that she ordered to her kitchens all the pistachio nuts produced in her lands. It was a crime to have them in one's possession.

A pistachio orchard is also, reportedly, a good place for a courting couple to spend a moonlit evening. Should they hear the audible pop made as the nut ripens on the tree, it's an omen of good fortune. The nuts are more than fifty percent oil; they self-heat if stored in large quantities, and can spontaneously combust. Like those lovers beneath darkened trees, placed too close to each other, the nuts create dangerous heat.

I sit on the safety barrier next to the road and happily munch these nuts. My heart and breathing slowly return to normal. I soak in the stark beauty about me. Beyond the dam, the road runs level as it follows the icy blue water of a huge reservoir. I'm still weak and take frequent breaks. Aching muscles are signs of a body that hasn't recovered. By late afternoon, I arrive at a small village and stop for a glass or two of chai. I could ask about a place to sleep, but am less comfortable with the people here. I leave, and soon darkness descends.

In the high mountains, it's hard to keep track of the sun and available daylight. An empty, narrow road climbing into darkened mountains worries me. Surely there is no place to sleep up there. The last light of day finds me cycling up into a rocky wilderness. I have no headlight. There's just enough light to show the occasional pothole. The road is cut into steep mountainside, so even a margin on which I could sleep is unlikely. The air smells of impending rain. I pedal on into the gloom. *What must I be thinking? Will I cycle all night in pitch black?*

The road curves to the left and I pass an outcropping of rock. I can just make out a darkened house on a narrow stretch of flat ground between road and river. Wary of dogs, I walk around to the back and find a door. I push and it opens. The house is still being built, but near completion. I laugh out loud. This is too good to be true. The floor is clean. The windows have glass in them. It's a perfect place to spend the night.

Waiting for sleep, I feel gratitude and wonder. Every night since my tent was stolen in Athens, I've either been invited to stay as a guest in someone's home, or have found a dry place to sleep. Well, mostly dry—but you get the point. Is it just happenstance? As if to test my faith, a place for the night often appears shortly before nightfall. Hardly a day goes by when I am not offered food. My basic needs have been met with little effort on my part. This was true even through the empty stretches. And then there was the accident two days ago in Teheran. Do we each have a guardian angel watching over us? I'm skeptical of cosmic babysitters, but the evidence does seem to be accumulating.

Before Greece, I focused on how far I'd traveled each day, and when and what to eat. The overriding need was to keep moving to avoid the impending winter. I'm no longer counting the miles. I'm happy to stop for a day or two. My impulse to control is relaxing a little. Whether I name it the universe, God, or a higher power, I trust it more. Here at the center of the Muslim world, beneficent intervention is in evidence. It manifests daily as people with big hearts. Each day brings a delicious sense of anticipation. There's wonder in what comes my way. I'm energized by this view of the world.

I awake at first light. Behind the house, gray mountainsides climb steeply away. They form a narrow V through which appear even higher mountains covered with snow. The river roars some yards from the house. I wash my hands, face and feet in the rushing water. My temples ache from the cold. From here, the road climbs up and away from the river. This is the ascent I've been steeling myself for. The map reminds me that the Caspian Sea lies on the other side. Three hours of heart-pumping, steady work bring me to the mouth of a tunnel. It's almost perfectly round, apart from the floor, which is the narrow road that's only wide enough for traffic to pass in one direction. It reminds me of a tunnel in the London Underground. There's no way to know if a car is coming in the opposite direction. What happens when two cars meet?

I cycle into the tunnel and find that it is straight and flat. The light behind me dims. There are no electric lights. I cycle slowly through absolute blackness. Creaks and rattles from the bicycle echo strangely. They mix with the sound of dripping water. The noise of my passing reflects off the tunnel sides and helps me steer clear of the walls. By listening attentively, I remain in what I imagine is the center of the road. The void continues and my mind plays tricks. I'm caught in a time warp, destined to live out my life cycling an unseen bicycle through a dripping nothingness. And I continue.

The thought occurs that I might smash into a fellow cyclist approaching unseen from the opposite direction. The idea balloons into a full-fledged fear. Convinced impact is imminent, I stop. But there's only the black and an echoing drip, drip, drip. I launch tentatively again into the dark. And then more mind games ensue. In the unbroken black appears a pale orange circle, like a dim full moon in a dark night sky. Slowly, this apparition becomes brighter. I am confounded; what on earth can this be? The orange turns to pale gold. Vague definition emerges in the tunnel brickwork and hewn rock overhead. All is sepia, as in an old photograph. Approaching the circular tunnel mouth, I realize the colors must be exhaust fumes left in the motionless air that filters the light. I emerge, squinting against the sun and snow.

The Kandovan Tunnel was finished in 1938. It lies at 9,517 feet and is an Iranian metaphor for struggle and resolve. Many workers were killed during construction. It's over a mile long and took three years to build. Winter snows make the road impassible for several months each year. This is one of the highest mountain roads in the world. It passes among peaks that range from 13,000 to 18,000 feet high. Nearby is the source of the Sofud River, on which Teheran is built. From here, the road drops dramatically all the way to the Caspian at 92 feet below sea level. That's 9,609 feet of downhill bliss.

I fly down the empty mountain road. From the cold of snow and ice, I soon pass into warmer air. The Elburz Mountains form a cloud curtain between the Caspian Sea and Teheran. Yesterday, I was in a dry plain on the southern side. Here on the northern side is a subtropical forest. I've passed from the plain that holds Teheran through subzero temperatures at the tunnel, into a lush climate that descends to sea level. The Iranians say there's no other place on earth where one can pass through these extremes in such a short distance.

The farther I descend, the greener the scenery. The road clings to the side of a deep river gorge. I glimpse waterfalls and wooded grottoes. Rounded outcroppings of weathered rock are topped with windswept trees. I recognize these as the natural formations depicted in Persian miniature paintings. A scarlet turbaned warrior on a white stallion would complete the scene. I marvel at the forces of nature that millennia ago pushed millions of tons of rock into these tortuous shapes. I stop to take in the grandeur; I will remember this as the most spectacular stretch of the journey. Was it really just a week ago that I was sick in Tabriz? I was ready to quit, certain I lacked the resources to continue. Yet here I am, in the sunshine and feeling fabulous. How is it that when all appears wretched, a world of hope is just beyond view? The inner landscape has changed with the outer, my desperation left behind in the dust of the Iranian desert.

I continue to barrel down. The road twists back and forth, following a ravine. The ride is exhilarating. At a small picnic area, I again stop to look back up at the way I've come. I'm relieved to be going in this direction. I don't even want to think about how tough it would be to cycle up this road. The cyclist I was sure I'd collide with in the tunnel must have given up and turned back.

I lie on a bench, looking through leaves at a gray sky above. The greenery, the drab sky and moist air create a very particular effect. For a moment, I'm back in England in familiar woodland. But among the beech trees large leaves of a fig tree bring me back to reality.

I arrive at Chalus, an agricultural village on the shores of the Caspian. The town is orderly and clean, the people pleasant. Walking around the market, I glimpse the Caspian Sea. I can view this journey as inter-sea sections: the North Sea to the Atlantic Ocean, to the Mediterranean, to the Adriatic, to the Aegean. The Mediterranean again, then to the Red Sea, back to the Mediterranean, and now to the Caspian. God willing, the next salty water I encounter will be the Indian Ocean.

I take a road out of town. It's a relief to be headed east once more, toward India. I'm cycling along a narrow coastal plain. The Caspian is to my left, and the Elburz Mountains, which I've just crossed, are to my right. The plain is fertile farmland. Beyond the fields, low wooded hills give way to mountainsides cloaked in dark conifers. The mountains disappear into low-lying clouds.

Residents of Teheran refer to the Caspian coast as "the north." Jackals, bears and wolves live in these wooded slopes. The area between road and water is the habitat of another creature. Large new homes are scattered here. Some aspire to be Italian villas, but they go overboard, stretching horizontally into sprawling complexes. They stand in stark contrast to the otherwise general poverty of the region. I see no dwellings for ordinary folk. I recall the dissatisfaction with inequality expressed by my student friends on the train to Tabriz.

My map shows that the road follows the coast for about a hundred miles and then turns southeast into the mountains again. I'm using a single-sheet map that shows the overland route from England to India. Although it lacks detail, it does show to which major city I'm headed next. There are so few roads in this part of the world that I don't actually need a map. I could simply follow Rudy's advice to "go in the good direction, where the sun rises each morning." From Turkey east, all one needs is a list of the major cities en route. I could just ask the way to the next city on the list, which is essentially what I'm doing. But I enjoy being able to see where I am, how far I've come and where I'm headed.

There's relatively little traffic. A car passes and pulls over up ahead. I'm disappointed because I was hoping to find a deserted spot with an unfinished house from where I could relish this beautiful setting. The young man who waves me down appears to be from India, and he speaks good English. There's a well-dressed woman at the wheel of the car. The Indian invites me for a cup of coffee, and I accept; I'm ever curious about what awaits after I accept any invitation for tea or coffee. At his suggestion, I follow the car. After a short distance, we pull off the road and head toward one of the large houses.

The impressive house has beautiful grounds. My hostess is the wife of one of Iran's top ministers. This is a holiday home; they have an even larger home in Teheran, and another in Paris. I accept her invitation to stay the night, as this will doubtless include a shower and some good food. The young man is from Sri Lanka. In front of Madam, he is the demure servant. He opens up when we talk in his downstairs room. He tells me about his employer, whom he calls, "my master." He explains that it's fashionable to have an English-speaking houseboy for guests to tip.

I awake early in the morning and join the lady of the house for breakfast. She offers me jam made from orange blossoms. It's clear, watery, and divinely delicious. It contains no fruit, only flowers. Rain falls steadily outside. I'll leave when it stops. I write in my diary and organize my things. The houseboy explains that in today's local paper, there's a "situations vacant" ad for an English-speaking houseboy. Now there's a fascinating possibility. I am low on money, after all. It would surely be an education. But it requires a one-year contract, and that wouldn't work for me. The rain stops midmorning, so I say my farewells and set out.

The road is flat and well paved. I keep a steady pace. I eat lunch on the beach. Gray sand stretches into misty nothingness on either side. This sullen weather reminds me of rainy days as a child on holiday by the sea in Norfolk. It must be beautiful here in the summer. One–eighth of the Caspian shore is in Iran, while the rest is in Russia. Iran sits at the extreme south.

In Iran, they tell a story of how the Caspian Sea was lost to the Russians. A minister came one day to his master, the shah of Iran. He reported that the Russians wanted the Caspian Sea. The shah asked his minister, "Is the water of this sea sweet or salty?" The minister replied that it was salty. "In that case, let them have it," said the shah. The minister added, "Yes, let us not ruin the sweet disposition of the czar of Russia over these salty waters." Little did they know that the waters of the vast Caspian, though brackish in the south, are almost fresh in the north, or that vast reserves of oil and natural gas lie below the waters.

The road continues along the shore. I take a break at a small café. A group of young men and women sit outside. One of the women asks if I'd like a glass of chai. Being invited by a woman to drink chai—that's a first. One young man in the group speaks English. He's studying in London and is home visiting. He offers an unflattering account of England, but invites me to stay the night at his brother's house nearby. Although I'd rather have a night on my own, I accept. I want to better understand his view of the English people and their culture. I'd like to hear from someone who has grappled with cultural differences from the opposite position to my own.

The brother lives in a huge villa directly on the beach. He's a property developer and clearly successful. I pass the early evening with a group of young men, drinking beer and smoking too many cigarettes. This is the first time I've witnessed alcohol being consumed in a Muslim country. New wealth brings with it new values, I suppose. The young men seem happy to pass the time doing not much of anything. We lay about on cushions, talk of inconsequential things, and play cards.

Through a window I can see the front door. Visitors arrive, most in new Mercedes. The guests are all male, dressed in formal business suits and ties. I guess that my host's brother is throwing a party for business associates. My host invites me to eat. Under the vaulted ceiling in the huge main room of the house, there are many more guests than I'd seen arrive. Some are eating, some drinking. On a table, every imaginable imported spirit is arranged. A group of men in one corner share an ornate water pipe. I eat and talk with a few men. Broken English limits the dialogue. This is no English-mannered dinner party. A man approaches and asks if I want some hashish. In my naïveté, I try to decline gracefully by saying that I'll try the pipe instead. Having said it, I realize that it's unlikely the pipe contains simple tobacco. Thankfully, he doesn't understand.

The evening grows stranger still. There are no women to be seen. My sun-dyed hair receives a lot of attention. A stranger suggests we go to bed together and smoke hashish. Another suggests that I try the pipe. He says it's very good, a kind of morphine. My host is nowhere to be seen and I feel abandoned. I recognize a well-groomed silver-haired man in his sixties whom I'd seen arrive earlier. He's dressed in a tan three-piece suit with a tie. I took him for a genteel doctor or lawyer. His tie now hangs loosely around a half-open shirt, and his hair is disheveled. He stands unsteadily and weakly attempts to greet me. His face is blanched and there's a wild look in his watery eyes. Another suited figure sits on the floor, propped against an armchair, jaw hanging open, eyes unfocused.

I firmly make my excuses and head to my room in another area of the house. I awake early the next morning, eager to be back on the road. My host is silent as we eat breakfast. It's awkward. What does one say after a night like that? I'm relieved to be back on my bicycle with the wind in my face. It blows from my mind the craziness of last night as I reflect on the stark contrast. One day, I'm in the glorious wild of the Elburz Mountains. The next, I stumble into a netherworld of the nouveau riche—stoned Iranians. God save me from such people.

The road continues flat and smooth, and the kilometers pass quickly. Turning away from the coast, I pass through rich farmland. I've reentered a world of real people, with humble as well as grander houses. There are small thatched cottages among the trees. Cows with long horns and humps move slowly across waterlogged meadows.

A farmer asks me to join him for tea. His cottage is similar to the simple farm homes I visited in Turkey. We communicate with gestures and the few words of Farsi I've written inside the back cover of my diary. He asks questions about money; it is a topic of great interest to him. The word "money" never entered into conversations with farming folk in Turkey and Syria. I compare my page of Farsi words with the page of Turkish words. Each was created with the help of a local who taught me the words he considered essential. Is it a coincidence that the Farsi page includes the word *money* and the Turkish page does not?

I leave and it's raining again. It's been many months since I was soaked to the skin. *Yuck. Not pleasant.* Night falls and I'm anxious; this isn't the weather for sleeping outside. It's dark when I come across a construction site: another luxury home for a wealthy transplant from Tehran. This is the perfect place to spend the night. I find tea, sugar, a dented aluminum teapot, and all that I need to make a fire. I sit close to the flames. My tea steams. I steam. In an upstairs room is an iron bed frame with a mattress. *Merci bien.*

When I awake, the rain has stopped. I get an early start. The road continues flat and is a joy to cycle. The day remains gray. Young men in villages catcall. This derisive mirth unsettles me. Do I misunderstand the sneers on faces? I want to give these people the benefit of the doubt and remain open, yet I feel threatened.

My map shows that the city of Gorgan is still a significant distance away, but the road is good, and perhaps I can push to get there today. The sustained effort is energizing. I think happy thoughts and stop periodically for a short break. Muscles warm and tired, I sit on the grass next to my bicycle. All is green and calm. The simple pleasure of the afternoon fills me. I arrive in Gorgan in the late evening. I've cycled about a hundred miles today—one of the longest days of the trip. People are helpful and no one tries to cheat me. Mohammed, a student at a local technical college invites me to sleep the night at the house where he stays. He and his friends are open and generous; they expect nothing in return. The relaxed atmosphere makes for an enjoyable evening. The best part is settling into a much-anticipated bed.

Gorgan, a park in the city: Mohammed and William.

Despite many hours of deep sleep, I awake still tired the following morning. Yesterday's miles were a huge physical effort. It rained heavily in the night, but the skies are clearing a little. Ragged patches of blue appear among the white and gray. But the promise of the sun's warmth doesn't materialize. I cycle most of the day through a light rain. It's hard to remain cheerful in this weather. I arrive in the evening at Shahpasand. A young man steps into my path, looking at me. I imagine he's playing chicken; this has happened before. With the heavy traffic, it's dangerous since I need to swerve into the road. On an impulse I raise my hand and wind up dealing him a hard blow across his face. I didn't mean to hit him, but I continue through the town without stopping, thoroughly ashamed.

As night falls, I can't find a place to sleep, and this adds to my nervous mood. In the darkness, I can make out a barn not far from the road. I approach quietly to check that it's empty. All is silent, which is a good sign. I peer around an open door and come face-to-face with a huge horse, which gives a start and seems as alarmed as me.

I continue to cycle through the dark, wet night. Dogs on farms go wild at my phantom passing. I stop repeatedly and throw stones so they'll retreat. I can make out their huge forms as they frantically bark. I'm frightened and on edge. I'm startled again as a large moth collides noisily with my arm. The dogs become still more frenzied. I get off the bicycle and walk, unnerved by the hounds of hell racing toward me out of the night. After a time, there's no more barking. Only darkness. I settle into a strange reality. No shape or sound reveals what's around. Only the texture underfoot tells me I'm on the road. I walk for a long time, passing through folds of black. I can't see my body or the bicycle. Perhaps I shall walk all night.

Car lights appear behind me. A van passes and stops some distance ahead, then reverses. The young driver asks with gestures if I am OK. I mime that I'm looking for a place to sleep. He motions that I should put the bicycle in the back of the van. We drive a short distance. From the main road, he turns onto a track awash with mud. We arrive at a small village. I'm ushered into a clean, simple house. My host has many sisters and brothers.

The familiar routine ensues. We drink tea. Through gestures and a few shared words, I answer simple questions about family, home and journey. I'm the evening's entertainment. We sit in the main room where there's a simple but large loom. My host's mother and several daughters show me how they weave fine linen. I fall asleep in an upstairs room to sounds of the loom shaking the house.

The following morning the rain comes down, steady and hard. I accept my host's invitation to stay longer. He lends me a pair of rubber boots and we walk around the village, splashing through puddles and soupy mud. This omnipresent ooze lends the place a gloomy atmosphere. The villagers appear oblivious to rain and mire. They go about their business dressed in neat clothes and shoes. They're surely wet and cold. A dog walks through the quagmire, its legs coated in mud and its belly a tangle of dripping, matted fur. It appears content.

My host suggests we visit nearby Gumbad-i-Qabus with a few of his friends. Gumbad-i-Qabus takes its name and fame from Qabus-ibn Washmgir, a local prince and patron of the arts. He completed a remarkable mausoleum several years before his death in 1012 AD. He wanted to be remembered for a long time. He used high-fired bricks—uncommon at the time—to build a remarkable tower. It's still intact. At around two hundred feet, my hosts tell me it's the highest brick tower in the world. Thirty-five feet of the base is buried in a man-made hillock. It is a ten-sided tower with angular buttresses that run from ground to roof. The interior is a gloomy void with a single small window at the top. The body of the prince originally hung inside a glass coffin suspended at the top of the tower; he must have felt the same as I do about the mud hereabouts. In 1933, Robert Byron took a ten-month journey that he describes in his book, *The Road to Oxiana*. Byron conceived the idea of his journey after seeing a photograph of this impressive tower; he felt compelled to visit. A restful day follows: sleeping, eating, and observing daily life on an Iranian farm. Rain permitting, I'll be back on the road tomorrow.

The following morning brings the gift of a cloudless sky, which is more than I'd dare hope for. I say farewell to my host and his friends. Today is Sunday. I go slowly and steadily to allow for the lack of power that will arrive later in this day of fasting. The morning sun picks out every sharp detail in the scenery. The rolling hills are a patchwork of chocolate brown and green. In the distance ahead, higher ground is covered with recent snowfall. Since leaving the Caspian, the road has followed a plain along the line of the Elburz Mountains on my right, to the south. Now, I come upon hills again. I'm heading up toward the Afghan plateau and mountains. The road passes into the Golestan National Park. It has been some time since I cycled along a tree-lined road with mottled shadows on the ground. I enjoy lunch by a river. Poplar trees above me stir in the breeze and sparkle with sunlight like sequined cloth. I rest here for most of the day. I wash a few clothes and myself in the river, clean the bicycle, and then lie on the ground and doze.

I'm back on the road by late afternoon, and the scenery is reminiscent of the Cheddar Gorge. It's as beautiful as any English woodland, yet it does not offer me the same comfort as home. I wonder when I shall see England again. What must it mean to a person to be forced from his homeland and unable to return? The lot of the refugee. Just the idea creates a tightness in my chest. And what is *home*? A few people I'm close to, damp green countryside, and a tribe of reserved people: these touchstones are at my core. I can't imagine life without them.

Shaking myself from mental meandering, I see again the trees, mountains, and the translucent glow of late afternoon. A car pulls over and several young men approach. Today, I find it easy to be open. As ever, my attitude is reflected straight back toward me. I ask for a cigarette, and they offer me a pack. They write out an address in Bojnord and invite me to stay with them when I arrive there.

As soon as I think about looking for a place to sleep, I catch a glimpse of a brick wall through the trees. I'd thought I might be sleeping outside tonight since I've seen few buildings here in the national park. An unclouded sky promises a dry night. Trees surround my shelter. Above them, on two sides, rises a high escarpment. On the third side, higher hills are powdered white with snow. On the ground all around me are small red tulips. Tulips as wildflowers! Don't they belong in neat rows among carefully tended beds in Hyde Park?

My home for tonight has no roof, doors or windows, yet it provides a sense of security that sleeping in the open cannot. To feel even safer, I construct an early warning system by blocking doors and windows with lengths of discarded pipe and dry branches. These won't stop anyone from entering, but if moved should make enough noise to wake me. I'd like a warning before I am murdered in my sleep. The sun goes down. The air becomes chilled and silent. I light a small fire for warmth and crawl into my sleeping bag. Above, a bright moon and countless stars shine. The distant murmur of a river is broken by the eerie call of a night bird. An occasional car passes. Other than this, silence.

I awake with numb feet. It was extremely cold last night. First light starts to flush darkness from the sky. I light another fire to thaw my feet and hands. I eat a light meal. When it's this cold, it's best just to get on the bicycle and move. I put on every piece of clothing I have, including woolen hat, scarf, and gloves. Each time I pass beneath a stretch of shade, it's so cold I must stop to warm myself in the next pool of sunlight. I cycle through a small village, alert for dogs. Some say the dog is a distant cousin of the wolf, but they haven't seen these dogs. These are the ill-tempered uncles.

The road rises steadily. By degrees, the trees thin until the surrounding hills are threadbare. In the space of a few miles, I've passed from dappled forest into dusty semi-desert. I'm again in an open wasteland of muted tones. The soft hues of ocher, sand and gray hold their own beauty. My surroundings will remain similar until I descend into Pakistan from the Hindu Kush Mountains. That's about fifteen hundred miles of rock and dust. The past week of cycling through greenery was a gift. The plain I cross now is as empty as it is dry. The road is a narrow gray ribbon laid across sandy earth. A shepherd herds a large flock of brown and black goats. He stares blankly at me as I pass. I am surely a stranger sight to him than he is to me.

I pass through two villages, each no more than a huddle of mud-walled cottages. A red, blue and white sign promotes Pepsi to the wilderness. This solitude is welcome after the heavily populated Caspian shore. Several large birds slowly circle above me. The carcass of a dead dog on the road has attracted a number of black and gray crows, as well as a huge eagle. I'm surprised to see this regal bird feeding on carrion. I approach, and it takes to the air as if in slow motion. A white band at the tip of each wing shows with each slow, strong stroke. His wingspan must be eight feet. He lands on a low rock at some distance and watches me pass.

Being alone on the road provides time for introspection. I think about the future: what will I do, where will I live, and what kind of a life do I want? On this empty plain, an intuition arises and grows stronger with time. My future wife awaits me in India. The idea arrives as a simple certainty. I don't doubt that it's true. She's in India, and I shall marry her. An exotic Indian spouse—how delightful is that? As I cycle through the barren landscape, I picture us together. We recline on silk cushions, drinking chai. Parrots screech in a mango tree outside. Café-au-lait-colored children play in the garden. It's a good life. It will be another fourteen years before I marry an American girl from Manhattan. But she is, indeed, in India at this time, and that's where we'll meet.

The road crosses a low pass, and then slopes steadily down. The wind whips tears from my eyes and I feel them pass along my temples into my hair. I relish speeding downhill on a silent piece of machinery that I can trust to carry me safely. The terrain settles into hills with moderate climbs and satisfying descents. I approach the top of a long ascent and become aware of something out of the corner of my eye. To my left, a little behind and above me, a patch of gray bushes is outlined against the sky. Odd, since scrub here stands no more than a few inches high. The bushes move and for a moment I'm confused.

Then I see it is a large pack of wild dogs. They're huge, with broad heads and shaggy, matted coats. There are fifteen or more, but I don't stop to count. I'm almost at the crest of the rise and they're some thirty yards away. There's no time for deliberation; I must try to outrun them. They rush at me as one, yowling wildly. Given their size, it's more galloping than running. My fear fuels extraordinary acceleration and speed. I race to the top and glance over my shoulder. They're in pursuit, with the leaders just a few yards behind. The giant in front has bloodshot eyes and huge yellow teeth. He's no more than fifteen feet from me. I pedal like a man possessed, down-shifting quickly from one gear to the next.

A mile passes before I dare to stop my frenzied pedaling. The adrenaline and my pumping heart roar in my ears. The dogs are nowhere to be seen. Another wave of shock passes through me. When I first saw them, I thought to face them. It would not have gone in my favor. Dogs gather in threes or fours. A pack this large is rare.

I later learn that these are Caucasian Mountain Dogs. These wild dogs, descendants of escapees from camel trains of the Silk Road, are legendary. The locals describe them as "tall as an ass" or "the bear who crushes wolves" because of the size and strength of their paws. This dog's massive face can appear like a bear's. Breeders caution against direct eye contact with an adult male, even if he's domesticated. The look may be taken as an act of aggression and could provoke an attack. The Caucasian is territorial yet trainable, so it makes an excellent guard dog. The Soviet government bred Caucasians in state-run kennels for service throughout the former Soviet Union. The Caucasian has a mythic reputation for aggression and fierceness. Indeed.

Toward the evening, I encounter a man whose motorcycle has broken down. Having once owned a motorbike, I understand his predicament. He speaks no English, but we share the language of temperamental engines. Together we tinker with the spark plug, leads, and carburetor until finally it sputters and starts. The *putt-putt-putt* of his motorcycle disappears into the distance as darkness spreads its cloak over the distant hills.

I'm loath to spend the night in such an open place. A river runs beneath the road and I scramble down the bank with my bicycle. The river has dried to a small trickle, and there's a large area of dry riverbed. I'm hidden from anyone passing on the road above. This is the most exposed I've been at night, but there's no other option. I must make the best of it.

I sleep well, but lightly. I'm awoken in the night by a sharp noise. I see nothing. Then all is quiet again. The nights are punctuated by unexplained noises that are alarming yet harmless—at least so far.

I wake again with a start. It's a little before dawn. There's a crouched figure some feet away in the gloom. He has my bowie knife out of its sheath and is testing the edge with his thumb. Scenes of horror play out before me—none with a happy ending. I struggle to get out of my sleeping bag. Heart racing, I get to my feet and prepare for the fight. I register the flat note of many animal bells. We are surrounded by hundreds of goats. The killer with my knife stands and smiles a toothy grin. His arms relax and drop by his sides. It's as if he's accustomed to waking foreigners beneath bridges in the wilderness with a drawn knife! He shows no sign of being aware that he's holding my property. He speaks, but I can't understand.

There are two other shepherds. Elaborate miming ensues. They're asking for tea. Tea? Tea! Should I scream or weep? Tea, the pleasant social drink enjoyed in a relaxed setting? Tea, a drink shared with friends over a plate of biscuits?

My heart rate slowly returns to normal. I dig out a small amount of tea that I've carried from Damascus. They make a small fire and brew it up. We crouch together on the dusty ground and drink steaming tea sweetened with misshapen crystals of sugar they provide. They show great interest in the knife. I've carried it from England, despite its weight and impracticality, but I've been thinking of getting rid of it. After some haggling, I accept one hundred seventy rials: one tenth of what I paid for it in England. Perhaps we should have made a day of it, drinking tea and bargaining back and forth. But this should be enough money to buy a pocketknife. The shepherd who woke me mimes how he'll use the knife to cut a sheep's throat. I imagine that's what they eat as they travel.

Tea consumed, business transacted, and slaughter theater complete, they leave. The discordant notes of tin bells grow fainter as the huge flock and their minders fade into the distance.

Bojnord and the invitation of a place to stay are only twenty-five miles away. So, I remain for the morning beneath the bridge and repair my clothes. Midday finds me on the bicycle. It's perfect cycling weather: warm sun with a cool breeze. This is probably a good time to cross Iran and Afghanistan, before the heat of summer sets in. I stop to take a break, and a truck pulls over. The driver offers me a cup of tea, so I join him in his cab. He speaks broken English, and we have a slow conversation. He says that Iranian men are all dark-skinned and black-haired. He adds with emphasis that I am very blond. I then understand he wants to share more than a cup of tea. I extricate myself. How does one decipher in this part of the world whether a man wants straightforward company or a sexual encounter? I imagine a local can, and it troubles me that I can't. I feel both foolish and threatened by these encounters.

In the late afternoon, an orange butterfly flies alongside me. I'm surprised. Surely butterflies need vegetation and water. There's neither of these here. I'm astonished when it manages to keep up with me. It appears intermittently over the course of an hour or more.

I arrive at the TV shop in Bojnord, where I've been invited to stay. I like the unassuming manner of the young guy who invited me, but his loud friends push him to the background. They are middle-class Iranians and live comfortably. They appear interested only in things American. Their company is tiresome. The night wears on, and I ask if it's OK if I retire. They tell me to remember "Iranian people's customs," and that to sleep would be an insult to my host. I'm angry to find myself again in a situation where I am treated as low-cost entertainment. An evening alone in an animal barn or under a bridge is infinitely more appealing. The lesson here may be to avoid invitations from wealthier people.

The next day, my hosts insist that I stay for the morning. We visit an old tomb and springs at Besh Ghardash, which means "five brothers." Local lore says five brothers fighting against the government took cover behind a rocky escarpment and disappeared, with five springs manifesting in their place. The tomb is of traditional Persian blue ceramic tile and is impressive. We swim in a deep pool out front, which is fed by the warm water springs. The water feels good and I thoroughly wash myself. A bath is a rarity in these arid parts. We sit in the shade of an old tree and share a picnic. The speed with which my young hosts do everything places a hurried edge on a relaxed morning.

I am back on the road by mid afternoon. Like most of the roads in Iran, the surface is excellent. It's perfectly flat and pothole-free. The wind at my back means that I fly. I'm crossing a vast plain. There's only the road, telephone poles that rhythmically pass to my right, and the sound of wind in my ears. This is mostly wasteland. There's an occasional farm, tiny fields of dust and stone bounded by rough rock walls. There's no sign of irrigation. It's unclear what is grown here, or how. The road runs roughly parallel with the Russian border, thirty miles to the north. What if I were to take a left turn toward Ashkhabad, the capital of Turkmenistan? Would they let me through at the border? But, there are no left turns. Nor right.

Another orange butterfly appears and flies alongside me. This is remarkable! I am traveling a steady sixteen miles an hour or so. He keeps pace with me, apparently with ease. I think he's gone, but then he reappears on the other side of me. Could this be the same butterfly as yesterday? It looks the same. How odd.

A deserted, open workshop on the outskirts of Shirvan offers a secure night's sleep. I cycle into the city the next morning. It's famous as a center for Persian carpets. The beauty of the carpets is not matched by the city, though. In the bazaar, I buy a compact penknife for forty-eight rials, leaving me a small profit. The road continues flat and arrow-straight. Overcast skies, a flat road, and an open plain take me back to that horrible stretch from Zagreb to Belgrade. I'm better able now to enjoy the empty miles. I discipline myself to neither look nor think too far ahead. If I look ahead to where road and telephone lines fade into nothingness, I'm disheartened. I keep my focus on the next fifty yards, and then on the next. This is a poor region; I imagine it's because of the lack of agriculture. I cycle through a village. Those I pass watch me with an expressionless gaze. No one responds to my wave and greeting of *salaa'am a lei'kum*. The very air tastes of aimlessness.

The sky clears. The sun and warmer air remind me that summer is coming. Toward evening, I again see a butterfly. I study him closely as we travel side by side. I'm sure it's the same butterfly as yesterday, and probably as the day before. I'm not sure why, but I think of this winged companion as being male. I'm amazed when he flies in circles around my head, even as we move along together. He flies in front of me, playfully close at times, yet never touches me. Incredibly, he flies a loop directly in front of me and then passes unscathed through the moving spokes of the front wheel. *How is that even possible?* After some more circles around me, he again flits through my front wheel, all while I cycle at a steady clip. What an extraordinary spectacle. A butterfly has never before flown alongside me, never mind danced in acrobatic circles. There must be some consciousness behind this behavior. It seems the creature is doing an aerial dance for my benefit, or to engage with me in some way. I remember; there were soft fluttering noises in the dark as I was going to sleep last night. I had supposed it was a moth. Now, I think it must have been this butterfly. Through the evening, my friend remains. Several times I think he's gone, but then he reappears.

Some distance from the road is a small building of handmade bricks and mud. It's barely high enough to stand up in, but it offers shelter for the night. It houses what must be an irrigation pump, and there's just enough floor space alongside the large pipe to accommodate my sleeping bag. I cycle some distance away to await nightfall and avoid being seen.

The butterfly appears and lands on my bicycle pack. He slowly opens and closes his wings. I speak to him and ask who he is. I tell him I'm delighted that he's here with me and thank him for his company.

I eat a simple evening meal of dates and dry bread. The sun sets in the west, directly over the road I've traveled. It throws shafts of light upward as it sinks beneath a bank of clouds on the horizon. The occasional vehicle passes. Unexpectedly, a large German coach goes by. I imagine they have showers, toilets, and air conditioning. Probably a plentiful supply of European food and drink. I wonder what their reaction would be to my tiny pump house accommodations. But I wouldn't trade places with them.

When it's dark and the road is empty, I return to my tiny home. I lay with moonlight near my face on the stony ground outside. Small wings flutter near me in the dark. The continued presence of this butterfly is sheer magic. The butterfly will become a symbol of this trip: my mascot.

Houses appear in the afternoon, on the outskirts of Mashhad. A day or two of rest here will be welcome. I've covered seven hundred miles in fifteen days and am deeply weary. I await my butterfly friend in the late afternoon. He does not make an appearance, though, and I'm disappointed. Maybe it's to be expected that he'd not emerge in the company of men. Did he mean simply to offer me comfort while I crossed a bleak stretch of road? I do not see the butterfly again. A construction site offers a welcome for the night.

I cycle into the city just before dawn. I want to be at the Afghan Consulate when it opens. I am focused on obtaining a visa for Afghanistan and plan no sightseeing. Maybe I can get my visa the same day. But, I imagine the glacial pace of Afghan bureaucracy is the same here as it was in Teheran.

Mashhad is built along the Hari River. It is one of the holiest places of pilgrimage for Shiite Muslims. Ninety percent of the Iranian population is Shiite. The eighth grandson of the prophet Muhammad, Imam Reza, was murdered here in 817 AD. *Mashhad* means "the place of martyrdom." A Shiite who has visited Mashhad is known as a *Mashti*. The city sits in a gap between two vast mountain ranges. The Elburz Mountains lie to the west, over and along which I've come, and the Hindu Kush range begins to the east. This twenty-mile gap is the convenient gateway through which trade caravans and invading armies have come. In turn, the Aryans, the Huns, Mongols, and other tribes have poured through to invade, rule over, and, in time, leave.

I arrive early at the consulate, but there's already a long line of people seeking visas. A fellow from Spain next to me in line explains that there's an education conference in Kabul from May 1 to 15. To ensure that hotel rooms in Kabul are available, all visitors must leave before April 30. Closing a country for a conference—only in Afghanistan! I now understand the expiration date on the Afghan visa I was given in Teheran—April 30. The one I get today states exactly the same. What a pity! I wanted to take my time in Afghanistan. Today is Saturday, April 22. Including tomorrow, I will have seven days to cross Afghanistan. I'll have to hustle; the border is a hundred miles away, and then there are five hundred miles of poor roads through mountains to contend with in order to cross Afghanistan.

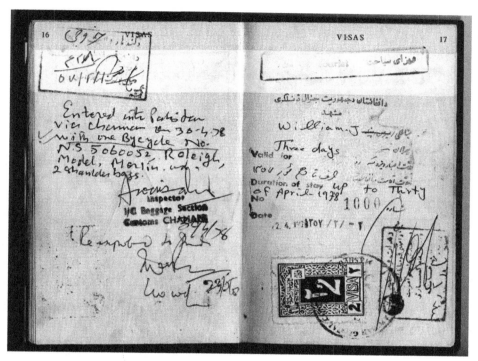

Visa for Afghanistan, valid "Up to thirty of April."

I set out from Mashhad a little after noon. My stamped passport is stowed securely in the leather pouch at my waist. Headed east from Mashhad, there's a fork in the fabled Silk Road. One route leads northeast, north of the Hindu Kush and on into Turkmenistan and Uzbekistan, then to China. The other trail stays south of the Hindu Kush and the mighty Himalayas. This southern route forks again at Kandahar in Afghanistan. The northerly branch from there passes through the Punjab and ends in Patna, India. The southerly route goes from Kandahar toward the fertile plains of the Indus valley. I will follow the southerly route through Kandahar toward the Indus River.

The Afghan deadline is already stressful; a strong headwind adds to the frustration. I'll feel better if I eat. I remove food from my panniers and flies swarm. Not thirty miles from here, there was but the occasional fly. They say that ten percent of the biomass in the Indian subcontinent is flies. Nearing Afghanistan, the land of the fly has begun. Two days of cycling to the border will mean two fewer days in Afghanistan, so I stick my thumb out for a lift.

My first is perched unsteadily atop a load of bricks in the back of a truck. The second is in a milk delivery van. A truck carrying powdered lime provides the third. After three rides, I'm fifteen miles from the border. I cross a wide plain. Pale green scrub stretches as far as the eye can see. The sun sets behind me. All is bathed in a surreal, rosy glow. Ahead, a full moon hangs pale above the misty mountains of Afghanistan. I stop. The evening is utterly silent. I sit motionless for many minutes in the dust by the side of the road. I wish I could share this sacred moment with friends and family.

A large culvert pipe crosses beneath the road. It's just high enough to fit the bicycle. Crouched low, I push the bicycle ahead of me. I brush away dried sheep dung to make room for my plastic sheet and sleeping bag. Fragrance aside, I couldn't have hoped for a better place to spend the night in this wilderness.

I awake early the next morning and quickly gather my things. Stepping out from my cylindrical motel, I come face-to-face with a young shepherd. He steps backward with a look of sheer terror on his face. How could I even begin to explain? He manages a stuttering *salaa'am a lei'kum*. As a child, maybe he was warned about demons that carry off sheep to eat—raw, bones and all. With a polite nod in his direction, I mount my bike and pedal off. I doubt his grandchildren will believe the story he'll tell them one day.

I arrive at Taibad and the Iranian border. Back home, I saw a TV documentary about this border post. The CIA financed the construction of the buildings and the training of the guards. It's here to stem the flow of drugs west out of Afghanistan. The TV program showed border police impounding an aging Volkswagen camper van. New screws in a countertop roused suspicion. Mechanics pulled the vehicle apart in a specially equipped garage.

They disconnected, unbolted or cut every part from its neighbor. An hour later, the intact vehicle was thousands of pieces arrayed on the floor. Bags of heroin were concealed within the countertop. The Danish driver and his girlfriend received twenty-five years in prison. And if a customs officer's hunch is wrong? "Sorry about your car. To what address can we ship these 1,723 pieces? Can we call you a taxi?"

Inside the border post, glass cases display some of the places drugs have been discovered: a pair of cowboy boots with hollow heels, an aluminum drinking bottle with a false bottom, the handle of a walking cane, a large crucifix, a truck's gas tank. For display, each has been cut cleanly down the middle. I wonder at both the creative concealment and the determination to discover. In a bar of soap, in a bar of chocolate, sewn into the lining of baggy underwear: given the sophistication here, I'm amazed anyone tries. There must be a lot of money to be made.

When my turn comes to meet a customs officer, I'm nervous. After my experience on the Caspian shore, am I a person of interest? The officer makes brief eye contact, smiles at me, and stamps my papers. He knows English naiveté when he sees it.

Cycling the short distance to the Afghan customs post, I meet an American walking the other way. We sit by the side of the road and share stories and a cigarette. He gives a bizarre account of losing his French girlfriend in Kabul. He doesn't know whether she was kidnapped or chose to run away with another man. I'm unsettled by his nonchalant manner. We're on a dusty plain, with the mountains of Afghanistan in the hazy distance. His story adds to the intrigue of Afghanistan. Even the mountains appear untamed. The fantastic contours end in sharpened summits. I proceed slowly but without problems through Afghan customs and immigration.

 Route though Iran: Tabriz, Maragheh, Teheran, Karaj, Nesa, Chalus, Nur, Sari, Beshahr, Kordkuy, Gorgan, Ali Abad, Minu Dasht, Gumbad-i-Qabus, Bojnord, Shirvan, Faruj, Quchan, Mashhad, Fariman, and Taibad.

Fourteen

AFGHANISTAN

April 23rd

JUST AFTER THE BORDER POST, a roadside shack offers chai. The floor, furniture and walls are caked in greasy dirt. A grimy tape player blasts Afghani music. The tones and melodies differ from the music of Iran. People are different, also. Skins are darker, and some of the men have square jawbones and look almost Russian.

I set out at noon. This is the primary border crossing in western Afghanistan, yet the road is almost empty. I've passed a threshold. In its own way, Iran was a developed and predictable place. I've entered a realm of mystery. I'm feeling both excited and wary. First impressions are of a vast emptiness. Parts of Syria were desolate, but none as empty as this.

The sun burns. I'm thankful for my *keffiyeh*, the black and white Arab head-scarf I bought in Damascus. I feel the effects of the heat; I am woolly-headed and fumble as I decant water from my large container into the bicycle bottle. It's an effort to arrange my thoughts logically. The muted clanging of tin bells announces a flock of goats in the distance. The heat dilutes the sound. The afternoon is breathless. The road crosses the Hari River, which flows west out of the Hindu Kush Mountains. *Ha!* This is surprising. How can water flow through this barren dryness and there be no green?

In the shade of the bridge, I wash my clothes and myself. I lack the energy to do a thorough job. It must be the heat on top of my Sunday fast. Even writing in my diary takes focused effort. I've felt a creeping lethargy these past few days. I'm finding today's fast difficult, yet I resist the bread and banana in my pannier.

Back on the bicycle, I feel lightheaded, but not hungry. A Citroen van is pulled over on the side of the road. I chat with the occupants, a French couple, also headed east. They tell me of an India-bound English cyclist they met some days ago. He's about a thousand miles behind me. He cycled from England to eastern Turkey in about six weeks. He has a goal of a hundred miles a day. Poor fellow. I've not cycled thirty miles and I'm drained.

I abandon my plan to cycle until nightfall. A small bridge over a dry river-bed promises shelter for the night. I sit on the dusty earth and enjoy the grand emptiness. I barely have the energy to set out my plastic sheet and get ready for the night. I can't continue doing full Sunday fasts under these conditions. I must follow Rudy's suggestion; start on Saturday afternoon and break the fast with a light meal on Sunday evening. I eat, yet my bone-deep weariness means I can manage only a few mouthfuls. The day wanes. I feel held by the empty vastness about me. A far-off group of brown skin tents are the only evidence of humankind. Snatches of sound float across the distance: a child's shout, then the jangle of a goat bell. The wind shifts and moans. An enormous orange moon rises above the road to the east. To the west, the first stars hang in the sapphire of day's end. I am completely spent, but at one with the world.

I have been marking my diary entries by date and place. This is no longer possible. This moonscape has no name. I set out early the next morning. A strong headwind slows my progress to Herat. I try not to be, but am stressed by my Afghan visa deadline. This fight with the wind is frustrating, but worrying about the visa doesn't increase my speed. I try to put it out of my mind.

Not far from the road, a camel caravan is headed in the other direction. It forms a long, slow-moving line. Women walk in front, wearing dark red and blue robes with fine embroidery. They lead the loping animals, which are laden with luggage and small children. Men follow in the rear; I suppose to watch over things. I'm headed east on my modern bicycle; they're going west on their gangly beasts. The new and the old on opposing courses, each headed into the other's territory—a metaphor for our age. What is their place in the modern world? I imagine the men wear wristwatches and the women use plastic containers. How long will these independent people maintain traditional ways? I feel sad. I'm observing an endangered species.

I pass a rise in the road. Ahead and below me lays a random sprawl of flat-roofed mud houses. Irrigated plots form fluorescent green patches among the mud houses. Beyond, the city of Herat has a dark green hue from countless conifer trees. It's a shock to come upon a large city in the midst of a wilderness. There was no road sign, no electric pole, and no clue of impending civilization. Since Turkey, I've come to expect a city perimeter of shoddily built warehouses and garbage-strewn roads. The outskirts of Herat consist of tidy fields and mud-walled vegetable gardens.

From the main road, I pass along a dual carriageway into the city center. This is a remarkable place. The absence of cars is the difference that makes all the difference. The busiest street in town has only an occasional bus or truck. The trucks are decorated with filigree metalwork and brightly colored, hand-painted panels of flowers and mountain scenes. Down the center of the street run two lines of conifers. These create an unbroken sunshade. This provides welcome relief from the intensity of the afternoon sun. The occasional honk from a truck doesn't disturb the serenity. Sounds of children from behind a mud wall mingle with the cooing of pigeons. The air is motionless and hot.

The city of Herat was established three thousand years ago. The Hari River is the reason the city is here. Atypical in this realm of dust, the river flows throughout the year. The city has a relatively moderate year-round climate. Winds from the mountains in the north bring spring rains and take the edge off the heat of summer days. Well, some days, but not today. The city lies at the other end of the same gap between mountain ranges as Mashhad. This position bestowed a history of repeated invasion, destruction and reconstruction. Old Herat is contained within massive walls atop impressive earthworks. The endless bazaar was once a vital center of commerce. Merchants traded silks from China, pepper and spices from India, lapis lazuli from mines in northeastern Afghanistan, and local glassware. A natural impurity in the local sand gives the glass here a clear blue color. Once the art of glassblowing was perfected, Herat glassware was in high demand in China. In 330 BC, Alexander the Great conquered both Herat and Kandahar. That year, both cities were renamed Alexandria. Historians report there may have been as many as seventy cities called Alexandria—good for his ego, bad for geographic clarity. My route from the Caspian Sea has followed Alexander's.

A few men are seated on the pavement outside a bakery. They're eating and invite me to join them. We converse in gestures as a mangy dog paces nearby, waiting for the occasional scrap of bread thrown into the dust. The dog is caked in dirt and has no hair except a small patch of fur on his back. Its pink and black skin makes ugly folds as it shifts position. *Am I the only one distracted by this unfortunate animal?*

The baker buys me tea. I struggle to use my few words of Farsi to give an account of my travels. The baker listens intently and explains in mime that he has a bad leg and could travel no more than one kilometer on a bicycle. We laugh together. I could sit here all afternoon drinking chai and enjoying the company. But I can't shake the thought that I need to get back on the road. I should stock up on food before I leave the city. A tour around the dingy shops reveals they are accustomed to tourists. Wild children with dirt-caked faces run at me and extend a hand for baksheesh. Shopkeepers quote prices I know are high. These people are poor; I'm relatively rich. They will milk me in any way they can, and I'd do the same in their place.

At a dried fruit shop, I ask for a kilo of dried apricots. The merchant places a piece of brick and an old carburetor on one side of his handheld scale. Nothing goes to waste here in Afghanistan—recycling as you've never imagined it. On the other side of the scales, he piles apricots. *Does he keep a larger piece of brick for local customers?* The merchant is surely a character in the nightmare of a British weights and measures inspector—those who certify grocery scales in England. I also buy raisins and scallions and load the food into my panniers.

An old man in a turban approaches. He explains my bicycle to a huddle of boys that has formed. With authority, he points in turn to different parts of this unfamiliar version of the bicycle. I suppose he describes the function of each. I can grasp a few words of his explanation. He points to the rear derailleur and states that this is the engine. *Ha! If only.* With the mountains ahead, a tiny engine would be welcome.

Checking my luggage, I discover that my bicycle pump adapter is missing. A kid in the crowded marketplace must have taken it. It's a simple, yet vital piece of equipment; nothing more than six inches of rubber tubing with a brass fitting on either end. It carries air from the bicycle pump into the tire valve. This is incredibly frustrating. The adapter likely has no use to the person who took it, but it's a big loss to me. I can't inflate my tires without it. Against the odds, I come across a bicycle repair shop. They have a few spare parts, including a pump adapter, but it doesn't fit my pump. I buy it anyway, in the hope that I might somehow modify it. Without a working pump, I'm unsure how I'll repair the next puncture.

Before leaving, I say goodbye to the baker. We share a bowl of chai. He and his friends show me pieces of hashish resin in plastic bags they produce from within the folds of their robes. Each has a supply that he openly displays and encourages me to buy. With the Taibad border fresh in my mind, I decline. The Afghanis understand the ready demand from young tourists, and there will be other opportunities to buy, should I wish. My experience with drugs is limited. Back home, nicotine and alcohol were the teen drugs of choice. My peers and I were fearful of other substances. Doing contract computer work in London last year, I worked with a team from a South African bank. They worked hard and played hard, as they often told me. I accepted their offer of "some of the best South African weed." That's my entire experience to date with narcotics. I've read about using consciousness-altering drugs to explore the nature of reality. I'm curious to try some hashish while I'm here.

I leave the city with a mushy front tire that I can't properly inflate. From Herat there are two roads east across Afghanistan. The direct route goes through the heart of the Hindu Kush, but that is a gravel road and is often closed. The other route loops in a huge arc south of the most extreme mountains. It's twice the distance, but overall it should be faster. From Kandahar, I will branch off directly east to the Pakistan border.

Afghanistan is one of the few countries in the world with no railway system. The few surfaced roads are a consequence of its strategic position. During the sixties and seventies, the US and Russia competed for Afghanistan's attention. The two admirers pursued her and demonstrated their ardor with lavish gifts. But Afghanistan was a two-timing girl. She accepted gifts from both, yet professed her love to each. And they, although they knew of the other's advances, felt this beauty was too vital to lose.

Games of passion, love and jealousy ensued. Ivan built roads north through the mountains to connect to Russian territory. "All the better to visit you quickly, my dear." The road north out of Kabul includes the famous mile-long Salang Tunnel. Conveniently, it's wide enough for tanks and armored personnel carriers.

Sam—Uncle Sam, that is—continued the Russian road southward from Kabul to Kandahar and Herat. The US Army Corps of Engineers built the Kandahar airport, and added an extension from there into Pakistan. To the west, Sam also built a connector road from Herat to Iran. Recall that Iran and Pakistan were Sam's buddies at the time. This is the road I used from Taibad to Herat. If Afghanistan felt any need to make a commitment, she never showed it. By 1975, Afghanistan had fifteen hundred miles of paved, quality highways. In a couple of years, rape will replace genteel advances. Soviet tanks and troop carriers will stream through the Salang Tunnel and down those convenient Russian and US highways.

I'm on the US highway. It runs southeast from Herat to Kandahar in a lazy loop and then heads northeast into Kabul. The road is excellent. The expansion joints between each concrete section provide a rhythm section to the whir of my derailleur gears. *Cha-chunk...cha-chunk...* I'm not many miles from Herat when the sun sinks behind me. Day drains quickly from the sky. An abandoned mud house will be home tonight. The crumbling walls offer some sense of protection. Night falls and brings the flicker of a far-off campfire in what during the daylight appeared a deserted plain.

The next morning, I fiddle with the pump adapter I bought yesterday. The end that screws into the pump is too small, and the other end is too large for the valve stem. I cut narrow strips of electrical tape from my tool-kit. I shim the gaps and half screw, half jam the adapter into place. I try the pump. Every few strokes, one of the connections pops apart. I contort myself trying to hold the pump between my knees. With one end of the adapter between my thumb and forefinger, I can just hold the other between little finger and palm. With difficulty I pump with the other hand. It's slow going. My impatience flares. I hear Brian's voice say, "But this is the adventure you wanted." *All right, all right!*

The tire eventually holds a bit more air—just enough to get me back on the road. The double line of conifer trees that started in Herat still run between the two lanes. The headwind I battled before Herat returns with a vengeance. The road is flat, but I must use a low gear and keep my head down. Anxiety descends: the wind, my delayed start, and four hundred miles to Kandahar. *I don't have enough time.* I stop by the side of the road and chew on a dried apricot. How can I free myself from this pointless tension? I don't want to be in this frame of mind for the next six days. I must choose and choose again to remain in the present moment. The avenue of trees ends a few miles later and there's a last chai shop. I enjoy a bowl of steaming green tea. The fragrant, sweet liquid provides a welcome break.

I set out again. Beyond the line of trees, the wind is free to do its worst. I drop to the lowest gear, which is usually reserved for the steepest hills. When it gusts, the unseen force stops me altogether. At the base of the surrounding hills, the wind picks up swirls of dust. I've been warned about dust storms. By midafternoon, I've cycled eight excruciating miles. Struggling against this invisible fiend is senseless. Beneath a large bridge over a dry riverbed, I find a nook between concrete support trusses. It's barely big enough for a person. I'm tucked under one end of the bridge into a snug corner on a steep earthen slope that falls to the dry watercourse below, partly sheltered from the wind.

I reevaluate my situation. Clearly, I can't cover the seventy miles a day required by my visa date limit. Sitting there under the bridge, it then gets worse. The front tire deflates suddenly with a sharp hiss. *Oh shit!* I curse the little bugger who stole the pump adapter. Bicycle tires have a mysterious rhythm. They go weeks without a puncture, but once disturbed, a series of punctures tends to follow. I panic; the bicycle is useless. I don't have enough water. I underestimated how much I'd need and didn't fill my container all the way. My map shows no village or town for a hundred miles. *Where do I go for help? For water?* The wind howls. Miserable setting. Miserable feelings.

And just like that, my panic fades. Acceptance emerges. This is how it is, and I must deal with it. There's always a next step; always something I can do to take care of myself. The next step may not be immediately apparent, but it's there. A sense of contentment arises. I eat some apricots and write in my diary. On the smooth cement of a truss, I write in pencil a short poem of mine, wondering if any English speaker will ever read it.

Up, then down;
here, then gone.
Endings not reached.
Point to point and on again.

I listen to the wind howl. It's now a full-blown dust storm and I can see only a few yards around me. Repairing the puncture is a painfully slow business. I repair it. It deflates again. My do-it-yourself pump adapter fails more than it works.

I munch on a handful of dates. A shepherd appears and herds several hundred goats under the bridge. He scrambles up the rocks to stand near me. Not feeling social, I offer him no welcome. He retreats a few yards and crouches on his haunches. He studies me with an expressionless stare. The bicycle is upside-down, the front wheel removed. Without air in one tire, the bicycle is a useless collection of ungainly metal parts. In proper order, it's a thing of function. Grace, even. These qualities are lost along with the air when I get a puncture. It's remarkable that these few pounds of steel, plastic and rubber have carried me so very far. Surely, there is no other machine that provides so much value for this small a quantity of raw material. Sitting in my little roost among the trusses, the absurdity of the situation hits me and I burst out laughing. The shepherd joins in. His laughter at a joke he doesn't understand makes me laugh more. He laughs more, too. Maybe the joke's on me. I'm helpless with laughter. Tears roll down my cheeks and my sides ache. I sense that my laughter is tinged with a little madness.

The wind yowls that it will grant me no passage. I persist with fixing the puncture. There's no alternative. After three hours I get just enough air in the repaired tire. The wind has died down somewhat, or so I hope. I wave goodbye to my buddy in laughter and set off. The wind remains intent on stopping any progress and I struggle on with a soft front tire. Still, I'm relieved to be away from that bridge and the prospect of spending the night there. I win a few yards at a time. Expectations are curious, shape-shifting beasts. My frustration at being unable to cover seventy miles is long gone. Under the bridge, I was sure I'd get no farther today. I pass the next five-kilometer marker stone and I'm elated at my progress.

The road rises into the Hindu Kush foothills. Ahead, craggy peaks fade into the distance. The road is headed straight into them. I'm worried about my supply of water. The few streambeds that pass under the road are all dry. There hasn't been a single vehicle on the road today. The only person I've seen is the shepherd with a sense of humor. There are few villages in the mountains, and my map shows the next town is Delaram, one hundred miles away. My grandfather once told me of a technique he learned as an officer during World War I, when he led a company of Indian foot soldiers through the mountains of northern Iraq. When they were short on water, they chewed on a button to relieve their thirst. I try this, and it helps a little, but by late afternoon I can hold out no longer. I drink the last mouthful of water, and struggle on with a dry tongue.

Without water, I'm in real danger. I imagine my bones picked clean by vultures, lying by a bicycle almost buried in blowing sand. I try the button again, but it offers no real relief. I struggle up a steep rise, my open shirt flapping wildly in the wind. The day wanes. Above to my left and below to my right, green-gray mountains with dramatic silhouettes are stacked in rows. They dissolve into the mist of distance. A pale sun sinks to the horizon, diffused behind a thin sheet of cloud. I continue through the dusk and fight both hill and wind. In the dregs of daylight, I scan the wilderness for a place to sleep. There are bandits in the mountains, so I need to be out of eyeshot of the road. I'm dehydrated and sleep will be difficult. I'm pretty desperate and at a loss. I pedal on; there's nothing else to do.

I hear noises on the road behind me. There's a truck barreling along, and not just any truck. It's a modern, European truck. I haven't seen such a truck since Greece. I haven't seen a vehicle of any kind since Herat. *Why on earth is this truck out here in this forsaken place?* I wave at the driver as he flies past, and then I see it has UK license plates and the TIR international trucking symbol. British license plates! I can't believe it. A few hundred yards ahead, the brake lights go on and the truck stops a little off the road. I cycle alongside and the driver's door opens. A head appears, and I'm greeted with a cheery, "'Ello there!"

Did I die of thirst? Who knew Saint Peter was a Cockney? His Holiness invites me to join him in the cab and serves me a cup of sweet, milky English tea. Just as I thought: heaven. I sigh and sit back, basking in the afterlife.

Turns out, his name is Gerry and he's from Southampton. He's driving empty from Teheran after making a delivery there. He's on his way to Kabul to collect carpets for Harrods in London. We chat about his family, and he shares his concerns about his wife's health. He offers me a meal of canned food, which he heats on a small burner: canned peas and canned Chinese noodles, made in Holland. Then there's dessert; canned peaches with condensed milk never tasted so good. My norm has become a meal that's eighty percent Middle-Eastern flatbread. This is way more to the right on the basic-to-gourmet food continuum. Gerry is the answer to all my present problems—no water, useless pump, no safe place to sleep, and a limited visa. He readily agrees when I ask for a lift to Kandahar.

Several men in flowing robes have materialized out of the night, so I ask for their help to lift the laden bicycle into the cavernous, empty truck. I don't like to think about how it would have been to sleep outside with present company roaming the night. They're helpful enough, but there's a decided shiftiness in their manner. I lash the bicycle to a tie-down rail that runs the length of the empty trailer and then join Gerry up front. He plans to drive nonstop through the night to Kabul, since it's cooler after nightfall.

Things just can't get any stranger. One moment, imminent death by desiccation: the next, milky tea in an air-conditioned cab. I munch on a McVitie's Chocolate Digestive biscuit. Leonard Cohen plays on the stereo. Eerie silhouettes of mountains slip by. As it happens, Mr. Cohen is perfect accompaniment to Afghan scenery by moonlight. Both are somber, both are dark, and neither varies much over time.

Gerry has been driving trucks to Asia for five years and has tales to tell. On his prior trip to Afghanistan three years ago, he delivered Afghan banknotes to Kabul. These are printed in south Wales, he tells me. His was one of a convoy of three trucks. A military escort of armored trucks met them at the Afghan border. The military vehicles broke down repeatedly and they were forced to stop while repairs were made. Each time they passed through the home village of a soldier in the convoy, it stopped to drop him off. By the time they arrived in Kabul, only drivers of the escort vehicles remained. Tonight, Gerry appears happy to have someone to talk to. The surface-of-the-moon scenery endlessly rolls by. We stop only once, and that is for the important business of making a fresh batch of tea over a camping stove. We arrive at the outskirts of Kandahar at dawn. An irrigated river plain of small, bright green fields dazzles me. The backdrop is a line of crazily shaped mountains. Each is tall and separate from its neighbor; they could be giant termite mounds. The early sun forces its presence through a stubborn mist. The city is headed to work; a huddle of people stands at a bus stop. Men on bicycles slowly pedal, their loose pants flapping. A boy leads a bony black cow. I ask Gerry to drop me here so I can be part of this enchantment. Curious faces watch me untie and unload the bicycle.

I say a fond goodbye to Gerry and the truck bounces away, raising a cloud of dust. Eighteen hours ago, I was under a bridge with a lame steed. I had little water and less hope. I was in real and present danger. And now here I am, blinking in the bright sun. It's seven in the morning, I'm fed and watered, and I'm in Kandahar, about seventy miles from the Pakistan border.

Memories of yesterday fade with the morning mist. I'm entranced by the surreal tranquility of the morning. People on the street pay no more attention to me than they do to one of the roadside cows. Afghan dignity does not permit that. A few schoolchildren in faded navy uniforms are the only ones who stare. At a roadside shack, I enjoy several bowls of that most delicious green tea. One of the other customers offers me hashish. I buy a small amount for about fifteen cents and then ride slowly into the city with my soft front tire. I match the measured pace of those around me. I sense a communal pact to not disturb the serenity of the morning.

Kandahar is the third largest city in Afghanistan and a center of trade. Its bazaar merchants sell sheep, wool, cotton, grains, dried fruit, and tobacco. It is one of the homes of the Pashtun people, and was once known as the Gateway to the East. The wide gap in those crazy mountains to the east explains why. Kandahar has played host to Alexander the Great, the Arabs, Genghis Khan, the Turks, and the British. In the eighteenth century, when Afghanistan was an independent state, Kandahar was its capital. The capital was moved to Kabul in response to the threat of the British, who were intent on pushing their Indian frontier into Afghanistan. The Shrine of the Cloak here houses a garment that's thought to have been worn by the Prophet Muhammad. I imagine the Prophet, peace be upon him, would approve of the cloak of serenity that lies over the city this morning.

I find a cheap and relatively clean hotel. Roses in the walled garden offer a heavenly scent. I sleep for most of the day to make up for my sleepless night. In the evening, I stroll about the city. It's noisy and crowded now that the heat of day has passed. There are few electric lights. Countless small oil lamps amplify the otherworldly atmosphere. Back in my hotel room, I eat half of the hashish and fall back to sleep.

I'm still floating from the hashish the next morning. I wander the streets and stop often to enjoy cups of that incredible green tea. I buy a replacement pump with its own adapter. But the merchants here know what most young Western travelers buy, and it isn't bicycle pumps. A brisk contemporary trade in drugs has replaced traditional Silk Road commerce. One insistent shopkeeper invites me into his handicraft store and offers me every narcotic I've ever heard of—and several I haven't. Do I want heroin, cocaine, hashish, opium or mescaline? *Excuse me, but how did cocaine and mescaline find their way here from South America?* He makes no mention of the handicrafts stacked about us on the shelves. Lower margins, probably.

In another shop, I accept an invitation to join the young shopkeeper for tea. He says he can pay me well. He shows me a pair of shoes with hollowed-out heels that he'll have made in my size. His face then lights up with inspiration. He will have my bicycle frame cut apart, filled with heroin and then reassembled. *Ha! I don't think so.* I've heard the tales of drug-smuggling Westerners languishing in disease-ridden Pakistani jails. Border police receive cash payments for catching drug smugglers. This has spawned a sorry scam.

Shopkeeper convinces unsuspecting Westerner to carry drugs across border. Shopkeeper alerts border police buddy with description and hiding place of drugs. Border guard nabs incredulous paleface. Shopkeeper receives share of cash payout from border guard. Whitey gets twenty to twenty-five years. Afghan government gets a pat on the back from US for stemming drug traffic. Enterprising—and sad.

I awake early next morning. I wash and repair clothes, then fix the adapter on my original pump so it will work reliably. I want the security of a second pump. I plan to have a last ride around the city this afternoon and then set out for the border. That will leave two comfortable days to cover the seventy miles to the border.

I leave my room around noon. At the lobby, I say hello to the hotel manager, who speaks good English. His news floors me. Last night there was a coup d'état in Kabul. This overthrew the government of Mohammed Daoud. Many thousands were killed, including President Daoud, his wife, children and brother. For a country in turmoil, things here in Kandahar remain oddly normal. There was an overnight curfew here that ended at eight this morning. I was completely unaware. Westerners who tried to leave the city earlier this morning were turned back by army roadblocks. Other locals appear reluctant to talk about what has happened and continue about their business. There's a remarkable lack of display of emotion given that a long period of stability in Afghanistan ended yesterday.

I later hear an Italian journalist's eyewitness account of the coup. The education conference was scheduled to open on May 1. The coup was likely coordinated with this period of few foreigners in the country. The conference will be canceled. Russian-made Afghan Mig aircraft strafed buildings in Kabul with gunfire and rockets; tanks careened down narrow streets, veering into buildings and rolling over street lamps. It appears that the drivers had little experience. My decision to leave Afghanistan from Kandahar is a fortuitous one. I might otherwise have continued with Gerry to Kabul and would have been there for all of that. I do hope Gerry is OK.

I flush what remains of the hashish down the toilet. That's not something to carry through checkpoints manned by jittery policemen. I leave the hotel in the early afternoon. I'm willing to take my chances leaving the city. I pass three army roadblocks and slow for each, making purposeful eye contact with the armed soldiers. Surprisingly, none makes a move to stop me. They stand motionless and watch me pass. I could be in a dream. I proceed cautiously past the barriers topped with barbed wire. I think of the rifles carried by the soldiers, and the muscles in my back tighten as I cycle away from each checkpoint. I dare not look back.

I get a puncture in the rear wheel, then a second. The sun sinks into the horizon. I am only ten miles out of Kandahar. Beside a field of green wheat, I watch the sun set. The grain sparkles as it moves in a light wind. A small bird darts in and out of this shimmering sea. Its wings catch the light with flashes of green and yellow fire. The disjointed mountains beyond are a line of discarded theatrical props on a flat stage. The sun sinks and they turn to dark silhouettes. I can see buildings, spires and trees in the rocky silhouettes. A terrestrial version of cloud-gazing. I ride on.

Not far from the road is a strange, tall building. Maybe it's for grain storage. It's out of place in this setting, yet it holds the promise of shelter for the night. I settle myself under an overhang in front of the locked door. Three soldiers materialize from the emptiness. I protest, but they make it clear that I can't stay. I'm then back on the road by the last light of day. A mile ahead, there are several high mounds of earth—likely left behind by a US bulldozer during road construction. These offer scant protection, but will have to do. I fall asleep under a sea of stars so bright they seem to crackle.

I'm on my way before the sun rises. My gurgling stomach of yesterday has settled, and my mood lightens. Unbroken blue overhead and the morning heat whisper that today will be a scorcher. My good checkpoint fortune of yesterday holds no longer. At a roadblock, a young policeman gestures for me to stop. His faded and patched uniform would suit an out-of-work car mechanic better than a representative of the law, yet his proud bearing communicates authority. His colleagues in the one-room office appear uncertain what to do with me. The senior officer makes several phone calls on an antique black telephone and has to shout to be heard. I ask what is happening, but the officer speaks only a few words of English. It requires twenty minutes of creative communication for me to understand that they have received orders to not let any foreigner pass. Specifically, any foreigner on foot, in a car, in a truck, or on a motorbike. But they have no instructions about one on a bicycle.

Three hours of amiable talking through miming, drinking chai, and waiting follow. They talk among themselves and appear to come to a decision. They again carefully inspect my passport, holding it upside down, and then wave me on my way. I later learn from the Italian journalist that all other foreigners were turned back at such checkpoints. They were required to leave to the west, back into Iran. Somehow, I alone manage to continue east.

I must continue through the heat of day if I am to be out of Afghanistan in time. Wearing my *keffiyeh*, I proceed steadily in the glare of midday. On either side, the sandy desert contains only the occasional scrub bush. I enjoy the empty stillness. It has its own particular beauty. An Afghan on a white stallion gallops by in the opposite direction, robes flapping. I'm in a scene from *The Lord of the Rings*: the desert, forbidding mountains, and now Gandalf on Shadowfax. This is as mysterious and wild a place as any visited by Frodo Baggins.

I arrive at a tea shack set in the emptiness. Happy to be out of the sun for a time, I enjoy hot, sweet tea. The few customers sit in silence and gaze out into the desolate plain. Countless flies buzz in the hot air. An old man coaxes music from a homemade instrument: an oil can as a sound box, nailed to a branch that supports two wire strings. The music is haunting.

Back on the road, I get yet another puncture in the rear wheel. It's time to change the tire. The one I remove is paper-thin in places. I changed the first in Greece. I wave down a passing truck and ask for the use of a water container. The driver hands me an engine oil can. The top has been cut off, and a rough wooden handle is fitted across the opening. Submersing the inner tube in the can of water, I locate a slow puncture. Once that is repaired, I continue in the intense heat. What will I do once I get to India? With the hot season and the monsoons that follow, it may be best to cycle into the Himalayas and stay there until the rains pass. Kashmir or Nepal, maybe.

The day wanes. The road passes between those crazy mountains. Oddly, up close they lose their sharp definition. They are indeed formed from extreme angles, yet the edges and angles are rounded like enormous globs of dark gray butter left in the sun. They are formed from huge boulders that appear to be welded together. Other large boulders have fallen away from the primary mass. These are scattered on and below slopes at the foot of the mountains. These boulders have eroded into bizarre shapes, and some have worn away, leaving a small foot on which they balance. I investigate further. Some have eroded so that a hollow has formed lower on the surface and hold the promise of some sort of shelter for the night. Up the slope is a huge one; from the road it appears solid, but from behind, I can see that it has a large indentation at ground level and three more high above. From some paces away, it resembles a giant human skull. I choose not to look for any significance in that fact, thank you very much. I bed down in the open mouth.

I'm happy that I do wake up the next morning. I scramble up a slope of scree above Skull Motel. The dun plain stretches out below me. Small plots of green wheat provide a startling contrast. The road cuts an arrow-straight line across the plain. It then slopes up into the mountains to my right, in the direction I am to travel. Far below me, Skull Rock hides my bicycle from the road. The air is clear and still. People appear from around the mountain on a dusty track. There are two on horseback, several on foot, and one on a motorbike. They are tiny in the distance. The silence is so complete I can hear gravel crunch underfoot as the walkers cross a dry streambed. The *putt-putt-putt* of the motorbike recedes.

I'm a bird watching the early morning unfold hundreds of feet below. A red glow in the eastern sky turns gold, then yellow. The sun emerges hot white from the mountains of Pakistan. The morning fairly sparkles with calm and clarity. It's a blessing to be here, at this moment, on this day.

I'm not far from the border. I have no need to rush on my last day in Afghanistan. I cycle slowly through Spin Buldak, the final village in Afghanistan. An old man holds a piece of fraying string, with which he leads a waddling pelican. The strange bird holds the attention of the locals. I pass by unseen. What an odd country this is. The formalities to leave Afghanistan proceed slowly, but without complication.

 Route though Afghanistan: Tir Pol, Herat, Gereshk, Kandahar, and Spin Buldak.

Fifteen

PAKISTAN

April 30th

I cross into Pakistan. A hand-painted sign informs me that I must now stay to the left. This holdover from the days of the British is disorienting. It's like looking at the road through a mirror. I've been cycling on the right since France.

The border police wear uniforms that are crisp and clean. Does this mean organized efficiency, as in Iran? Ah, no. I complete many forms, and each is processed at a ponderous pace. Among the many details, I must enter the serial number of the bicycle. They record the bicycle in my passport. If I do not leave Pakistan with it, I'll be charged three hundred twenty-five percent import duty. The officials speak passable English. The fact that I am English seems to impress them more than the fact that I cycled here *from* England. They remember with fondness the time of the British Raj. The British left behind the pandemonium of partition, the separation of Pakistan from India. But here in Chaman, there's only jolly good cheer for all things British.

Lt. Col. Muhammad Salim of the Pishin Scouts invites me for tea in the customs office. He has the shocking orange hair that some Baluchis inherit; even his impressive moustache is orange. His uniform is immaculate. He speaks with an Oxbridge accent, like an English country squire, though a Pakistani accent or phrase periodically intrudes. He's jovial and animated as he pours tea from a teapot into my cup. It has a matching saucer, just like at home. Milk and sugar are offered; Lt. Col. Salim has measured manners. I work to not smile in response to the plumminess of his speech. "Absolutely, old boy." "Would you care for some tiffin, old fellow?" Surely these are echoes of the time when local military men served under British officers in the Indian Army. But it's all a bit threadbare. The teacups are chipped. The painted walls bubble and peel in places.

The good lieutenant colonel explains that Chaman was a terminus of the British Indian rail system. Through a feat of civil engineering, a rail line climbs from the Indus River valley through the mountains and over a pass of nine thousand feet. It ends here in the Afghan plain, not two hundred yards from the Afghan border. Stiff resistance from the Afghans prevented the British from extending the rail line or their control any farther.

After my leisurely tiffin—morning tea with biscuits—I set out into Pakistan. Five minutes later, an army jeep overtakes me and stops. It's Lt. Col. Salim with a driver. During our conversation, I had mentioned that I have twenty afghanis to change into Pakistani rupees. He took this to mean that the twenty afghanis were my total wealth. He insists I take the fifty rupees he hands me. I explain the misunderstanding, but he'll have none of it. He says, "You look as though you need the money." Perhaps it's my weekly fast. Either way, he's uninterested in my thanks. The jeep does a tight U-turn and speeds back to the border, kicking up clouds of dust.

Rudy's definition of a far-off place is one where they call you *Sahib*. So, I must be somewhere far-off. In the town of Chaman, every child that sees me runs at me with right hand extended. "*Sahib—baksheesh! Sahib—baksheesh!*" Each repetition is more frantic than the last. The town is dirtier and noisier than Kandahar. A similar mix of Pashtuns and Baluchis live here, yet Pakistan is another culture. In the space of a few miles, the restraint of the Afghans is gone.

A tourist office sign points to a small shopfront. Inside, there are no telephones, no brochures, and no posters on the wall. A young man behind the single desk asks how he can help me. Half joking, I say by letting me sleep on the floor. If he's surprised, he doesn't show it; he asks me to return at eight. I pass the early evening in a nearby chai shop. Each customer wants to shake my hand and talk. They're inquisitive and informed. It's an enjoyable evening, and bodes well for my time in Pakistan. I meet my friend at the tourist office as agreed. He brings a mattress, a pillow, and a sheet. The nights are warm and there's no need for a blanket. He arranges a bed on the floor. Way more helpful than a color brochure.

My host brings chai in the morning and we talk. The curtains remain drawn against the already intense sunlight. The breathless morning promises a day of honest-to-goodness heat. A grimy fan turns slowly overhead, but does little to relieve the oppressive air. We're in a scene from a black and white movie of British India. My host leans slowly back in his large chair, exhales a long sigh, and says, "My God, but this is a dull country." With local tourism in the hands of my host, Chaman may be destined to remain an unknown backwater.

From here, the road rises steadily. It proceeds toward an unbroken wall of mountains. How can a road possibly cross such terrain? These mountains formed the border between Afghanistan and British India. The Pashtuns, famed warriors, countered the might of the British Army with guerilla warfare here. The British called them an "impudent bunch of goat herders." Impudent or not, these herders of goats were never beaten. The British civil servant Mortimer Durand negotiated the frontier with the Afghan emir, Abdur Rahman Khan. The Durand Line ignored tribal boundaries. It sliced through the ancestral area of the Pashtuns, the Baluchis, and other ethnic groups.

It's a long, slow climb. The road crosses back and forth over a twin-track rail line. Road and rail line form a two-stranded, twisted thread. That a road was built here is remarkable. More remarkable still is that a rail line was pushed through such inhospitable mountains. The railway passes through tunnel after tunnel, and the stonework at each tunnel mouth reveals a style that would be more at home in the English countryside. The road crests at 8,881 feet in the Khojak Pass. The rail line passes nearby through the two-and-a-half-mile-long Khojak Tunnel. The emir of Afghanistan was wholly opposed to construction of the rail line. He said the cutting of the Khojak Tunnel was like a knife in his vital organs. Speaking of, the rail line is vital to modern Afghan trade. It transports fruit grown in the few fertile Afghan valleys into Pakistan.

I work my way slowly up each turn of the road. This climb is similar to the one through the mountains of northern Greece. There, I made the mistake of looking at the road high above me. It was that knowledge that made the going so tough then. Now I don't look ahead, though the temptation is great. I focus on the next few yards, then the next. I enjoy how the struggle keeps me present. I focus, I climb, I breathe. I could go on like this forever. I focus, I climb, I breathe.

After some hours of steady uphill labor, I reach the pass, and there's a twinge of disappointment. I'd begun to enjoy this. The road descends from the pass, but less than I'd climbed. I'm on an elevated plain—still dry and dusty, but with an occasional knot of trees. Their green stands in contrast to the ocher surroundings. The quality of the light, the heat, and these trees offer what I imagine is a foretaste of India.

During the days of the British Raj, this was part of India. It was only in the 1940s that Pakistan was conceived. As the British planned their departure from India, the Muslim leader Muhammad Ali Jinnah advocated for a separate Muslim state. Mahatma Gandhi disagreed. His vision was for Muslim and Hindu to live side by side in harmony, as most had done prior to the arrival of the British. Jinnah's politicking succeeded. British India was partitioned into two separate countries: India, with Hindus as the majority of its residents, and Pakistan, with Muslims the majority of its population.

Partition caused one of the largest migrations of human beings in history. Before the British left India in 1947, Hindu residents of what was to become Pakistan, and many Muslims in what was to become India, feared discrimination or worse. The partition of the country was announced, but then later moved up so that there were only weeks to prepare. Ten million people left everything and set out to relocate to a new country favorable to their faith. It was a period of horrific turmoil. Every available train, ship and vehicle was crammed full of people. Many more had to walk hundreds of miles. Hindu and Muslim convoys attacked and killed each other when their paths crossed. Fear and animus reigned. More than one million people were killed. After Partition, there was an East Pakistan and a West Pakistan. A thousand miles of Indian territory separated the two halves of this single nation. This untenable situation was resolved in 1971 when the new state of Bangladesh was formed from East Pakistan. West Pakistan became simply, Pakistan.

I wash my feet in a small stream. A group of men sit on the bank. The not uncommon smell of burning hashish hangs in the air. They beckon for me to join them and I share a joint with a stately old gentleman. He has a magnificent white beard and moustache.

Twenty minutes later I'm cycling across a salt desert. I'm blissfully unaware of a bicycle beneath me. I float a few feet above the road; its surface fascinates me. The passing textures and colors are just so beautiful. With a twinge of anxiety, I wonder how long it has been since I last looked where I'm going. The road surface again draws my attention. I'm intrigued to realize that I'm on a bicycle and that the bicycle is still on the road. At the top of my lungs, I belt out a Simon and Garfunkel song to the emptiness. The richness of my voice moves me. *Whoa. That was good stuff.*

My high slowly wanes, and then nature provides a different show. Over the past few days, I've seen a number of dust tornadoes. These tall, opaque columns move slowly across the plain, even when the air is still. Today, I see smaller twisters twirl into being in the desert. In my semi-stoned state, I'm fascinated by the remarkable display. One passes directly over me. Its edge is windy and extremely dusty. It blows fine sand up my nose. My mouth remains closed, yet I somehow end up with grit between my teeth. All around me, a curtain of brown dust extends far into the sky. I'm in the center of a swirling tube hundreds of feet high and can see nothing beyond the billowing walls. The center is strangely calm and very hot. Then, more dust flies into my orifices as the other edge passes over me.

Something in the corner of my eye catches my attention. I turn, and half a mile behind me, a wall of dust extends from earth to sky. Unlike the twisters, this forms an unbroken, wide curtain. The top edge is beyond sight. It's downright eerie. The light takes on a greenish hue, then dims. A brisk wind gathers momentum. I'm in danger and need to get out of the way.

I bind my *keffiyeh* tightly about my head and leave only a small slit for my eyes. I pedal hard, but the towering wall gains on me. The wind pushes me forward with a visceral force that I feel as a firm pressure on my back. I pick up more speed. The storm is moving perhaps thirty miles an hour and is gaining on me. The sky darkens further. The village of Saranan should be close. The sun is now blotted out. The temperature drops. The lack of visibility is the same as it is in a pea soup English fog; in this case, the soup is orange-brown lentil. A howling wind pushes at my back even more forcefully. I enjoy the thrilling speed.

I arrive in the village. Wooden stores with verandas line the road, as in an old Western movie. Windows are shuttered and doors are closed. A gate swings and bangs in the wind like a thing possessed. A dog walks slowly across the empty street.

I startle the huddled occupants of a chai shop as I enter with my bicycle. The door slams shut violently and shakes the whole building. *Wow, that was a close call!* I'm relieved to be inside a closed building. The air is thick with hashish smoke. There's no light inside and it takes time for my eyes to adjust. A pale orange glow shows through cracks in the shutters. Shadowed faces peer at me through the gloom. The wind wails and whistles outside. The window shutters shake frantically. The proprietor will take no payment for my tea. One of the patrons insists he buy me a meal. Mohammed Ebrahim is a laboratory assistant in a Quetta hospital; he invites me to be his guest tonight. The wind dies down somewhat. Outside, the air is still dusty. There's enough light to see, yet there's no direct sunlight.

Mohammed's village is a few miles off the main road. I cycle behind him along a raised causeway. His old bicycle lurches and creaks with each turn of the pedal. His house is simple and wonderfully clean. Shy children with large brown eyes and long lashes hide behind their dad's legs. He's a charming, generous host. I'm humbled by this openhearted generosity from someone with so little. My journey and its motivation fascinate him. He tells me of an Englishman who bought a donkey in the village for about thirty dollars some years ago. He traveled with it through the mountains. "You can sell it at the end of the journey," he explains. Maybe for my next trip to Pakistan, I say.

Mohammed leaves early next morning to catch the bus into Quetta. I'll meet him there later in the day. Before I leave the village, I visit the chai shop. I'm bought numerous bowls of sweet green tea. Many of the older men speak good English; it's curious to hear quasi-Oxbridge accents emanate from gnarled, walnut faces. One old man is interested to hear about my family and asks questions about my background. I guess he is locating me within his 1940s Anglo-Indian understanding of class-bound English society. I explain that my father is English and my mother is French. A look of sympathetic understanding comes over his animated face. As if it were a secret never meant to leave present company, he lowers his voice, leans forward, and says, "Ah, yes. I see... a half caste." The onlookers appear confused by my burst of laughter. Well, I suppose I am. I've just never thought of it in that way. My questioner takes no offense at my laughter, and I'm struck anew by the easygoing nature of these people.

I'm under the weather: probably my gurgling, raw stomach. I ride the bicycle and my mental cobwebs clear. Around me, the heat mounts until I'm close to fainting. I stop to lie in the shade of a tree. Back on the road, bus and truck drivers make me angry. They drive perilously close. Many sound their horns just feet behind me. This makes me start and sends a bolt of pain through my temples. Twice, they pass so close I'm forced off the road and bounce down the dusty embankment. They appear to do this intentionally, and I'm livid. My map shows that this is the only road. I've no choice but to persist.

I arrive in Quetta too late to visit the post office. I'd hoped to collect my letters from home today. My prior *poste restante* stop was Teheran, so I'm eager for news from home. Mohammed's laboratory is also closed, so I'll return to see him tomorrow. Quetta is a large, noisy city. There are remnants from the days of the British Raj; signs indicate the governor's residence and an ordinance depot. Flowerbeds with stands of hollyhock grace the entry to an army barracks. A policeman directs traffic nearby. He stands atop a small circular platform in a busy intersection. He makes graceful, sweeping movements with his hands and arms, as fine and coordinated as any dancer. He even turns like a dancer. He has no visible effect on the flow of cars. It's one unbroken stream of honking traffic. Like bees flying around a hive, each somehow passes without collision. That cop must have given up any hope of influencing the traffic and now performs for the sheer joy of it. If there are ballet troupes in Pakistan, here's someone they need to audition.

In a flyblown restaurant, I eat a plate of heavenly curry and *chapattis*. I find a small hotel for twelve rupees a night. Even this is a stretch for my meager budget. Unprompted, the manager tells me stories of random police drug raids. For the second time, I flush hashish down a toilet.

The next morning, I enjoy a leisurely breakfast in a chai shop. The momentum of the city builds. Bright sunlight gives sharp definition to the morning. I collect my letters from the main post office: one from my mother, one from Rudy, one from Brian, and a couple of others. I'd expected some books to be forwarded from Israel, but I suspect the parcel has been stolen. Theft by postal clerk here is a given. Each of my letters has been opened, then resealed with lumpy brown glue. I imagine they've been read as well as checked for valuables. I've been told about this and expected it to happen. Still, the violation of my privacy makes me angry.

At a restaurant with a walled garden, I enjoy the letters. Dappled sunlight plays across the white marble tabletop. In a small flowerbed, blue cornflowers and yellow roses are vibrant in the sunlight. I order English tea. I immensely enjoy the familiar padded tea cozy, hot teapot, cube sugar in a bowl, milk in a small jug, tea strainer, and the fine teacup and saucer. It doesn't get any better than this. I consume several pots of tea over a few hours. I read and savor each letter. Reading letters from home and writing long replies has become a ritual, a way to reconnect to home and things familiar. I decorate each letter with small drawings I make with the colored pencils I've carried from England in lieu of my watercolors. I describe my travels and again feel blessed. Dangerous situations have worked out in my favor time and again. I'm grateful to all those who have shown me goodwill.

I visit Mohammed at his office. In the evening, I return to the restaurant near my hotel. A young man asks if he can join me at my table. He's a geologist and well-educated. He has many questions, and we talk late into the evening, attracting a large circle of listeners. I enjoy having an audience. We discuss religion, Islam, the role of women in Islam, and life in England. I describe my experience of the cultures I've passed through. I paint myself as the understanding, wise traveler. I omit any description of my aggressive responses when I felt threatened. I present the narrative as if my actions, thoughts and feelings made complete sense. I do not describe how messy it has been at times, or that some situations brought out the darkness in me. I leave with a creeping recognition that I've been disingenuous.

I've become fast friends with the man who brings tea to my room and does odd jobs around the hotel. He's a dwarf with an impressive white beard. He's a casting director's dream for a role in the Pakistani version of *Snow White and the Seven Dwarves*. He reacts the same way each time we meet. His face wrinkles into a huge smile. Arm extended, he walks directly up to me so we can shake hands. Smiley speaks not one word of English, yet when our eyes meet, we laugh together at some unexplained joke. I suppose I'm as strange a creature in his world as he is in mine.

I'm reluctant to leave the relative comfort of the hotel but I want to get back on the road. After just two nights in a bed, I'm feeling a tad anxious about living by my wits again. I'm back on the bicycle the next day, and it doesn't take long to rediscover the rhythm.

A few miles from the city, I sit on a rock by the roadside and enjoy my current favorite delicacy: a sandwich of sliced white bread and ripe banana. *Mmmm.* My stomach is a little better, but my ears hurt a lot. I think it's due to an ear infection in each ear. I cycle on and pass several nomadic camps, each some distance from the road. As in Afghanistan, each camp is a cluster of black or brown skin tents. Several huge dogs bark frantically at my passing. Thankfully, they are tethered and can't come after me. A young nomadic girl standing by the road flashes me a smile. Her sparkling eyes and simple sweetness lift my spirits. I'm happy to be on the road again.

The nondescript terrain provides a good setting to consider last night's conversation with the geologist. Is Western freedom of thought and speech oversold? How free are we really, in our thinking and in our speech? How much of what we think and say is the product of upbringing, environment, social conditioning, the company we keep, and the media we consume? Do our daily schedules and what we eat influence our thought and speech? Can we perceive our own conditioning, the lens through which each of us sees the world? Is there any part of us that is free of outside influence? Is there a freedom to be gained from our baser nature? Is freedom for an Englishman the same thing as freedom for a Pakistani?

I discover that I've left my maps behind at the hotel in Quetta. Ha! So here's a certain freedom from others' view of reality. No matter—they were mostly for reassurance. There are so few paved roads that I need to ask for directions only occasionally. A rail line runs parallel with the road. A strip of bright metal atop each rusty rail shows that the line is in use. I'm headed south-southeast toward the Indus valley. This is a fairly direct route to India, although I'm unsure where the border crossings into India are.

The road rises and parts company with the rail line as I head up to the Bolan Pass. This is a final reaching for the sky before the road descends to the Indus River plain. Night falls before I can find a place to sleep. This is an inhospitable stretch of mountain. There are no trees, no vegetation of any kind. I'm unhappy to be so exposed. In the dark I can discern a shallow depression in the dusty earth. It's a hundred yards from the road, so perhaps it offers marginal safety from nighttime surprises. I've seen no one all afternoon, so it should be OK. There's nothing here except rocks, scree, and the road.

I fall into a deep sleep. At some point in the night, I dream that the earth rumbles and shakes. The dream feels so real that I awake in terror, only to find that the earth is indeed rumbling and shaking. A blinding light is headed straight at me with the deafening roar of an enormous diesel engine. I panic. There's no time even to stand, so I roll frantically along the ground, away from the bulldozer. I'm about to be crushed. *What? How?* A bulldozer in the wilderness, in the dead of night!

My brain struggles to piece things together. Coursing adrenaline now has me wide awake. Behind a low rise, twenty feet from my sleeping spot, is the railway line I'd seen earlier in the day. I had not seen it all afternoon and just assumed it was some distance from the road. I'm shaking. A diesel locomotive roars slowly by. In the dark, I can make out a long line of freight cars. I move a hundred feet away. Instinct tells me to move no farther into the dark night. I lie beneath a field of the brightest stars, but sleep doesn't easily return. Rumbling freight trains wake me two more times.

I wake well before dawn and feel lethargy in every joint; this tells me that I'm still sick. Who knows with what? I start again with the first light of day and soon reach a stone marker for the Bolan Pass. The pass is in fact a series of narrow valleys that stretches fifty-six miles. During the British Raj, it was known as one of two Gates of India. The second is the Khyber Pass, which is hundreds of miles to the north.

After the Bolan Pass, the road drops 5,400 feet to the Indus valley. The road and rail track follow the dry bed of the Bolan River. Road, railway and river cross over each other in a long braid that descends out of the mountains. There's fine stonework at each of the rail tunnel mouths. Many have castellated tops. A name is engraved in the stone above each tunnel entrance: MARY ANN, then later, WINDY CORNER, 1894. Names for cottages on the Isle of Wight, perhaps, but they're out of place in the Brahul Mountains of Pakistan.

The stonework is wonderfully intact. It's a testament to the English masons who labored here under a fierce sun. Probably wishing to be with Mary Ann, and far from this windy corner. There are low bushes with fleshy leaves by the road. The sandy mountains are otherwise utterly bare. The road is in poor repair.

I speed downward, and the rough road rattles the bicycle. My arms, head and ears throb with pain, but I continue down. The temperature rises further. A caravan made up of several hundred camels works its way up the dry riverbed: vestiges of the historic Silk Road that runs from India. I pass a clump of palm trees, out of place here in the bone-dry mountains. Trucks appear on the road. The truck drivers are demons. Absolute demons. They allow no space as they pass me, even where they could. Several times, the slipstream causes me to lose control and veer off the road to avoid going under their wheels. The worst are those who come from the opposite direction. Several intentionally drive over to my side. I make eye contact and see a sneer or outright laughter from the driver. *Fucking bastards!*

I drink a chai at the first roadside shack I encounter. It's midmorning and already unbearably hot. I'm about halfway down to the Indus valley. A young man explains that long-distance truck drivers smoke hashish to stay awake. They drive for days without sleep so they can earn a living wage. I need to be cautious. I don't want to be roadkill for a strung-out, latter-day bullock cart driver.

I continue down out of the mountains and the day becomes hotter still. The wind feels like it comes from some gigantic hair drier on a high setting. The air is unpleasant to breathe. The asphalt of the road is now molten. My tires make the same noise as they do on a wet road. Asphalt sticks to the tires, which then pick up tiny pieces of stone. This isn't good. I worry that hot asphalt is a solvent for tire rubber.

Incredibly, the riverbed now runs with a little water. There's a clump of trees by the bank. I stop. Even in the shade, the heat is intolerable. A pool has formed at a sharp turn in the river. The deep water turns slowly in a blue-gray pool. I dive in, fully clothed. Muslim brothers probably lurk unseen, and there's no need to offend any sensibility. I swim back and forth across my tiny private swimming pool. The cool water refreshes and revitalizes me. Out of the water, my clothes dry on me in minutes. I can't trust the river water, so I drink what I carried from the tea shack. I've already drunk some thirteen pints today. I've been sweating profusely from pores I never even knew I had—on the inside of my wrists, for example. My water supply is low. I must push on despite the heat. I dive into the water one more time; I want to start out wet and cool. Then I soak my *keffiyeh* and tie it about my head. Even so, the heat makes the blood pound in my temples. There's a slight pain with each pulse. I stop occasionally to allow a fainting sensation to pass.

I stop for water and a cup of chai at a roadside shack. It's no more than a large, filthy box by the road. People crowd about me, touching the bicycle. This attention is sheer torture. I feign incomprehension. I'm rude. I make fun of their poor English. Still, they won't leave me alone. The educated people I met in Quetta were a joy to be with. Here, I'm grab-it-while-you-can entertainment. They meet my unpleasantness with sneers and mockery. The only way I can handle my anger is to go back into the sun and continue cycling. I simply don't know what else to do.

The trucks continue to drive perilously close, horns blaring. I'm again forced off the road several times. I'm at the limits of my emotional endurance. I've faced each obstacle, each fear on this journey. But now I face an impregnable wall, and, it's inside me. I feel threatened to my core by this witch's brew: intense heat, filth, pervasive flies, a persistent sickness, mocking people, and unhinged truck drivers. I lack the inner resources to deal with it. It's simply too much.

I emerge from the mountains onto the plain. And plain it is—as flat as a billiard table. I pass through an irrigated area with many shades of bright green. There are stands of palm trees and lumbering water buffalo. Here is the Indian subcontinent, exactly as I'd imagined it. But I soon leave the fields behind and pass into a sandy desert, where I see not a soul. The sun sinks toward the mountains behind me. My long shadow races next to me along the flat ground. The sky and even the very air are orange. The setting sun shimmers in folds of heat rising from the desert. I keep my head down and my legs pumping. I want only to get through and away from this inferno. The last light of day fades.

I come to a junction. A huddle of low buildings lines the road. They are made from rickety wooden frames with patchwork walls of warped, flattened oil cans. There are restaurants and shacks selling cigarettes and Coca-Cola. I devour a large plate of potato curry and freshly made chapattis. I'm near Sibi, Baluchistan Province. I ride into the darkness in search of a place to sleep. I look for some shelter or camouflage in the open expanse, but there is none: no tree, no building, not even a small rise in the land. I see a thorn bush fifty yards from the road and make a bed on the ground, keeping the spindly bush between me and the road. It provides the merest hint of protection.

It's an hour after the sun has gone down, and the world is still a blast furnace. *God! Is there no escape from this heat?* Lying on top of my sleeping bag is too hot. I lay fully clothed, directly on my sheet of plastic that I've laid on the stony ground. Inside my sleeping bag, I at least have the illusion of security; I've never felt this exposed at night. Exposed to passersby—if, indeed, there are any in this godforsaken wilderness—and to the creatures of the desert. I'm keenly aware that this is the realm of snakes and scorpions.

I wake well before dawn. I'd kept my shoes on as I slept, so departure is a truly simple affair. Fold and stow the plastic sheet, swallow a few mouthfuls of dry-as-toast *chapatti*, gulp as much water as my belly will hold, and I'm on the road before the first light of day. I can already tell that in this heat, it will only be possible to cycle before dawn and perhaps a little in the evening.

I'm crossing a perfectly flat, perfectly empty desert. The stony ground stretches away to an unbroken horizon on either side. The road runs alongside a single-track rail line. Road and railway run arrow-straight. Welcome to my world. A strip of asphalt, a rail line, a line of telephone poles, and me, cycling steadily with a blessed wind at my back. There are only a few trucks. As they say in these parts, God is great.

The telephone poles pass. The rhythmic rise, fall, rise of the telephone wires is hypnotic. I force myself to focus on something else. Mile markers count off the distance to Bel Pat, the next town. By nine in the morning, I've cycled the forty miles to Bel Pat. The sun is a demon, intent on villainy. It's already far too hot to continue. I must find shade.

Bel Pat consists of a rail station and a huddle of grimy shacks that serve truck drivers. This really is the heart of nowhere. But *heart* is the wrong word to describe this place. I order a chai at a tea shop—*tea shop* being another wrong word. It's more a tin box. The shopkeeper does not wash my cup. He wipes it with a greasy cloth so filthy that a car mechanic would throw it away in disgust. The owner's clothes are as dirty as the rag. It's impossible to tell what color they once were. He scratches himself vigorously and constantly. Grass matting on the earth floor is caked with greasy dirt. A dog lies in the shade, so still it may be dead. Hundreds—and I do mean hundreds—of flies settle on me whenever I stop moving. The lethargic customers appear not to care about the pervasive grime and flies. The scorching air stinks of shit. Patrons relieve themselves directly behind this row of shacks, using water and their left hand in place of toilet paper.

I am suddenly overcome by the pervasiveness of the filth. An Austrian traveler I met in Teheran told me, "Beware people who do not keep themselves and their houses clean." But there's no escape. The next village is thirty miles away, and I simply cannot venture into the furnace outside. I've seen no train on this line, so I can't escape by rail. In England, I did volunteer work at a local mental hospital. I was curious about the nature of mental illness and felt thankful for my emotional steadiness. Not here. I'm in a hell-world from which I can't escape. I'm at the brink, close to a meltdown. I close my eyes to find some escape.

I'm in my grandparents' back garden in Cambridge, England. I know of no cleaner, more ordered world than this. I'm seated on a wooden garden bench on a paved area that's two steps below the lawn. It's time for afternoon tea. My grandmother pours tea from a porcelain teapot decorated with small forget-me-not flowers. The teacups, saucers, sugar bowl, and plates all match the teapot. Each teacup makes a reassuring ta-chink as Grandma places it on a saucer. As she carefully pours the tea, her hand trembles a little. Her hands have shaken now for a number of years. I take two spoons of sugar using a small silver spoon my grandfather won at golf. He's a keen golfer. A cabinet of silver trophies attests to his dedication. We sit in the shade of a brick and flint wall. The upper half of the wall is covered with creeper, and there are small berries on the plant. A sparrow hops about somewhere in there. The bird knows there will be crumbs on the ground when we're done. The birds can count on this afternoon ritual as surely as they can count on daybreak.

I take a slice of the rich fruitcake. My grandmother makes this on her weekly baking day. The combination is heavenly: hot, sweet tea and rich, moist cake. We discuss the garden, of which my grandfather is so proud. Perennial beds are arrayed with tall hollyhocks at the rear, ranging down to a neat line of white baby's breath along the lawn. My grandfather declares his lawn the best in all of Cambridge—and there are many fine lawns there. The lawn is his labor of love. If a patch becomes even a tad bare, he transplants individual shoots of grass that he finds among the perennials. He uses a matchstick to make a hole into which he carefully locates the small root.

Will I ever again have afternoon tea there? If so, I'll relate the story of crossing this desert. It'll be a good yarn to tell from the safety of an English garden. I'll wipe a crumb of cake from my chin and laugh at the memory.

The trip to Cambridge pulls me back from the precipice. I have an idea. The rail station opposite may have a waiting room—and indeed it does. I'm the only one here—not surprising, given the lack of trains. I enjoy the cool concrete of a solid bench that runs along one wall. The stark simplicity is soothing: whitewashed walls, a high ceiling, and an unmoving ceiling fan. The exposed electric wires to the fan are coated in a thick fur of coagulated, greasy dust. I write letters.

A young Pakistani man of my age enters. His hair is matted and wild. He's dressed only in a small, faded red cloth tied loosely around his middle. Around his neck and shoulders is a harness-like affair. It's made of rough jute string. A length of string goes from this down to his waist, around, and on down and around one ankle. I can think of only one explanation for this strange arrangement: a spiritual device for mortification of the flesh, like a local version of sackcloth and ashes. In one ear he wears a huge hoop earring. Onto this are tied small pieces of dirty cloth in hues of red and brown. Also on the earring is a small playing die. He walks straight up to me and speaks excitedly in what sounds like Pashto, but I'm not sure. I remain motionless, both curious and fearful.

He drops to his knees before me and repeatedly kisses my ankles and shoes. I put a hand on his shoulder to lift him, embarrassed. He jabbers on and appears to experience many emotions as he speaks—excitement, enthusiasm, anger, sadness—and each with great intensity. The show is spellbinding. *Am I in danger?* But his clear face and eyes reveal no bad intent. I warm to this strange encounter. *What is this otherworldly behavior, and where is it going?*

He speaks more excitedly still as he roughly tears away the strange harness, throwing it to the ground. My penknife is on the bench next to me; I'd just finished cutting up a tomato. He takes my knife to cut away the cloth pieces from his earring. He motions for me to remove the wire hoop from his ear. It's tricky and he moans with pain. He asks for water and I give him some. He also accepts the chapatti and tomatoes I offer. He eats the bread dry and squeezes the tomatoes above his open mouth to eat only juice and seeds. He throws the remainder down with the discarded harness on the floor.

He hands me the die from his dismantled earring and gestures for me to throw it. I throw an impossibly high percentage of sixes—maybe two out of every three throws. He lets out a cry of delight with each six I throw. After some minutes, he retrieves the die and then sits in relaxed silence for some time, looking about. I finish my food. He stands and leaves without another word.

Was that bizarre show just for my benefit? The earring removal was so difficult I doubt it's something he repeats often. I discover that my penknife is missing. Was it all an elaborate ritual to relieve me of the knife? There were more valuable things he could have taken, and there are simpler ways to steal a knife. He asked for no money. India is known for its *sadhus*. These wandering mendicants devote their lives to the pursuit of inner peace through austerity. *Sadhus* carry with them what little they own. They live off alms and spend their years walking from one holy site to another. They wear red or orange, often no more than a cloth around the waist. Was this young guy a Hindu *sadhu*, here in Pakistan?

I spend the rest of the day in the waiting room. I visit a roadside shack opposite the station to buy Seven-Up, ginger ale, and Coca-Cola. I spend three days' food budget on this sugar water. I rarely buy these, but today my system welcomes the cool, sparkling beverage. I fill my water containers at a hand pump outside the waiting room. Even at rest in the shade, I drink several pints of liquid an hour. *How do people survive in this heat?*

Among the shacks is a barbershop. A customer at the Coca-Cola shack tells me that he's not a good barber. For what I've in mind, that's of little consequence. I wait while a young boy has his hair cropped. His father tells me that the boy has bad head lice. The barber doesn't clean his dirt-caked tools between customers. No matter. Five minutes and one rupee later, my head is shaved. My best value haircut ever: clumps of sun-bleached blond hair contrast with the mat of black hair on the unswept floor. Back at the station, I strip to the waist and take a soapy shower. I crouch low under the water pump to awkwardly work the handle and wash at the same time. *Wow, that feels really good.* I run my hand over the suede-like smoothness of a newly shaven head.

I take my chances at half past four. The heat hits me in the face like a Pakistani cricket bat, but I have little choice; I must get out of here. I wrap the *keffiyeh* around my head and neck. The horizon fragments in the heat. Wide, shining bodies of water appear in the distance. I know they're a mirage yet I can feel the draw to cycle off the road and toward them. A group of laborers work by the road. Several sit cross-legged on the ground in the full sun. With handheld hammers, they break football-sized rocks into smaller pieces. What desperate work—it's a scene from Dante's *Inferno*. As the sun sets, I remove the *keffiyeh*. The shadow of my head is noticeably smaller than it was at the same time yesterday evening. Still fierce, the orange fireball sinks into the desert on my right. Tomorrow it will rise and repeat its dreadful cycle.

After sundown, I arrive in Nuttall. There's a huddle of small houses along the road; they appear cleaner than the buildings in Bel Pat. I'm relieved. I stop for a chai. A truck driver insists on buying me a Coke, which is four times the price of a chai. I wonder what prompted this act of friendship from the enemy tribe of truckies.

An old man with white turban, white robes, and a flowing white beard sits down at my table. Only a nut brown, wrinkled face and thin hands break this vision of pure white. His measured manner and soft voice lift my spirits. I'm grateful for his company. He explains that we are in the Sindh desert and that it's the hottest place in all Asia. And this is the hottest month of the year. Apparently, it's also unusually hot this year. So, it's not just me. He says that the monsoon rains will arrive in one month. Then things will be cooler. I don't plan on sticking around to find out. He asks me to write to him from England. I shall.

The railway station is my best bet for the night. As in Bel Pat, the waiting room has a cement bench along one wall. I lay out my plastic sheet and sleeping bag for some padding. I lean the bicycle against the bench, inches from my face, and make my bags as thief-proof as possible. If someone enters in the night, I'm not sure I'd awaken. I'm exhausted. But I do wake in the night several times, and my sleeping bag is drenched with sweat. Sleep in this heat does not refresh.

It's Sunday. I'll stay here for the day. There's no way I could fast and cycle in this heat. The oven outside mounts a coordinated campaign against the waiting room. Even here inside, the water in my containers becomes almost hot enough to make tea. I have a bad stomach and continuing diarrhea. I'm woolly-headed, weak and irritable. I lack the energy or will to write letters, which is my primary activity when I'm not cycling. The persistent intrusion of locals is maddening. I just want to be left alone.

I eat a small meal in the late afternoon and set out at half past five. It should be cooler now than in the middle of the day, but I really don't think it is. Trucks return to torment me. These have loud klaxon horns, which the drivers sound as they draw level with me. The noise sends a shooting pain through my ears. I place cotton wool in each ear, but the agony is almost unbearable. A blast of hot, dust-swirled air as each demonic vehicle roars by adds to the misery. I am so angry; I'm close to tears. The road's dust and stone margin is too rocky for a bicycle, so I must stay on the road itself. It's essentially a single-lane highway. As trucks pass one other, each partly leaves the road, raising clouds of dust. I rant internally.

The trucks should be on roads that can accommodate them. They should have proper silencers. They don't need to sound their horns at bicycles. The drivers should work reasonable hours. They shouldn't drive beyond endurance in a drug-induced haze.

And so on. I'm miserable. My only respite is to imagine causing pain in return. If I could, I most surely would. I again visit my grandmother in Cambridge for afternoon tea. That shady corner of the garden, that rich fruit cake, that serene ritual. The scales tip back a little toward inner stability.

In the early evening, a line of trees appears in the distance. It's a tree-lined canal that runs through the arid landscape. This is the Pat Feeder Canal, which carries irrigation water from the Indus River. The canal starts one hundred fifty miles to the north, at the Guddu Barrage on the Indus River. I cross the canal at Dera Murad Jamali and enjoy a delicious tomato curry with rice at a roadside shack. The rail station beckons.

I ask for permission at the stationmaster's office to sleep in the waiting room. He graciously shows me to a private room with a door that locks. The electric fan in the ceiling works. I go to bed well fed and feeling cared for. I'm relieved that my dark anger has passed and happy to be in air that moves. I've upgraded from a traditional oven to a convection oven. I bake evenly throughout. My sleep is restless. When I awake, my sleeping bag is again stained dark with sweat.

For breakfast, I share a kettle full of milky chai with the assistant stationmaster. All is tranquil at this early hour. I'm on the road before first light. I relish the relative cool of the hour before dawn. A glow in the sky brightens. The air vibrates with a warning of impending heat. The sun is benign as it rises in a rose sky. Within thirty minutes, the heat and glare are intense. The twenty-two miles to Jacobabad pass steadily and easily. There are irrigated fields now in the dust of the plain. Near the town, the road is lined with trees. A group of women form wet cow dung into flat cakes. They slap these onto the side of a low wall to dry in the sun. Most cooking is done on a fire of dried dung. Few trees here mean a wood fire is a luxury.

Jacobabad is the only city in the Indian subcontinent named after an Englishman. John Jacob was a nineteenth-century general in the Indian Army. He established a cavalry regiment of local soldiers known as Jacob's Horse. His approach differed from most of his countrymen in that he respected Muslims and Hindus as members of esteemed cultures. He wrote, "I do not propose to govern them by force or fear. I will govern them by appealing to their higher, not their baser attitudes." During the Indian Mutiny the men under his command remained loyal. To this day, locals tend his grave with care.

Jacob was from Somerset in England. One could not imagine a place more different from England's West Country than Jacobabad. This district is famous for its summer temperatures. It holds the record for highest temperature in Pakistan: 127 degrees Fahrenheit in the shade. Jacob died of brain fever as a result of excessive heat. Line drawings from his day show a leafy, pleasant place. Today, it's a filthy warren of narrow streets. It stinks of shit, and the heat is overpowering.

At the post office, I send the letters I've written these past days. An old gent sits outside at a small desk under a black umbrella. For those who can't write, he pens letters and fills out forms for a fee. He invites me to join him for lunch. I agree to return at noon. At a bank, I change a traveler's check into Pakistani rupees. The young clerk Muhammad invites me for dinner and to sleep at his place. He insists that I should be his "honorable guest." The Muslim hospitality is predictable and welcome. I return to the post office and join my scribe friend for lunch. He speaks good English. The restaurant is air-conditioned, and it is pleasure without bounds to be out of the heat. We eat vegetable curry with *chapattis*.

I buy a newspaper printed in English: my first since Teheran. The heat wave is front-page news. Yesterday the temperature in the shade was 122 degrees. The lead story is that a number of people have died of heatstroke. The heat is killing the locals—and pushing this visitor to the very edge of madness.

In the late afternoon, I return to the bank and walk with Muhammad to his home. The dirt and heat assail me. The heat is a hot, dry blanket wrapped close about. It is a pressure on my face, on my neck, on my arms, and on my hands. On each side of the street is an open drain; the stench from these is overwhelming. My host doesn't appear to notice. I leave my bicycle at his house and we brave the heat for a tour of the town.

A man holding a cloth bundle approaches. He seizes my hand and shakes it. In an elaborate ritual, he adjusts and taps his sack. He plays a strange-looking flute, which emits a vibrating note; the sound is deep and haunting. He sits cross-legged on the ground in front of the sack as he plays a droning tune, swinging to and fro. I lean in to confirm my theory that this is all theater and there is no snake. He whips the sack away. A cobra springs up with a malignant hiss. I jump back, unsettled by my naiveté. The snake's hood flares slowly in and out; a small tongue flicks nervously in the air. The charmer now has my attention. The snake sways, matching the movement of its owner. The music ends with a sudden blast, at which the snake flinches. The charmer passes his hand in front of the snake, yet it makes no attempt to strike him. My host assures me the snake has its fangs. He says that cobras are easily found in the desert I've just crossed. And slept in.

Muhammad and I visit a barbershop with several tiled stalls at the rear. For three rupees, I receive three buckets of cool water. I follow my host's lead. I strip to my underwear and crouch in a stall. I use the provided plastic jug to pour water over my head. It's not truly cold, but what a delicious sensation!

Refreshed, we return to Muhammad's house to collect his small motorcycle. I sit on the back of the bike, and we drive around town. A blood red sun sighs onto the horizon. My host buys me a *paan*, a sweet and spiced concoction placed within an edible leaf folded into a small triangle. It's a sort of post-meal digestive that locals seem to enjoy at all times of the day. I've heard it's habit-forming. Following Muhammad's lead, I place the small packet in my mouth. I let it sit whole for a time inside my cheek. When I chew, a medley of flavors emerges—menthol, sweet, spicy and bitter. It requires fifteen minutes of chewing to break down the lumps of betel nut inside. The *paan* leaves me with aching jaw muscles, a fresh mouth, and bright red teeth.

We return to Muhammad's house. His family is seated in a circle on the floor around my opened bicycle bags. They are reading my letters and diaries. They show no sign of shame; it's as if this were acceptable behavior. I silently take my things from their hands without making eye contact. No one says anything about this over dinner. Their eyes reveal that they've already forgotten it. I guess personal privacy in a place this crowded holds a different meaning. The family has a television. Many neighbors arrive after dinner to watch *The Avengers*, a British TV show. I'd rather talk, but no one asks, so I watch.

Muhammad knows how difficult the heat is for me. He suggests that I sleep under the stars. I thank him for his thoughtfulness and imagine that he means I should go up on a roof. I'm surprised when he leads me outside to the street. He has placed here for me a *charpoy*—a wooden frame with a netting of string on which to sleep. I lay on this bed, out in the middle of the street. The day slowly falls quiet. I fall asleep on my back, adrift in a sea of countless stars.

As a child, I had a delicious fantasy. I pictured myself in a bed placed on the sidewalk of a nearby road. I imagined bedclothes tucked tight under my chin against the cold, watching in comfort as cars and people went by. Fantasy is reality the next morning. The day has started in this wide city street. A boy leads a water buffalo past me. Staring men on bicycles pass on either side of the bed. Another boy drives a herd of floppy-eared goats. They bleat objections at this unexpected island in their path. I pretend to still be asleep and lie motionless to relish the moment.

My host invites me to spend the morning at the bank. He counts enormous stacks of new rupee notes. They come in sealed bundles, only to be counted again as they arrive in the bank. Unthinking work to support an unthinking process. Good for employment levels, I suppose. Muhammad is markedly less friendly this morning. I ask if I've done something to offend. He says that there's nothing wrong, but his behavior belies this. If he won't tell me, there's nothing I can do. Was it my searching questions last night? I'd queried at length the separation between men and women in Muslim countries. Or maybe it was my silent reaction to the family reading my papers. Who knows?

It's the same pattern I've faced with other educated Muslims. We talk, exchange ideas, and develop a rapport. But true understanding requires more than good intention and substantial conversation. It needs time and shared experience. Hours of committed enquiry were needed to resolve cultural misunderstandings between Rudy and me. And those were differences between two similar European societies. Culture is a slippery creature—hard to grasp, yet exerting a profound force.

After the bank closes, we go in search of a map of Pakistan. We find a locally produced map that shows good detail. The white void where India should be reveals where the map was made. There's no recognition of the neighbor to the east. Muhammad explains that this ill will means little access between Pakistan and India. Rail lines that once crossed the border were dismantled or fell into disuse after Partition. Since those fateful times in 1947, families have been unable to see their relatives in villages across the border. Neither side will grant a visa to residents of the other. There are two thousand miles of border, but only a single border crossing. I will need to make a five hundred-mile detour to the north. Could I shorten the time in this heat with an illegal crossing to the southeast? Muhammad explains that would require crossing the Great Indian Desert. With an absence of roads, this is possible only by camel. So, I have no choice. I must head north to the sole border crossing.

In the late afternoon, we visit the stalls at the barbershop again. Who knew that joy came from a bucket in the form of water that's not warm? Refreshed, I say my goodbyes and set out toward the next town, Sukkur.

After some hours, I arrive at a road junction and have a choice of route—my first in many, many miles. Should I take the east or the west bank of the Indus River? The western road runs through officially designated Tribal Territories. This area is known for its lawlessness. Several people in Jacobabad warned me against traveling through the Tribal Territories. I was told that the police barricade themselves in their stations each night. The hours of darkness belong to gunrunners and smugglers. At daybreak, police control returns. The east bank is more heavily used, so there will be more trucks on that road. My options are being peppered by a tribal, or pancaked by a trucker.

I take a twenty-five paisa coin from my pocket. The side with flowers means east bank. I flip and...no flowers. Good, I'll be happier with the light traffic on the west bank. I'll take my chances with the wild folk. There's another bridge across the Indus seventy miles to the north. Should I need to, I can cross there to the other bank. Since the Caspian Sea, I've been heading steadily southeast. I will now follow the Indus River northeast toward the Whaga border crossing into India.

Day's end brings a sunset that sets the sky afire. I enjoy the magnificent solitude. Two locals happen upon me. I offer no greeting. I want to be alone. I leave the road by the last light of day. I find a corner of a small field, sheltered from view by banked irrigation ditches of dry mud. This will serve as a clean home for the night. I fall asleep below a stand of darkened trees.

I'm on the road before sunup. The road here follows a wide canal. A line of shade trees between the road and the canal softens the bite of the heat. At least, I'd like to think it does. It's hard to be sure. I'm traveling along an irrigated emerald ribbon laid across the desert. Crags of the Hindu Kush Mountains threaten from the west. Between the trees, I glimpse a sharp edge where luminous green meets light-sucking ochre. I know that to the east, beyond the river, lies the Thar Desert.

Several water buffalo escape the heat and stand motionless in the canal. They splash the murky water with a periodic flick of an ear. The top of a head and two points of bony rump are all that show of each animal. Several young boys take turns climbing onto the largest beast and using it as diving platform. The children shout and laugh, skinny brown bodies glistening in the sun.

I reach the busy city of Kandhkot before noon. I buy a penknife to replace the one lost to my strange friend in Bel Pat. I'm surprised to find a large public library—an ideal place to write in peace. But a large troupe of boys follows me inside. They stand close in a ring around me. They stare and repeatedly intone, "Speak Eenglish?" I keep my eyes down and continue to write. If they get no response, surely they'll leave. Most do, but a librarian then tells me that the library will close in ten minutes. I explain my case to the young man. I want a place where I can sit in silence and not be badgered. He says that yes, he understands perfectly, and suggests the rest bungalow across the street. He assures me that complete silence and privacy await me there.

I cross the street, gathering a fresh batch of curious onlookers. An attendant at the rest bungalow reassures me, "Yes, yes, silence and privacy is here." He firmly sends the children away, and announces with pride that I now can have silence. He shows me to a chair and table. Pulling up chairs, he and the other attendants form a seated circle around me: front row seats to the show. They ply me with questions. After twenty minutes, I acknowledge the inevitable. I beg their pardon and take my leave. There's hurt in one of the young men's eyes when I decline an invitation to visit his house. There you can most surely write in silence, he declares. As in Syria and Iran, there's a fuzzy line between welcoming a guest and enjoying low-cost entertainment. Once I accept an invitation, I'm fair game. I don't seem to register in the equation as an individual with needs.

I discover the perfect alternative to Coca-Cola. For half the price of one bottle of Coke, I can buy a huge watermelon. The challenge is securing it to my rear carrier. In the late afternoon, I scan each side of the road for a private place to enjoy watermelon number three. But there's always a person to be seen. I am now most surely out of the wilderness. I take a dirt side road. There's not a soul in sight, and I'm aware that I'm holding my breath as I install myself unseen behind a nearly solid hedge of cactus.

After three minutes, I hear approaching voices. A group of young men appear. They have nothing else to do, so they stand in a knot and stare, waiting for the show to begin. I turn my back and ignore them. I eat my watermelon, but it's hard to enjoy it. They talk, giggle, and make silly noises. I pack up and ride off without looking at them. Catcalls follow me. I want time alone, but that's going to be tough to find. This seeming emptiness conceals idle eyes. A rail line again runs parallel to the road. There's a station. I'll ask if I can use the waiting room.

I push the bicycle over stony ground and gather a crowd of followers. These boys and young men initiate a game of trying to touch my bicycle and bags. I mount the bicycle to ride away, but the ground is too stony. They laugh and shout at my unsuccessful attempt to lose them. I feel weak and deeply unwell. This is a waking nightmare. Once again, I'm being pushed beyond the bounds of my sanity. A huge crimson sun sets behind the belligerent crowd standing on a rise above me. They appear only in silhouette. Something inside me snaps. I pick up a handful of stones and launch a volley at the throng. Tears stream down my cheeks as I yell, "Go away! Leave me alone, you miserable fuckers! Just leave me alone!"

The response is immediate. The return fire of much larger stones comes my way. Some barely miss my head. Adrenaline pumping, I jump back on the bicycle and ride furiously away, jolted by the stony ground. I cycle out of the village, but don't want to go too far. This morning, a young man delivered in a grave tone a "most serious warning." Bandits who are beyond the law, he said, control the road between here and Kashmor. Even if you have nothing to steal, they'll kill you just for being there. That's why I wanted to stay in the rail station. I've just eliminated that option. Evening is now almost night. Along the road there are brick works. House-sized stacks of bricks smoke in the firing process. Next to these smoking mounds is an open, dusty area.

By the last light of day, I can see that several paths cross this area of stony dirt. I'll be safer tonight close to the village. I choose an area away from the paths and lay the bicycle down. It will form my one low wall of shelter tonight. I lay my plastic sheet on the ground next to the bicycle and settle down to sleep. I lie awake and listen as sounds from the village slowly die down. The clear sky shimmers with stars. I'm exhausted and fall asleep, despite my resolve to remain attentive.

I awake with a start. The position of the stars has changed, so some hours have passed. Wild dogs howl in the distance. They might be wolves; they live in the desert here. I try to suppress the persistent cough that started a couple of days ago. Tears roll down my cheeks as I cough again and the noise is met with more howling, nearer now. A sliver of moon casts just enough light to make out the dim shapes of the brick stacks. I stare hard into the dark. It offers up no clue of what's out there. Even the slightest movement causes the plastic sheet below me to crackle like fireworks in the silence. I hold my breath because my wheezing sounds so loud. I sense that the animals are both smelling and listening for me. I want the assurance of my bicycle pump in hand, but dare not move or make more noise.

I'm sick with fear. I expect that a pack of wild animals will rush at me out of the dark at any moment. Instinct has me remain motionless on the ground. I wish I were lying on my stomach rather than on my back; I'd be less exposed. At least I have the bicycle to one side of me. If Rudy were here, he could tell me how to react to the dogs—if that's what they are. The howls continue, mixed with some barking. They're on all sides now, maybe a few hundred yards away. I grope for the pump in the dark. Slowly, ever so slowly, I pull it out of the sleeping bag in which it's rolled. Paws pad across the hard ground and an animal pants. I lie motionless, every muscle taught, poised for the fight that will come at any moment. *Please, God, don't let them find me.*

The howls and barking continue around me—in one place, then in another. I lie motionless for ten minutes, then half an hour, then an hour. The howls die down. Slowly, I allow myself to relax. Next thing I know, I awaken again. It's just before dawn. In the first light of day, the place is innocent enough. It bears no resemblance to the realm of dread that I inhabited last night. I quickly gather my things and leave.

It's another scorching day. I make slow progress into the afternoon. Two hundred yards away, parallel to the road is the wide, tree-lined canal. It's a likely place for my afternoon siesta. I lie on the ground below the canopy of plane trees. The gray-green leaves shimmer as they twist in the breeze. A camel caravan passes on the opposite bank. A dirt road along the canal appears deserted. The cooing of a pigeon completes the scene.

But I can't relax. I anticipate spectators. Just a few days ago, in the mountains, there were three fellow humans per square mile. Here, there are one thousand three hundred. That's a person every fifty yards in any direction. My feelings toward these people are as turbulent as my stomach, and the overpowering heat amplifies my every frustration.

Between the dirt road and the line of trees, there's a grassy area with concrete tables and benches. The hand of foreign engineers is apparent in the design; World Bank funds paid for the canal. I take a long siesta in the sweltering shade, and I awake feeling heavy. I sit at a table to write letters. A teenage peasant boy approaches and stands a few feet away. He remains motionless and studies my every move. I glare and shout at him, gesturing for him to go away. He retreats a few yards, stands, and continues to stare. *What is it with these people?* I shout and curse at him, yet he remains fixed to his spot. A wave of pure anger rushes through me. I grab my new knife and run at him, yelling wildly and waving the knife. This he understands. I'm thankful he runs faster than I do. I'm at the limit of my physical and emotional endurance. I'm floored by the power of the cocktail of dark emotions that swirl within me, not to mention ashamed and drained.

The road continues parallel to the line of trees that shade the canal. I arrive at the Guddu Barrage midafternoon and have my first sight of the famed Indus River. The name Indus comes from the Sanskrit word *sindhu*, or "trembling body of water." The river trembles here a mile wide. It glitters in the afternoon sun. The barrage is a water flow and flood control barrier. It's quite the feat of engineering. It has a series of sixty-four bays, each sixty feet wide. Each has a gate that can be raised or lowered. It also has a wide lock for shipping. It feeds four large irrigation canals, one of which I've been traveling alongside. It provides critical flood control during the rainy season. A road runs across the top.

I'll cross the river here; I've been having second thoughts about remaining in the Tribal Territories. I cross and then make my way down to the water. I remain here for the afternoon. I bathe and wash my clothes; my shirt is stiff from dried sweat. I wash everything, even things that don't need it. I clean away more than dirt. I imagine the desert, the heat, the filth, and the flies eddying away into the mighty Indus. My clothes dry in the sun. The constant flow of swirling water soothes me. The surface of the water is broken by a series of small heads—turtles basking in the shallows.

As I buy *chapattis* in a small village, a young man introduces himself. He works for a government road contractor and invites me to spend the night at his work compound. It's seven miles away, and we can ride there in his truck. My bed for the night is out in the open, but within a walled enclosure. I join the workers for a simple and tasty evening meal. As soon as I say my goodnights and turn in, the workers start a game of cards and turn a cassette player up to full volume.

In the morning, I thank my host. He says that I should not thank him since I am his guest. I've been told this before, and I ask him why he says this. He relates a story. Some years ago, he met an English couple traveling through Pakistan. They were waiting for a bus, not far from his house. It was late in the day, so he invited them to stay in his house that night. They replied that they would not, because he was a Pakistani. This is his account, though I doubt anyone English could be that direct. He brought tea and food to where they waited for their bus. He disliked them and their refusal to stay in his home, but he offered them food and drink because it was his duty. So, duty is required and is no grounds for gratitude.

He provides detailed directions for a series of smaller roads that will keep me off the main highway for a while. A late start, so I'll cycle today until the heat stops me. I pause often to douse myself in water. It feels good, though the relief lasts mere moments.

Here, the Indus valley has a serene beauty. It shimmers in every hue of green. There's no hint of the desert that lies some miles to the east. A sturdy farmhouse of brick and timber sits in the shade of two spreading mango trees. The trees are as huge and noble as any English oaks—surely they're hundreds of years old. Three water buffalo lie in the shade, munching at a pile of hay. Several large crows perch on each bony back. Thin cattle stand nearby, motionless in the heat. A large flock of parrots fly low across the sky. They flash bright green and yellow in their passing, and their individual tails show up as short, distinctive horizontal lines. Shrieking and twittering, they disappear into the mango trees

Channeled water crosses over the land. Sparkling canals flow into streams and then into narrow ditches that carry a few inches of gurgling, milky brown water. A farmer uses a broad-blade hoe to divert water into a field, coaxing it into tiny rivulets between each furrow of earth. The dry field is the color of the desert. The water turns it to a rich brown. Only the low *whump... whump... whump* of a distant diesel irrigation pump disturbs the breathless midday silence. Another farmer guides a pair of buffalo pulling a plough through the rich soil. On the next farm, a tractor works the land. This must be a wealthier area.

I've had no problems with dogs chasing me for some weeks. Most lie listless in the heat. So, I'm surprised when two rush at me, barking wildly. There are no stones to throw, so I wield my pump and run at them. This makes them even crazier. I stand motionless. Eventually, they wander off. They may have been rabid; I must be more cautious. As I did in France, I'll carry a pocketful of stones for such encounters. By eleven, the heat is intolerable. A broad shade tree offers respite for a siesta. I write in my diary and repair a rip that's appeared in my pants. I fall asleep for an hour or two. Again, I wake heavy and lethargic. I continue to cycle in the late afternoon. A rose red sunset flashes through the trees to my left. It sinks in a sky the color of blush wine. The light floods everything in a translucent glow. The scene is sacred and timeless. No wonder expatriate Pakistanis have a gleam in their eyes as they talk of home; I fall in love just passing through.

I arrive at the so-called National Highway, Pakistan's primary road. It runs south to north from Karachi to Lahore, then on to Peshawar. Accordingly, it's also called the KLP Highway. I plug my ears with cotton wool and brace myself for the trucks, but I'm delighted. The road isn't as busy as I'd expected, and it's wide enough that trucks don't threaten my existence when they pass. The road is lined with trees where it passes through a village. Every few miles, there's a huddle of shacks: teahouses, mechanic shops, and other services for the trucks and buses. People here are accustomed to travelers. While I still draw a crowd, it's less intrusive here than in the remote areas.

The Great Indian Desert lies fifteen miles to the east, and the Indian border another seventy. A tantalizing thought, but I must travel several hundred miles north to the Lahore-Amritsar crossing into India. A building by the road has a white perimeter wall. Black letters several feet high announce, KNOCK FOR HELP. I do need somewhere to sleep tonight, so I prop my bicycle against the wall and knock for help.

The man who answers speaks not one word of English. He does not understand when I point at the sentence adorning his home. After some confusion, he understands my mime of sleeping. He offers me a bed with covers and a pillow. *Ah, what luxury!* I do not learn the reason for the sign on the wall, nor why I am offered the bed. One does not always need to understand. I feel deep gratitude for the small and large acts of kindness I am shown each day. I don't know how I could ever repay or even properly acknowledge what I receive.

Though the bed is wonderful, I sleep poorly. I'm weak and in a sour temper the next morning. The miles pass easily enough, however. I take my siesta at a stand of palms trees. There's a bed of soft, green grass below. I wake soaked in sweat from a long, groggy sleep. Back on the road, each stop I make for water, food or watermelon is a trial. Jeering youths surround me. Their faces and tone of voice are scornful. They chant in Pashto some word that I guess is the equivalent of *whitey*. This is how Pakistanis in England must feel when taunted with the label *Pakki*. I'm surprised to be on the receiving end. It's a paradox that I also receive hospitality and friendliness. Several clumps of palm trees a good distance from the road offer a good place for the night. I'm glad for the end of the day and the chance to sleep again.

Back on the road before the sun rises next morning, I'm keenly aware of how weak I am. Even on this flat terrain, I proceed slowly. In addition to the heat, I must still be sick. I have to coax myself to eat since my stomach doesn't call for food. The fertile plain continues: irrigated fields, bunches of palm trees, small villages, and farms shaded by spreading trees. There are few towns, no cities, and no sign of industry. I wish I felt healthier, to better enjoy this glory. Today is Sunday, and I'm intent on doing a partial fast. This may be a bad idea, but the heat is scrambling my brains. I don't learn until later of the need to replace body salts when in the heat, especially if one has diarrhea.

By late morning, I'm ready for my siesta. I lie on a patch of grass beneath a spindly tree not far from the road and fall directly into a feverish sleep. I awake a few hours later. I'm soaked with sweat and have a pulsing headache. I'm helpless due to a lack of energy. I must break my fast. I eat a couple of dry *chapattis* and two bananas. This tasty combination is easy on my raw stomach. The sleep did not reenergize me as it should have, though. These past few days have contained six hours of slow pedaling, two hours of writing, resting or eating, and sixteen hours of sleep. A lot of sleep, and still I am limp as a rag.

I fantasize about familiar food. I'm seated on a wooden bench outside a pub in England. It's Sunday and a slow game of amateur cricket is underway on the village green in front of me. I sip at a pint of cold lager and lime. Better still, I knock it back in three swallows. Then I'm sitting on a wrought iron bench in the same village green, enjoying chocolate ice cream on a cone. I lick the melting ice cream where it overflows. Then comes perfection. The prodigal son has returned home. I've refused the fatted calf. Instead, I'm seated at the kitchen table, eating my mother's homemade apple pie with creamy, sweet yellow English custard.

At a roadside chai shack, I exchange my final Pakistani coins for a glass of sweet chai and some fudge-like goo that sits beneath a layer of black flies. It's a poor substitute for apple pie and custard, but it satisfies my craving for sugar. I have a pack of Pakistani cigarettes with six remaining. The storekeeper trades these for a second piece of the flyblown confection. I last changed money in Jacobabad. I've unsuccessfully tried banks in the small towns I've passed; bank clerks here don't know what an American Express traveler's check is. Or, they tell me they don't know the exchange rate. My supply of local currency has dwindled. I am now paisa-less. I have four US dollars in cash, but know from experience that these are not accepted outside of large cities. But Pakistani generosity is dependable, so there will be food and a place to sleep, no matter what coins my pocket lacks. This stands testament to the sociability of Pakistanis of every stripe. In which Western nation could one feel no anxiety when penniless?

And then I hurtle from appreciation to its opposite. A pressing, in-your-face crowd gathers. An unbroken wall of humanity bears down on me. They touch the bicycle, my things, and one tugs on my shirt. I tell them, "Fuck off, you bloody animals." I push my way past sneering faces, fit one foot into its toe clip and angrily pedal away. Night falls and I enjoy the relatively cooler air. By the light of a half-moon, I ride through the dark. I pass through pools of total darkness where roadside trees canopy over the road. Fireflies dance and lend magic to the warm night air. I concentrate hard, peering into the dark, trying to discern the inevitable potholes. I hit one or two, but nothing too bad.

Two hours of cautious cycling brings me to the village of Shaher Sultan. A sign on a large brick building announces it's a police station. It looks solid, clean and welcoming enough. *What the heck—they can only say no.* I lift my bicycle up the stone steps. With difficulty I open one of the two massive wooden doors. I push my bike past the cells. In one, a half-naked man lies motionless on the bare stone floor. His expressionless eyes follow me as I pass. The officers on duty agree to my request for a place to sleep. They bring me tea and ask if eggs for breakfast will be OK. They offer me the chief of police's office with its wooden desk so I can write in my diary. They turn on the ceiling fan and ask if I'm comfortable. The generous heart of Pakistan reasserts itself into my addled brain. A wooden bench in an empty room is my bed for the night. This opens up a whole new realm of possibility. I'd not previously considered police stations as homes for the night.

I'm up and ready to leave early in the morning. There's no one about. I leave without the promised eggs. Might be as well, given the state of my stomach. The motionless watcher in the cell tracks my departure with his eyes.

I ride into a small village and see a communal water pump where I can fill up. I stand the bicycle using the kickstand and remove my water bottles. A few teenage boys gather, speaking loudly and jeering. I try to ignore them. I want only to quickly fill up with water and be on my way. They move in closer, snickering. I motion for them to back off. They share a sly laugh and I become angrier. I shout at them to go away and leave me the fuck alone. They stare at me and move not an inch.

Accumulated anger from the heat, the filth, and the personal intrusion wells up. I rush at them, grab one by the throat and push him to the ground.

In that moment, the bicycle stand sinks in the soft earth. Bilbo topples slowly. The front wheel and panniers fall into a small pond that catches the pump runoff. The pond contains evil-smelling black slime.

I pull the bicycle out. Stinking gray-black sludge drips off my bags. More join the crowd to mock me. I seethe with fury, yet am forced to remain. I remove the front panniers, empty their contents, and painstakingly wash each item. Cleanliness is critical both to my state of mind and to protect my health. Who knows what horrors lurk in this vile muck? I've seen pools like this in many villages. There's no sewage system, and these open pools of waste ferment in the tropical sun. Their stench permeates the air for hundreds of yards in every direction.

This is the last straw. I'm teetering at the brink, close to breakdown. I walk some distance from the pump. Newcomers join the crowd, curious and less belligerent than the youths from earlier. An older man joins the crowd and approaches. I am not civil. He has kindly eyes and asks me in English if I would join him for a cup of chai. A little reluctantly, I agree. I finish washing off my things as best I can and join the old gent at a table outside a chai shop, on the dusty margin of the road. He buys me chai and a kind of toasted biscuit. He is the local *mullah*, or priest. In limited English, he asks the usual questions. What countries have I visited? How many miles have I cycled? Where is my family? He's interested in every small detail.

The conversation turns to religion. I ask about the separation between men and women in Islam. He explains that the Prophet Muhammad told his followers to "keep your women away from yourself." To avoid the possibility of sin, the *mullah* explains. Of the sexual variety, I assume. He invites me to become a Muslim, which I respectfully decline. Then he asks me why I'm going to India. I'm surprised by the simple reply that springs from some-where within me. "To find God."

He's silent for several long moments at my response and looks at me intently. He then stands and turns to the gathered crowd, raises his arms in the air, and says something in Pashto. There are some fifty men and boys gathered. As one, they fall to their knees in the dust and bow their heads. The *mullah* leads them in a rhythmic incantation. After some minutes of this, they fall silent. All are motionless, heads bowed. Gray and green robes move slightly in the morning breeze. Traffic on the road is oddly absent. This worshipful stillness seems to last some minutes. The *mullah* turns to face me again and says, "We have just said a prayer that your soul might find God."

I say my goodbyes with handshakes and smiling eye contact. I leave the chai shop both chastened and full of gratitude to these people. A familiar minestrone of emotions splashes about within me. In a moment, it all shifts, then shifts again—like having a set of randomly moving wickets in some weird Pakistani game of cricket, where others know rules I can't grasp.

How can I reconcile the dichotomy I've experienced in every Muslim country—openhearted generosity along with jeering animosity from young men? I believe that genuine human caring is part and parcel of Islamic culture. On the other hand, the sour reactions are exclusively from young males. From conversations with these young men, I've concluded that this is caused by economic disparity and maybe the aftereffects of European colonialism: a tension between the have-mores and the have-lesses. I am hugely privileged. I can travel how I like, where I like. I can return home and with reasonable certainty find work and earn the money I need for a comfortable life. Such freedoms are beyond all hope for many here. Just my presence, with my sophisticated bicycle, must act as a sore reminder of this inequality. If I were to cycle through an oil-rich, wealthy Muslim state like Saudi Arabia, I'm guessing there'd be no sneering animosity.

At a bank in town, I try again without success to change money. The bank manager explains that in Multan, the next large city, I'll be able to change my four dollars. In my eagerness to reach Multan, I cycle out into the early afternoon heat. I stop after two hours of pedaling and feel my knees ready to buckle under me. I've pushed too hard.

I lay in the shade of a tree, thoroughly spent. My body feels as if it's been immersed in hot water. I'm dizzy and trembling. A crowd of onlookers gathers.

One is a young man who speaks good English. I explain that I'm ill. He invites me to rest at his college dormitory. I accept gratefully. The tidy gardens that surround the dormitory buildings are a soothing and welcome sight.

The young man insists that I take his bed in the room he shares with three others, then leaves me alone to rest. He returns shortly after with several friends. They invite me to join them so they can "entertain me in the town." I explain that the best entertainment they can offer is some silence and sleep. There's hurt in their eyes at my reply. *Why this bloody nonsense again? I'm just too weak to deal with this shit.*

Begrudgingly, they agree. Instead of taking me into town, they sit on the surrounding beds and ply me with questions. One is insistent in his questions about "free sex" in England. The conversation follows a predictable pattern. They're about my age, but their naiveté surprises me. I try to describe how things work between young men and women in my society. They lack both context and sophistication to understand. They seem intent on maintaining their belief that in England any girl will allow you to sleep with her. My questioner repeatedly returns to the subject of sex. He twice reminds me in a reproving tone that, "Islam says men and women should remain apart until they are married."

These young men conform to the conservative values of Islam, yet are exposed to modern Western culture: all the titillation with none of the outlet. Better would be a full and contented participation in one world or the other. I'm grateful not to be in their position, caught in this cultural crossfire. They do finally allow me to rest. I sleep long and deep. I set out early the next morning and arrive in Multan before noon. The city is known for its mosques, mangoes, ceramics, carpets, bazaar and beggars. I don't have it in me to relate to any of these. I pause only long enough to find a bank and change my cherished four dollars.

Local lore claims that Multan is the place where Alexander met his stiffest opposition. He was wounded here, and for the first time in battle lost hold of his shield. Three years later, he died of those wounds. Given my desperately difficult time in Pakistan, I wonder if I've lost hold of some shield of mine. I cycle beyond the city and look for a shady place. I need a break from the contradictions of Islamic hospitality. I find a sheltered spot some distance from the highway. An elbow of two earthen banks at the corner of a parched field in the shade of a large eucalyptus tree will do nicely. I'm fairly sure no one saw me push my bicycle here. I place my plastic sheet on the dusty ground and settle in for an afternoon sleep.

From beyond a line of trees an old man dressed all in white appears. Odd, since there's no farm or dwelling in sight. He's tall and thin, with the white cotton turban of a local farmer. He carries a tray, which is covered with a cloth. He wishes me *salaam e lei'kum* in a soft voice and sets the tray on the ground in front of me. He says nothing more and removes the cloth. The tray contains a number of dishes, each in its own small stainless steel bowl. There is salad, several different curries, warm *chapattis*, and a yogurt dish with diced cucumber. I make a halfhearted show of protesting. Without words or eye contact, he gestures for me to eat. I do, and he retreats a little. He rests on his haunches and waits, wanting nothing from me. The food is utterly delicious. I savor each mouthful.

I finish and he approaches to take the tray. He pays no attention to my thanks. He says nothing and slowly walks off across the dry field. He disappears among the trees from whence he came. Allah to William: *Young fellow, please give me a break from your judgments about what Islam is and is not.*

Back on the highway, trucks and buses hurtle along. They sound their horns and pass perilously close. The vehicles are intricately decorated—but large and heavy. The drivers don't touch their brakes unless they absolutely must. Instead, they relentlessly sound their horns and expect all in their path to get out of the way. When two trucks head toward each other, each holds to the center of the road. At the last possible moment, each moves over just enough. They pass in a solid wall of noise, both wailing long, solid notes on their horn. Absolute madness, yet the drivers seem to enjoy this dance with death.

I pass the aftermath of a head-on collision between a truck and a bus. The mangled remains of both vehicles have been dragged to one side of the road. I have no sympathy. The only surprise is that there aren't more such carcasses along the road. At a chai shop that evening, I prompt an invitation to stay at the home of a young man. We cycle together to the small village of Kohi Wallah, located a mile off the highway.

I'm pulled from a deep sleep in the night by the amplified chanting of a *muezzin* in a nearby mosque. A long sung note is followed by an animal-like yelp. Another long note, and another yelp. This continues with no end in sight. After some time, I fall back to sleep. The sound weaves itself into my dreams. In the morning, I join my hosts in doing nothing. This takes several hours. The waste of time frustrates me, but I know it is the expected behavior of a guest. Today I comply because I lack the energy to do otherwise. To avoid more of the same, I resolve to sleep out in the countryside until I reach India.

I manage to leave around midday. I cycle through the heat of the day. I stop at a chai shop in the late afternoon. A young man approaches and sits at my table, without asking if it is OK. He insists on buying me another chai. As if it were the normal thing to do with someone you've just met, he asks me for a gift. I have an extra pen and give him that. He plies me with questions and wants to know why I am "wasting my time, money and energy on such a foolish endeavor." I explain that I don't see it that way. His English is good, yet I struggle to provide an explanation that makes sense to him. We each lack the cultural context to understand the other. Given this morning's idling about, wasting time is most surely in the eye of the beholder.

In the evening, a railway station at a short distance from the road promises shelter for the night. The stationmaster reacts cautiously when I ask for permission to sleep in the waiting room. He says that this small station has no waiting room, but he relents, and his assistant sets up a *charpoy* bed and blanket for me on the sole platform. I arrange my things on the concrete bench alongside. I enjoy the light meal the stationmaster also provides. Local children gather around to stare at this strange sight. This is the first time in Pakistan that I've seen young girls mixing with boys. Their

English is limited, yet I enjoy talking with these guileless children. I fall asleep as the last light of day leaves the sky.

The next morning I awake at a quarter to five. An early start is now a habit; it allows me time to get ready, gather my things, and be on the bicycle a little before daybreak. I can then make the most of the one or two cooler (but it's all relative!) hours of the day. The assistant stationmaster on duty invites me to join him for breakfast. Abdul Rashid Mazza is in his fifties. His faded uniform belies the cultured man within. We talk for several hours, and I'm happy to delay my departure to enjoy his company. He's deeply religious, warmhearted, and wholesome. It's clear that he finds spiritual nourishment in his faith. It's just as clear that he's risen above the dogma. Had Abdul Rashid been born a Christian in Mississippi, he'd surely be the same man—delightful, kind and thoughtful.

We talk at length about Islam. I feel I can ask him any question about his faith and not risk insult. He explains things in a simple manner. He starts by saying, "Love for others is more important than any religion." He talks about the need to eat pure food and to discipline the mind and senses. He says it's a man's duty to take complete responsibility for his actions. He explains that the Five Pillars provide an easy way to understand Islam. These are the five duties that shape the routine of the Muslim. Both Sunni and Shia follow the Five Pillars.

The First Pillar of Islam is the declaration of faith, the Shahada: "There is no god but God. Muhammad is the messenger of God." To my ear, the Arabic sounds like a small fountain bubbling in the courtyard of a mosque— la ilaha illa Llah. There is no god but God. Ilaha means god, without the capital g. This is anything that can be put in place of God: wealth, power and the like. I imagine that the Shahada helps explain the Muslim's aversion to the excesses of Western capitalism. For the devout Muslim, pursuit of wealth without commensurate pursuit of the spiritual is a wasteland to be shunned. The declaration of faith continues: Muhammadun rasulu'Llah. "Muhammad is the messenger of God."

The Second Pillar is ritual prayer, or Salat—the prayers a Muslim offers five times a day. Abdul Rashid explains that Salat are always verses from the

Quran in Arabic. Prayers are said at dawn, noon, midafternoon, sunset and before bed. They determine the rhythm of the day. Life thus revolves around remembrance of God. I tell Abdul Rashid about my time in Damascus, when I sat under the veranda in Sultan Salim's mosque. I witnessed the noon prayer, he explains.

A principle of Islam is that all things belong to God. Human beings therefore hold wealth in trust. This helps explain the Third Pillar, Zakat. The word translates as both purification and growth. By giving to those in need, the Muslim purifies his wealth. Each year the devout give away two-and-a-half percent of their net worth. They give to the poor, the needy, those studying or teaching Islam, and travelers in need of help. As Abdul Rashid talks, I wonder if this pillar is at the root of the remarkable hospitality I've received in the Islamic world. It may explain the frequent response when thanking my Muslim hosts, "But it is my duty."

The fourth Pillar is fasting, or Sawm. This is observed once a year in the month of Ramadan, the ninth month of the Islamic year. For the entire month, Muslims fast from first light until sundown. They abstain from food, drink, smoking, and pleasures of the senses, including sexual relations. The primary reason for fasting is to purify the spirit; the physical effects are a side benefit. Perhaps I can consider my Sunday fasts as very short Sawm.

The final Pillar is Hajj. This is the pilgrimage to Mecca. Every able Muslim hopes to make this journey once in a lifetime. It is believed to be the most important act in a person's life. Each year, several million travel to Mecca. This is the largest annual gathering of people on earth. Pilgrims wear simple garments to blur distinctions of class and culture. I ask Abdul Rashid if he thinks that the European idea of pilgrimage has the same intent. He agrees it probably has.

Many I've met talk of Islam in dogmatic terms: keep women away from you, do not expose bare skin, and so on. Abdul Rashid explains his faith in simple terms I find easy to understand. Having experienced the great hearts of these people, I can see how Islam at its core is not so different from Christianity.

By early afternoon I'm back on the road. Pakistan soon serves up a sharp contrast to Abdul Rashid's vision of peace. A man in a cart pulled by a donkey mercilessly whips the struggling beast. I am appalled at the savagery of his actions and shout at him to stop. I can see that he understands my gestures, but he looks at me as though I'm from another planet. I suppose I am. He whips the thin animal with yet more determination. I yearn to intervene, but I'm physically spent.

By mid afternoon my chest is tight and the wheezing of my breath is at its worst yet. I stop at a roadside chai shop. Maybe my breathing and the knot between my shoulders will ease. I sit down, and it becomes worse rather than better. My chest tightens further, and there's a sharp pain when I take a full breath. I either gasp for air or cough uncontrollably. I'm seated at a table in the dust near the road. The few other customers move to a table further away from me. Tuberculosis remains a common and deadly threat here. I've seen TB clinics in many towns. TB is highly contagious and is spread by coughing. My coughing fits therefore worry the other patrons. The chai shop owner won't approach when I motion for another chai. *Ha! Have I finally stumbled on the secret to solitude in Pakistan?*

Things go from bad to worse. The only way to breathe is by standing, bent over, hands propped on my knees. When I sit or try to stand up, my breathing seizes completely. I experience the same panic that I had as a child with asthma. I must not let the panic take hold or I shall choke. Thinking that it might help, I try to vomit, but I can't. I feel oddly calm, yet recognize that if I don't get medical help, I'm in real danger of dying. But I can't ride the bicycle, and these people will not come near. There are no phones.

My mother told us children something many years ago. If you face a danger and have done all you can to help yourself, you can call on your guardian angel for help. This long-forgotten memory now comes to mind. As best I can, hands still on knees, I half turn to look up at the dark sky. The stars seem appropriate recipients of the prayer I'm about to offer. *I don't know who you are, or what your name is, but I need your help. Please help me.* I have no doubt that this is a significant action, and it will summon help.

But nothing happens. No angel. No celestial trumpets. I'm deeply disappointed. A few moments later, I remember a Vicks inhaler that I bought in Greece. It's at the bottom of one of the panniers. The size of a lipstick, it's designed to fit up a nostril. If I put that into boiling water and inhale the steam, it might ease my breathing. I empty each pannier, taking one item out at a time and placing it on the table. Each small effort leaves me fighting for breath. After removing each item, I must rest for some moments before I can continue. I do all this bent over, left hand on left knee.

Twenty difficult minutes later, I have the inhaler. My few words of Pashto are enough to ask the chai shop owner for hot water. I have no breath to raise my voice enough to be heard, so this requires several attempts. Tears roll down my cheeks from the effort. I need to pause and look down every few words. He finally understands and places a bowl of steaming water on a nearby table, visibly unhappy to get so close. I drop the inhaler in the water and stand bent over the bowl. I use my Arab headdress as a canopy to catch the steam (it is indeed a handy piece of apparel). After ten minutes, my breath eases just a little. The sense of panic passes. I can lie down and still breathe.

I lie on one of the *charpoy* beds provided for customers. As best as I can, I massage my back. I use a relaxation technique I learned from my mother. I start with my toes and work slowly upward. I tense then relax in turn each part of my body. I've tried this once or twice in the past, but this time the effect is profound. My body does indeed settle down, but more than that, it relaxes to the point that I lose all awareness of having a body. I can no longer feel it. By the time I reach my head, I am just awareness. There's no physical sensation or form. I'm aware there are a myriad of stars above, but I am no longer thinking; I simply am.

I come to. The stars above have rotated considerably. Five or six hours have passed. I feel fantastic. Not just good, but great. I lie looking up at the stars. Then I remember what I was doing here. I'm astonished that my breathing is free and relaxed. Not only that, but each in-breath brings a pulse of elation and well-being. All restriction and pain in my chest are gone. I sense that dawn is near. The chai shop is shuttered and deserted. I slowly gather my things and leave. The sense of well-being continues.

Pakistan: a roadside tea shop with *charpoy* beds outside.

The first light of day seeps into the sky. I feel settled and at ease. My mind is clear and serene. Cycling away below an arch of plane trees, the leaves shimmer. They are utterly beautiful; they take my breath away. The world is all beauty and grace. I've no idea what happened last night, but this remarkable feeling lasts all day. I am lit from within by a profound sense of joy. It's an extraordinary natural high.

I'll later recognize this as my first experience of deep meditation. I'll come to treasure the accompanying sense of clarity and well-being. Today, I get carried away and push myself too hard. By evening, my breathing is again labored. The cough returns. I lack the energy to find a place to stay. I lay my plastic sheet in the corner of a field just off the road. I try the same relaxation steps, but they do not work as they did last night. But my breathing isn't as bad, so I'm OK.

Oh boy, am I ready to leave this country. I've had enough of the heat, the dirt, this sickness and these people. I literally ache to be home in familiar surroundings. At this point, I want only to get to India as soon as possible. The border is another one hundred miles. It's going to be tough with these breathing problems. There's nothing to be done other than to continue, and continue I shall. It's a fitful night. My own coughing repeatedly awakes me.

I feel terrible from the moment I awake. Dawn breaks and I'm discovered by a group of youths. They see me and run madly across the field, laughing and shouting. The circus has arrived in town. They form a circle and study my every move as I pack. I'm close to screaming. Being watched like this is so painful for me. I'd hurt them if that would make them leave me alone.

On the road, I'm weak and unsteady. My progress is slow. Oddly, when I'm cycling, my breathing is a little freer; it gets worse when I stop. A demonic bus driver passes close—so close I see the front wheel nuts within inches of my arm. I'm livid with rage, and this fuels my pursuit. I follow the bus into a town. It pulls into a bus stand and I catch up. Shaking with fury, I yank open the driver's door and pull the guy from his seat. He falls from the bus onto the ground. I now see he is large and well built: not the scrawny fellow I'd unconsciously assumed. He's now as angry as I was a minute ago and lands a solid punch on my chin. I'm no match for him, so I make do with screaming at him, "You wild dog; you miserable animal!"

A large crowd gathers. They are on my side. Some saw him hit me. The crowd shouts and threatens him. All are focused on the bus driver. No one notices as I quietly take my leave. I've seen how disputes are settled here. After a lot of shouting, things will die down, and the bus driver will go on his way. I'm ashamed, but feeling better. I've vented the anger that's been building these past two weeks.

Back on the road, I want to cover some miles. I try another strategy for handling the harsh reality outside and within. I look down at the road and focus only on the passing surface. In my mind, I'm cycling in France. On both sides of the road are green fields with happy cows. Wildflowers offer a hint of scent to the pleasantly warm air. A pretty girl waits behind the counter at a *boulangerie* in the next village.

Time passes, and it works. Sort of—the pretty girl was a stretch. At the small town of Raidin, a roadside sign announces that there's a Catholic church nearby. I'll ask for a bed for the night. I simply can't face another night outside. The church and school are part of a mission run by two Belgian priests, aided by several Pakistani nuns. I ask to visit the church, and they unlock it for me. The familiar surroundings and quiet, cool atmosphere are a comfort. I say a few prayers before joining the two priests. They show me to a room with a stall to take a bucket bath. I bathe, and when I see myself in the mirror I'm shocked by how thin I am. My ribs protrude and there isn't an ounce of fat anywhere on my body.

I put on clean clothes and join my hosts for dinner. *Ah, what pleasure!* Sitting at a real table covered with a clean linen tablecloth and eating with a knife and fork. Two nuns serve us. There's a local curry, but served with Western white bread. I enjoy the intelligent conversation, though my hosts are distracted by the TV they leave on during dinner. They share their informed perspective on Pakistani history and culture. I ask about the sneers and mockery I've endured. They explain that during the Raj, the British treated the locals as inferior people. A lone white male offers an opportunity to demonstrate that they're no longer beholden.

There's a tension in the air as we eat. The priests are polite to each other, yet avoid eye contact. Each talks mostly with me, while only rarely addressing the other. It dawns on me that the two are angry at each other. They have been together here for twenty-five years, and like some old married couple with hurts that run deep, they've developed an uncomfortable truce. I admire them, living here for so long. I can't even imagine what personal sacrifices they must have made to adapt to this culture. I ask about their work, and the picture that emerges is a life of bureaucracy. Not what I'd expected of a "mission." They maintain birth, baptism, marriage and death registers for the Catholic population in a large rural area. They administer funds from Catholic foreign aid agencies. They make no mention of conversions to Catholicism. Perhaps the flock they shepherd is large enough.

Another difficult night. My breathing once more becomes labored. I adopt again the standing-with-hands-on-knees position for an hour before I'm able to sleep. I join my hosts for breakfast and settle for a cup of coffee with plenty of sugar, since today is my fast day. I decline the bacon and eggs. Silly, really— that could have been just what I needed. I'd be happy to stay a day or two and recuperate, but neither priest offers, so I leave after breakfast. Lahore is thirty-five miles away. I mentally plan the day. I'll look for a place to sleep before Lahore, then cycle through the city tomorrow. That will mean another day on a three-rupee budget, chai in a flyblown teahouse, and a night with my plastic sheet on lumpy ground. Just the thought of another night like that leaves me feeling nauseous. This is no good. I need to take care of myself. I want to buy some fruit, stay in a hotel and meet some other travelers.

A change of plan is in order, so I cycle steadily all morning and reach Lahore a little after noon. My last seven rupees buy apricots, bananas, and two mangoes. I've never eaten mangoes before and my first are decadent, sensual, and utterly delicious. It's Sunday and the banks are closed. There's a YMCA in the heart of the city. The desk clerk says I can stay tonight and pay tomorrow, after the banks are open. A place on the roof comes with a locker, a bedroll, and sheets. I meet Alan, a young British naval officer. He's taking the long way home after a two-year posting in Hong Kong. We share stories about funny things that have happened to us in strange places. He explains that Chinese script is pictorial. The word for woman is a stylized picture of a seated woman. He asks me to guess the word for discord; it's three of these symbols together.

I laugh long and hard at his stories. He laughs at mine. I tell as comedies events that were not the least bit funny at the time. It has been weeks since I even smiled. To laugh now is a release and a joy. Alan buys me a lavish meal and we talk late into the night. We lie on the roof looking up at the stars. Like-minded, hopeful company is medicine indeed.

In the morning, the world is new. Alan says goodbye. I've been at rock bottom, perhaps close to death. Self-confidence, joy and steadiness had all but deserted me. In the space of a few hours, life works again. It needed only caring company, some good food, and a break in the routine. Thank goodness for human resilience. I feel goodwill toward the locals. My demon is back in its bottle. I'll celebrate the passing of a living nightmare with a day of rest in this ancient city. I cash a traveler's check. I enjoy ice cream, fruit, and whatever takes my fancy.

Lahore was the capital of several Mughal rulers of India. The Mughals built grand mosques and monuments. The British then added heft with granite and soaring pillars. The solidity of the buildings is strangely comforting. I visit the Shalimar Gardens some miles from the city center. Shah Jahan was born in Lahore, and it was he who laid out these gardens in 1642. I enter along an impressive avenue lined with royal palms. There are terraces with shaded walks, fruit trees and flowerbeds. It was known once as the most magnificent garden in the subcontinent. Still grand, the gardens are in need of a little maintenance. A group of young men follow and taunt me. I'm able to remain civil. Back at the YMCA, I struggle to carry my bicycle up the tiled stairs. Rest and time will be needed to regain my health.

I'm up and away by dawn the next day. I weave through the bustle and fumes of morning traffic. It's a whirling flow of self-absorbed pedestrians, cyclists, motorcyclists, trucks, and buses. Above the tinny horns I'm astonished to hear from behind me a very English voice.

"Hello there!" It is Mike Hoffe, the English cyclist I was told about in Afghanistan. Mike will make the Guinness Book of Records for his trip, cycling four thousand eight hundred direct miles from England to India in forty-five days. Despite this furious pace, he appears to be an easygoing fellow and his company is a pleasure. We take it gently as we cycle side by side toward the border. With India so close, maybe Mike is no longer in a hurry. He plans to head north in India, then do some mountaineering. I can't even imagine, but I wish him well. He'll push on ahead of me once we cross the border. The process to leave Pakistan takes four hours. The forms and delays are many. Having a bicycle is a major complication. I keenly feel the texture of the day as it passes. My destination is close.

Route though Pakistan: Chaman, Quetta, Sibi, Jacobabad, Shikapur, Kandhkot, Kashmor, Sadiqabad, Uch, Aipur, Muzaffagarh, Multan, Sahiwal, Okara, Pattoki, Lahore and Whaga.

Sixteen

INDIA

May 23rd

I ARRIVE AT THE INDIAN BORDER POST at Whaga. It has been eleven months, one week, and four days since I left home. I've cycled more than eight thousand miles through thirteen countries. I've worn through four tires and several pairs of shorts. I've fixed countless punctures, many broken spokes, and several buckled wheels. The road has taken me 1,300 feet below sea level at the Dead Sea in Israel and 9,517 feet above sea level at the Kandovan Tunnel in Iran. I've crossed desolate wastelands. As if in a dream, I somehow side-stepped a coup in Afghanistan. I've passed through the hottest place in Asia, during the hottest time of year, in the grip of a heat wave. I have faced a personal hell. I have received the best and the worst of human nature. And given the same.

My immediate plan is to find cooler weather by heading north toward the Himalayas. From the border it's fifteen miles of flat, arrow-straight road into the center of Amritsar. India is all I expected and more. Chaotic and crowded, occasionally serene, dirty, yet magnificent. I take a bus from Amritsar to Jammu in the Himalayan foothills. My cheap hotel here has a mirror in the room. The whites of my eyes are the color of ripe pumpkin. I recognize this as a symptom of hepatitis, likely from infected water in Pakistan. This now explains my dire sickness.

I will return to England. I can stomach no more of the Orient—figuratively or literally. Another bus takes me to New Delhi. In Connaught Circus, a young Indian man approaches to ask me questions about the bicycle. He's planning to ride a bicycle from India to England. We chat over several glasses of chai. His father is the surgeon general of the Indian Army and an authority on hepatitis. *Ha! Being taken care of again.* He invites me to join his family for dinner, where his father diagnoses my case as severe. To prevent permanent damage to my liver, the treatment is to rest, drink lots of fluids, and foreswear alcohol. I book a seat on an overland bus to London. The relay team of two Turkish drivers will complete the trip in thirteen days of nonstop driving.

Two days before the bus is to leave, I meet a Canadian man at the campground where I'm staying. We talk of our travels. I tell him of the recent incident in Pakistan, how I was so ill, called for help, relaxed, lost consciousness, and experienced a profound serenity—and that it was unlike anything I'd experienced before. He states that this is a classic meditation experience. He tells me of an ashram—a residential center of yogic study—near Bombay. He claims that he and others at this ashram have had similar experiences. I'm intrigued and write in my diary that the pull to visit the place he describes is strong—so strong that if I were to sit on a chair and refuse to move, the chair would move toward Bombay. I cancel my overland bus ticket and buy a rail ticket for myself and the bicycle to Bombay.

From Bombay, another train ride and fifteen miles of cycling past dry rice paddies take me to the ashram. I expect a sixties-style community. I imagine ponytailed Westerners wielding hoes in dry fields beneath a windmill. Initially, I want to leave because the reality is so different. It is organized and efficient, structured around an unchanging daily routine. It is quite unlike the self-directed lifestyle I'm now accustomed to. My head objects, but my heart says stay. I have meditation experiences; some have the same extraordinary quality as that in Pakistan. A week turns into a month, but it is six months before the hepatitis clears and I regain my strength. I'm able to get the rest that the doctor ordered.

India: a quiet moment outside the local temple.

I dismantle, refurbish and paint the bicycle. It was not recorded in my passport when I arrived in India, so I'm able to sell it to a pharmaceutical sales rep from Bombay. The proceeds provide me with two years' worth of bananas, biscuits, and overseas postage stamps. I come to love the Indian seasons—hot, monsoon and cool. My favorite time of day is the early evening, which brings a world infused with that honeyed light of the tropics. Periodically, I wander on foot beyond the high stone walls of the ashram to explore the neighboring rice paddies, small villages, and wild countryside beyond.

I live in the ashram for three years. I follow the daily schedule of rising early, chanting, meditation, and a few hours of work. This is the communal, spiritually oriented life I had sought. If the journey was a time of adventure and living by my wits, this is a time of predictability and serenity. This is the happiest period of my life, and a story of its own.

Spirituality is an inextricable part of life in India. It's a land of revered teachers and mendicants who wander in search of higher truths. They say there that a saint is a person who's overcome all forms of desire. Even today in India there are hundreds who are accepted as having reached that spiritual state. The man on the street confers sainthood through belief and devotion. When a person says, "I'm going to visit a saint," no one raises an eyebrow. Most here accept holy men, miracles, and other notions that might curl a cynical Western lip.

I've been living in the ashram for about a year when one day I visit the nearby village. At the center of the village is an impressive marble shrine where the local saint is interred. I join an elderly man at a table in a small tea shop. We sip hot chai as the old man speaks with simple faith. He recounts stories of his teacher, this local holy man. He knew the great man personally. This teacher looked after the welfare of all around him, the storyteller explains. Devotees told of protection at times of danger. To this day, the saint takes various forms to protect those who travel here. He may take the form of a tiger to protect a pilgrim en route, or sometimes a dog. The old man relates all this as simple fact.

He's silent for a moment, and then he adds, "And sometimes he takes the form of a butterfly."

AFTERWORD

MY QUEST WAS TO FIND MEANING—to find meaning *out there*, in a place far from home. What I found, a treasure far sweeter than honey, was closer than I could ever have imagined. It was with me from the start of this journey. It never left me. It is the present moment. No more, and no less.

I stumbled on the first clue as I worked my way up a French mountainside. The Taurus Mountains and the Hindu Kush reinforced the lesson: *focus only on this turn of the pedal, now this turn, now this.* I resisted the tendency to think ahead, to look up at the steepness of my immediate future. Focusing on my solar plexus and on my breathing kept me tethered to the here and now.

Hours of featureless desert nudged my awareness forward. Scenery lacking in detail failed to engage my thoughts. I caught a glimpse, then, of a deep truth about the mind. It ceaselessly jibbers and hops about like a monkey. I observed my mind. At times, I was able to witness its meandering, rather than just being carried along on its flow. And perhaps for the first time, through this witnessing, find distance from the chattering mind. I found relief. I had some agency over my thoughts.

My daily diary entries logged my experiences. As I wrote or reread my own words, insight seeped between the scrawled lines. Over time, I became more familiar with the still place that resides within, the place where my mind is not hauling me into the past or the future.

In India, I learned to use conscious breathing to settle my mind as I sat for meditation. I focused on the small details of the in-breath and the out-breath: the sensation of air moving in through the nostrils, the conscious, deep breath in and the slow, purposeful exhale. Focusing on the finer points of the breathing cycle kept me engaged with the present moment. There was no space for yesterday or tomorrow. Only now.

I learned that meditation is the gym of the mind. Through this daily discipline, I built mental muscle that allowed me to remain longer in the moment. As I meditated more, I found I could choose where my mind lingered. I was better able to focus on the task at hand. In the ashram, this was known as *one-pointedness*. I could feel the power of the one-pointed mind. It was like a powerful spotlight I could direct wherever I chose.

And what's the big deal about living in the present moment? Simplicity and wholeness await there. The notion of freedom that Abud and I passionately debated in Damascus? I believe it is just this: freedom from the tyranny of the mind. If that's right, then it can be found in Memphis just as easily as it can be in Mumbai. This is not at all what I had expected when I started my journey. And yet... And yet it is not entirely surprising. Lodged deep within, some part of me may already have suspected this: that freedom resides in the present moment, in the here and now.

The Indo-European word *dei* means "to shine." *Dei* was originally used to describe bright days and heavenly spirits. *Dei* is the root for several English words: *deity, journey* and *diary*. This journey, my diary, and my destination are bound together in some mysterious manner by a certain thread. I like to think of that thread as deity, as the god of the present moment.

ACKNOWLEDGEMENTS

THIS ACCOUNT STARTED as my detailed diary. So, I must first thank Rudy, my friend and traveling companion, whose example in this I followed. Because I kept a daily written record, the many details were not lost to the mists of Afghan mountains.

The finished book would not exist if it were not for my wife, Chaya. She started me off by typing out the many pages filled with my tiny handwriting—a strategy to reduce the number of written volumes I carried on the bicycle. The raw manuscript then remained in the doldrums for too many years. To finish this book was harder for me than reaching any distant border. Thank you to Peter Jordan, my first reader and welcome critic.

The book would lack polish without the encouragement, coaching and skills of my fine editor. Thank you, Margaret Bendet. And to Laura Ricard for a late-stage read through. Thanks also go to Katelynn and the folks at DartFrog for providing a steady hand to guide me across the finish line.

Most of the reflections here are my twenty-two-year-old self's, though I did not resist the urge to sprinkle in some insight from my older self.

ABOUT THE AUTHOR

ORIGINALLY FROM THE UK, William Spencer is a Fellow of the Royal Geographical Society. He has traveled, lived and worked on several continents. After spending seventeen years going back and forth to India (subsequently by airplane), he settled with his wife and two young children in New Jersey, USA.

His work with Fortune 1000 companies focuses on making the workplace more human through participative learning and employee-centric change. His curiosity about other cultures persists. His quest for meaning continues.

Email: WilliamSpencerAuthor@gmail.com

READER FEEDBACK

WHAT DOES AN AUTHOR STAND to gain by asking for reader feedback? A lot. In fact, what we can gain is so important in the publishing world, that they've coined a catchy name for it.

It's called "social proof." And in this age of social media sharing, without social proof, an author may as well be invisible.

So if you've enjoyed *Far Sweeter Than Honey: Searching for Meaning on a Bicycle*, please consider giving it some visibility by reviewing it on Amazon or Goodreads. A review doesn't have to be a long critical essay. Just a few words expressing your thoughts, which could help potential readers decide whether they would enjoy it, too.

BOOK CLUBS

Use these questions to guide your book club discussion:

1. What do you think led the author to leave England? When in your life have you left behind something familiar and safe, and what drove you to take that leap?
2. What would you have taken with you on this journey that the author did not? Why?
3. The author describes his two companions and what they meant to him as they traveled the globe together. How important is the support of your friends in your own life's journey?
4. Where have you traveled, and what insights did those trips grant you?
5. The author experiences culture shock on more than one occasion. Why do you think simply visiting a new place can be so challenging for us?
6. The author describes male-female dynamics that he observed in Muslim countries. In what ways did this account surprise you? Or, did it?
7. In what ways has this book informed or changed your view of Islam?
8. If you had been on this journey, what might you have done differently? Why?
9. The author survived many different kinds of dangers. Was he just lucky, or do you believe there was someone or something looking after him?
10. If you had been on this journey and experienced everything exactly as the author describes in the book, what life lesson would you have taken away? Is there a lesson the author shares that he could have discussed in more detail?
11. How might this journey look different had it been organized and taken by a woman instead of a man?

Made in the USA
Las Vegas, NV
13 March 2022

45553627R00184